WITNESSING ANDRÉ MALRAUX

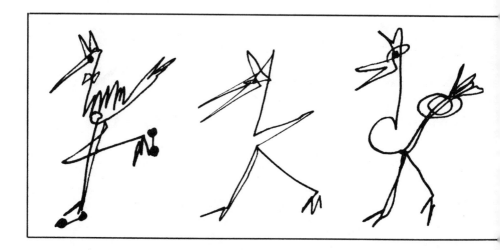

Essays in Honor of
Wilbur Merrill Frohock

WITNESSING ANDRÉ MALRAUX

Visions and Re-Visions

Edited by
Brian Thompson and Carl A. Viggiani

WESLEYAN UNIVERSITY PRESS ✠ Middletown, Connecticut

Grateful acknowledgment is made to the Editors of the *Romanic Review* for permission to reprint "Malraux and Tragedy: The Structure of *La Condition humaine*" by Bert M-P. Leefmans; to Grove Press Inc. and Random House Inc. for permission to quote from *Man's Hope* by André Malraux, translated by Stuart Gilbert and Alastair MacDonald.

All inquiries and permissions requests should be addressed to the Publisher, Wesleyan University Press, 110 Mt. Vernon Street, Middletown, Connecticut 06457

Distributed by Harper & Row Publishers, Keystone Industrial Park, Scranton, Pennsylvania 18512

LIBRARY OF CONGRESS CATALOGING IN PUBLICATION DATA
Main entry under title:

Witnessing André Malraux.

  Includes index.
    1. Malraux, André, 1901–1976—Criticism and interpretation—
Addresses, essays, lectures. I. Thompson, Brian.
II. Viggiani, Carl A.
PQ2625.A716Z957 1984 843'.912 83-19647
ISBN 0-8195-5096-5

Manufactured in the United States of America

First Edition

CONTENTS

Dedication   vii
Preface   ix

INTRODUCTION: MALRAUX'S QUEST
Brian Thompson   1

MALRAUX CRITICISM: TWO EXEMPLARY MODES
Norman Rudich   16

ASIA OUT OF FOCUS: DECODING MALRAUX'S ORIENT
Mary M. Rowan   30

MALRAUX'S SAINT-JUST
Sergio Villani   40

MALRAUX AND TRAGEDY: THE STRUCTURE OF "LA
CONDITION HUMAINE"
Bert M-P. Leefmans   48

MALRAUX, FAULKNER, AND THE PROBLEM OF TRAGEDY
Haskell M. Block   56

MALRAUX AND SARTRE: DIALOGUE ON THE
FAR SIDE OF DESPAIR
Mary Jean Green   62

MALRAUX AND CAMUS 1935–1960:
MASTER AND DISCIPLE?
Carl A. Viggiani   73

BEFORE "L'ESPOIR": MALRAUX'S PILOTS FOR
REPUBLICAN SPAIN
Walter G. Langlois   89

AUTHORITARIANISM AND ESTHETICS: THE PARADOX
OF "L'ESPOIR"
Nicholas Hewitt   113

"L'ESPOIR" AND STALINISM
Robert Sayre   125

MALRAUX'S WOMEN: A RE-VISION
Susan Rubin Suleiman   140

FROM FASCINATION TO POETRY: BLINDNESS IN
MALRAUX'S NOVELS
Brian Thompson   159

MALRAUX'S SHAMANISM: INITIATORY
DEATH AND REBIRTH
Mary Ann Frese Witt   169

ON DREAMS AND THE HUMAN MYSTERY IN MALRAUX'S
"MIROIR DES LIMBES"
Ralph Tarica   179

APPENDICES
A. Major Works of André Malraux   191
B. Books in English about André Malraux: A Selection   193
C. Notes   195
D. Contributors   217

Index   221

DEDICATION

We dedicate this book to Wilbur Merrill Frohock, distinguished scholar, critic, and teacher, Professor Emeritus of French and General Education at Harvard University. For the countless undergraduate and graduate students at Brown, Columbia, Wesleyan, and Harvard universities who were privileged to take courses or do research with Professor Frohock between 1935 and 1976, the serious study of literature often began with their encounter with him. However brief that encounter, they remained marked, not only by his personal qualities —his warmth, wit, good humor, rocklike integrity and honesty, conscientiousness, and even his not infrequent outbursts of puzzled impatience with certain human frailties—but more importantly, by the highest standards of teaching and scholarship, which he exemplified. His courses were models of careful and thorough preparation, the products of long research and thought, presented with clarity and organization, but also with wit and a saving touch of modest self-irony. He took more seriously than most of the enormous responsibilities of teaching the young and of training those who themselves would later teach. It is not too much to say that many of us owe him our careers.

Professor Frohock's contributions as a scholar and critic place him in the first rank of his generation. His many essays and books— which continue to appear, six years after his "retirement"—have often been pioneering studies. *The Novel of Violence in America*

1920–1950 (1950) provided a method and a concept for a new look at post–World War I novelists. *André Malraux and the Tragic Imagination* (1952), the first systematic study of that author, remains today, some thirty years after its publication, a basic text for further reflection on Malraux as well as a model for biographical, historical, and critical analysis of modern French writers. It established Professor Frohock as the acknowledged dean of Malraux scholars. His wide-ranging interests have also given us studies of most of the major figures of modern French and American fiction, from Gide to Bellow and the New Novelists; of Rimbaud and other French and American poets; and of the picaresque tradition in European and American fiction.

Both a theoretical and a practical critic, Professor Frohock came out of the tradition of historical and sociological criticism founded by Sainte-Beuve and Taine. Without abandoning that humanist tradition, he moved quite naturally into the development of the American New Criticism and became one of its finest practitioners, integrating its formalist methods into the social and historical context. While giving the most rigorous attention to the formal elements of each text, he has always been deeply sensitive to the extraordinary violence and tragedy of the human situation in this century, and has sought as well to reveal the *human* beauty and value embodied in the formal elements—for example, the love, hope, generosity, and compassion embedded in Malraux's finest novels. For all that he has taught us, and for other, more personal gifts, we dedicate these essays to him in gratitude and affection.

PREFACE

With the exception of the late Bert M-P. Leefmans' "Malraux and Tragedy: The Structure of *La Condition humaine*," the fourteen essays included here were written especially for this volume and in order to honor Professor Wilbur Merrill Frohock. We are very happy to reprint Professor Leefmans' pioneering study of the great novel as a tribute both to him and to his mentor, Professor Frohock, who originally proposed the subject of the essay to him many years ago. We are very pleased that the essay will once more come to the attention of readers of Malraux and in addition be more easily available.

We wish to express our gratitude to Russell Young, Director of the Camargo Foundation, and Michael Pretina, Associate Director, for the encouragement they have given us in our effort to produce this volume. We thank the Camargo Foundation for its grant in support of this volume and our colleague Professor Walter Langlois for his permission to use Malraux's drawings and the photograph of Malraux. To the University of Massachusetts and to Wesleyan University, our thanks for the support that made it possible to bring our work to fruition. To Marie-Claude Thompson, Jane Mead Viggiani, and Natalie Frohock we give most special thanks for their help, encouragement, confidence, optimism, and many labors of love.

B.T.
C.A.V.

WITNESSING ANDRÉ MALRAUX

Brian Thompson

INTRODUCTION:

MALRAUX'S QUEST

André Malraux is one of the most complex and fascinating figures of modern French letters. For over half a century his works have alternately or simultaneously intrigued, scandalized, astonished, disappointed, enraged, and inspired his audience. His life was as active and multifaceted as his pen; his actions provoked a range and intensity of reaction similar to that his writings elicited. The essays in this volume bear witness to Malraux's continuing impact. The questions that he raised and that he pursued so persistently and intensely throughout his life have lost none of their relevance; the powerful novels and poetic meditations in which he embodied these questions reward repeated careful readings. But despite the many autobio-

graphical elements in his novels and memoirs—perhaps even because of them—the man himself remains something of an enigma.

Malraux was born in Paris in November 1901. Little is known of
his childhood, which he apparently hated, at least in retrospect: his
parents' divorce, the apartment above his grandmother's grocery
store in suburban Bondy, undistinguished studies in less than first-
rate secondary schools.[1] And yet with no academic training beyond,
perhaps, a few courses at the Musée Guimet or the Ecole du Louvre,
by the age of twenty-one Malraux had managed to acquire a solid,
wide-ranging, and eclectic literary and artistic culture; he had more
than a passing acquaintance with a number of the leading poets and
artists of the day; and he had published a number of articles as well
as several pieces of curious surrealist fiction.[2] Clara Malraux's account of her first meeting with Malraux at a literary dinner is fascinating; its almost immediate result was a marriage that was intended by both parties to last six months. In fact, each had found a
worthy partner (and occasional adversary) for a good while longer.

Two years later, in 1923, after some reverses on the stock market,
Malraux mounted an "archeological" expedition to Indochina. After
a successful trek through the jungle to the temple of Banteay-Srei, in
Cambodia, Malraux, Clara, and their companion were arrested in
Phnom Penh and charged with theft of bas-relief sculptures; Malraux
had apparently intended to sell his finds to American collectors to
recoup his losses. Clara was soon released, and she sailed home to
France to arouse public opinion. Petitions signed by the major artists
and writers of the day helped obtain the suspension of Malraux's
three-year prison sentence. What had begun as a less than disin-
terested adventure was to play a decisive role in Malraux's life and
work, however, for in Indochina he had seen for himself the corrup-
tion and injustice of the colonial regime. Within a year the erstwhile
Parisian dandy was back in Indochina working with the anticolonialist Jeune Annam movement. With his friend Paul Monin he founded
and published an anticolonialist newspaper, *Indochine*. When his
biting editorials attacking the governor general led to the paper's suppression, Malraux managed to locate and smuggle in printing type
from Hong Kong to resurrect the paper, rebaptized *Indochine enchaînée*. Although the episode was hardly conclusive politically, Malraux's bout with colonial "justice" and his entire experience in the
Far East were to profoundly alter his perception of himself and of the
world. His adventure supplied him with the settings and raw material for several of his major works.

It is probably true that Malraux's first departure for Indochina was
already a quest for something more than a quick profit. Coming to

adulthood in the shambles of post–World War I Europe, already knowledgeable about oriental art, the young Malraux no doubt turned to the East as a foil for his own rapidly disintegrating civilization. The first results of Malraux's reflections were characteristically set down in dialogue form, as a fictional exchange of letters between Ling, a Chinese visiting Europe, and A. D., a European discovering China, under the title *La Tentation de l'Occident*. Malraux portrays, on the one hand, the Western obsession with the personal identity of the individual, against a background fading away into nothingness, and on the other, the Eastern spontaneous acceptance of life within the larger human community, absorbing the individual into the whole. Characteristically, too, there is no resolution: the questions remain. Malraux's quest for the meaning of the human adventure led him to a lifelong passion for the arts and civilizations of the world. His approach remained comparative, inclusive, eclectic; his mode of thought remained interrogative.

In the meantime Malraux also set about exploring, in fiction, the ramifications of twentieth-century man's loss of a center, of an identity. Earlier and more profoundly than most, he realized that if, as Nietzsche proclaimed, God is dead, then man—man as he has always known himself—is also dead. At the very least, man must rediscover who he is and what the meaning of his existence in the world might be. For what is man in a world in which the only certainty is death, in which even that death is of no apparent significance; in which the dominant feeling is of the absurdity of the entire enterprise? As one of his characters succinctly puts it, in *La Condition humaine*: "What good is a soul, if there is neither God nor Christ?"[3]

The three novels set in the Far East portray a number of possible responses to the dilemma. Garine, in *Les Conquérants*, flees the absurd by throwing himself into the revolution in China, although he admits he has no love for the poor. But revolutionary action can at best keep the absurd at bay for a time; once the revolution succeeds, the questions once more arise and must be faced. Perken, the aging adventurer in *La Voie royale*, attempts to counter the feeling of the transience and meaninglessness of all things human by "leaving a scar on the map." He fails, and despite further flights into eroticism and opium, dies a painful and solitary death from gangrene. There are no answers to the dilemma, but there are some very powerful images: Nicolaïeff casually brushing dead mayflies ("éphémères") off his desk, thus mirroring the sudden death of a spy interrogated by Garine; the oppressive, insect-infested jungle, indifferent if not hostile to man's undertakings; the blind, enslaved Grabot, in his degradation and dependency a painful "image of the human condition."

Beneath the political or adventure-story trappings, this is Malraux's real subject matter; the title of his third and most ambitious novel, *La Condition humaine*—winner of the Prix Goncourt in 1933—could well be extended to cover the entire corpus of his works. The novel chronicles a crucial phase of the Communist insurrection in Shanghai and brings into play a complex and variegated cast of characters, largely Europeans or other "displaced persons"; each is working out his destiny or frantically trying to escape it, against a backdrop of violent political upheaval. The overt results are not very satisfactory: the insurrection is brutally crushed and most of the main characters die. And yet the final tone is not one of despair. The "virile fraternity" among comrades, the deep relationship between Kyo and his wife, May, Katow's gift of his poison—"more than his life"—and willingness to accept an atrocious death in another's stead, these are new tones in Malraux's palette and they counteract the apparent negative conclusions of the narrative. As Katow states, "If you don't believe in anything, *especially* because you don't believe in anything, you have to believe in the qualities of the heart when you come across them, it's obvious" (*CH* 333–34).

Malraux's novels were widely taken for reportage, for thinly disguised accounts of firsthand experience. While the novels clearly have their basis in experience—certain aspects of the Kyo-May relationship, for example, are surely autobiographical—Malraux did not participate in the insurrection in Shanghai, nor was he in the revolution in Canton narrated blow by blow in *Les Conquérants*. Although he did reply to Trotsky's criticism of this book (Garine and the author both need "a good dose of Marxism")[4] by pointing out that it was first of all a novel and not a chronicle of the revolution, Malraux did little to squelch the rumors and legends that surrounded him. Indeed, being something of a mythomaniac, he seems to have started or at least encouraged some of them. It was no doubt he who provided the information for the afterword of the German translation of *Les Conquérants* to the effect that he had been acting director of propaganda in Canton.

All legends aside, Malraux's literary and extraliterary activities were impressive enough, long before *engagé* became a fashionable catchword. In the thirties he presided over the Comité mondial contre la guerre et le fascisme. As president of the Comité Thaelmann, he traveled with Gide to Berlin to deliver to Goebbels petitions on Thaelmann's behalf. His 1935 novel, *Le Temps du mépris*, was an early outcry against the torture and oppression of the Nazi regime. Once again, human fraternity and communion are affirmed in the face of humiliation and death. In the important preface to the novel,

Malraux seems to be moving toward an integration of East and West: "It is difficult to be a man, but no more difficult to become one by deepening one's communion than by cultivating one's difference."

The outbreak of the Spanish civil war in 1936 provided an opportunity for a fully active role in the struggle against fascism, and Malraux immediately offered his services. He was instrumental in founding and equipping the Republican air force, and he personally commanded the Escadrille España during the first year of the war, flying numerous missions as a machine gunner. Wounded in action, he embarked the following year on a speaking tour of the United States to garner support and to raise money and medical supplies for the beleaguered Republican forces. By the end of the year Gallimard brought out his monumental novel, *L'Espoir*, based in part on his personal experience in Spain and presenting an eloquent and compelling witness for the Republican cause. Beneath the action at hand, beneath the conflicts between being and doing and the necessity of "organizing the apocalypse," runs the current of Malraux's constant quest. As the old art historian Alvear states, "mans reasoning must be given a new foundation." (E705) As for Malraux, he continued his work in Spain, shooting a film on the conflict at the request of the government under siege. Working under the most difficult of conditions, Malraux and his crew finally left the studio in Barcelona the day before the fall of the city. The film was never quite completed as planned, although some scenes were later shot in France. Finally released in 1945 to critical acclaim, *Sierra de Teruel*, rebaptized *Espoir*, was awarded the Prix Louis Deluc.[5]

Upon the outbreak of World War II, for which the Spanish civil war had provided a dress rehearsal, Malraux enlisted in the tank corps. He was taken prisoner (without, apparently, having seen any real combat), managed to escape, and made his way to the unoccupied zone in southern France, where he settled down with Josette Clotis and their sons.[6] There he received Gide, Sartre, and others, but he remained for some time withdrawn from the fray. Malraux was not entirely inactive, however: in 1941 Skira published *Les Noyers de l'Altenburg*, a reflective, wide-ranging novel bridging two generations, two world wars, France, Germany, Russia, and the Near East. This novel was the remains, according to Malraux, of a still broader work entitled *La Lutte avec l'ange*, which had been destroyed by the Gestapo. The novel as published continues the search for "fundamental man," for the meaning of human existence across time, space, and cultural differences. The question debated at the Altenburg colloquium is the question Malraux had been debating with himself and the world: "Are there . . . any data on which to base the notion of man?" The walnut trees of the title are only one of the images of continuity that hint at the "enigma," the "secret," the "mystery" that haunts narrator and author alike, and that is occasionally grasped or experienced intuitively.

After two years of relative tranquillity on the Riviera—a strange interlude in Malraux's life, perhaps "the rest of the warrior," perhaps depression over successive defeats in Spain and France—Malraux finally contacted the Resistance networks in southwestern France. Malraux was a born leader with combat experience in Spain, and he soon became "Colonel Berger," commanding Free French forces in three departments. Wounded in a German ambush, he was captured, interrogated, and stood before a firing squad; they shot over his head, one of Malraux's many close calls with death. Freed from prison by the Allied invasion, he then organized and commanded the Alsace-Lorraine Brigade. Death continued to hound him, however: both his brothers were killed, and Josette Clotis slipped under a train and died before Malraux could reach her bedside. Rejoining his troops, he participated in the liberation of Dannemarie, Mulhouse, and Strasbourg. His fearless and inspiring leadership earned him the Légion d'Honneur.[7]

The same year, 1945, marked the first meeting with General de Gaulle, an encounter that would largely determine Malraux's political commitments for the rest of his life. Many have seen Malraux's unfailing allegiance to de Gaulle, in season and out, as a betrayal of his antifascist and anticolonialist past. In an era still marked by the internationalist dream of the nineteenth century, he had espoused the proletariat; now he espoused France: "for me there is no difference or rupture of any kind [. . .] there is above all no difference in behavior. The profound bond is the same."[8] And for Malraux, the values he associated with France were precisely those he found incarnate in de Gaulle: freedom, honor, and above all the dignity for which Kyo, Katow, and the heroes of *L'Espoir* were willing to fight and die. Indeed, for Michel Cazenave, "It is because he is faithful to those who died at Guadalajara that Malraux is a Gaullist."[9] Malraux's supposed defection from the Left is thus a fidelity to the *values* the Left had embodied: "For us, the Left is the presence, in history, of the generosity by means of which France has been France for the world."[10] For Malraux, "France's vocation is for all men."[11]

Putting his considerable talents as an orator to good use, Malraux served as Minister of Information in de Gaulle's first government in 1945. When de Gaulle came back into power at the height of the Algerian crisis in 1958, he again called upon Malraux, first as Minister of Information, then, from 1959 on, as Minister of Culture. It is

perhaps in the latter role that Malraux's impact was most manifest, from the cleaning of monuments and buildings in Paris to the
establishment of numerous Maisons de la Jeunesse et de la Culture, decentralizing and disseminating culture opportunities through
France.[12] Equally important, however, was his unfailing support for
de Gaulle throughout the Algerian conflict, despite his own earlier
condemnations of colonialism and the use of torture, despite bitter
attacks on his person, both by word and deed (years later he would
still recall with grief a little girl almost blinded by a terrorist bomb
intended for him): for Malraux, politics was not what one *desires* but
what one *does*, and he saw in de Gaulle the man who could best accomplish what had to be done in the real world of possibilities. This
fidelity did not come cheaply, as Shinichi Ogasawara points out:

If he did not renounce political life, if he remained faithful to de Gaulle
during what was no doubt the bitterest period of his life,[13] it is because
his commitment depended precisely on the decision he had made to live
out fully the tragedy of politics. This tragedy does not reveal itself in the
politician, nor in the born man of action, nor in the intellectual who
flirts with politics—it is embodied in the man who has committed himself to the point of betraying, in order to realize it, the very idea he has
advocated as a man of truth.[14]

Jean Lacouture has compared Malraux's role here to that he played in
conjunction with the communists in the thirties: "In each case one
sees this volcano adapt its explosions to the necessities of a situation,
according to remarkably realistic analyses."[15] Lacouture also hy-
pothesizes that this self-imposed mutism perhaps contributed to
Malraux's astonishing productivity during the latter years of his life.

Malraux's quest had not, of course, come to a standstill when he
joined forces with de Gaulle, although it no longer found its expression in the novel. It seems that the intuitions expressed in *Les
Noyers* of the continuity of man across time and space, associated as
they were with artistic creation, had in a way liberated Malraux and
sent him off on an exploration of artistic creation that would last the
rest of his life. As Françoise Dorenlot puts it, "Malraux stops questioning his conscience in order to question the world's civilizations."[16] Art was hardly a new concern for Malraux—witness his
early articles on painting, Claude's discussion of metamorphosis in
La Voie royale, and the definition of the role of art in the 1935 preface
to *Le Temps du mépris*: "Try to make men aware of the greatness in
them." But Malraux seemed to have exorcised certain demons, to
have come to a kind of certitude. He could now say, "I am in art as
one is in religious life."[17]

Art and artistic creation are for Malraux man's means of affirmation in the face of destiny—in the face, that is, of death, solitude, humiliation, dependency, "tout ce qui impose à l'homme la conscience de sa condition."[18] Hence the central affirmation of *Les Voix du silence*: "Art is anti-destiny" (*VS* 637). For Malraux, the artist never transcribes reality, he rivals it. He transfigures the "real," which is but his raw material, in order to attain the absolute, the supernatural, the "unreal." Hence the titles of some of Malraux's major meditations on artistic creation: *La Monnaie de l'absolu, L'Irréel, Le Surnaturel*. In a 1974 interview with me Malraux stated with no little force, "Everything that I have written consists in posing the contradiction between the realm of appearances, in the metaphysical sense— that is, what one could call life—and the realm of the absolute, whatever it might be." This is, of course, a never-ending quest; one never quite "attains" the absolute, but "at bottom, the whole question is, beginning with reality, to attempt to attain the inaccessible."[19] It is less the answer that counts than the question. The human species is the only one that questions itself and its world; for Malraux the most profound mode of thought is interrogative:[20] "Do not forget that what one could call my inquiry into art represents something absolutely interrogative. The key to my entire effort is questioning considered as a value in and of itself."[21]

Malraux's questions were embodied in novels and in meditations on artistic creation; beginning with the publication in 1967 of his *Antimémoires*, they also took on form in a series of volumes— occasionally reworked, combined, retitled—which combine memoirs (of sorts), fiction, dream, the real, and the unreal in what will perhaps be seen as Malraux's greatest and most original work.[22] The early pages of the *Antimémoires* indicate the underlying object of this continuing search: "Man does not reach the depths of man; he does not find his image in the extent of the knowledge he acquires, he finds an image of himself in the questions which he asks. The man you will find here is one in tune with the questions which death addresses to the meaning of the world."[23]

Death no longer has the final word, however, even if there is no clear, unequivocal answer. Through successive volumes—*Les Chênes qu'on abat . . .* (after de Gaulle's death), *La Tête d'obsidienne* (after Picasso's death), *Lazare* (after his own near death, prolonged coma, and "resurrection")—Malraux continued his quest, guided by certain key intuitions, key experiences that seemed to throw a morning light on his evening years, in which life and death were chords in a mysterious harmony behind the appearances of the real world. T. Jefferson Kline has shown that Malraux's portrait of Picasso—like all his other portraits, no doubt—is really a self-portrait; it is a portrait of an artist whose passion is "burning self-interrogation,"[24] whose permanent quest is never over.

What is astonishing in the portrait of the artist offered in *La Tête d'obsidienne (Picasso's Mask)* is that it summarizes not only the problematics of the composite hero Garine-Perken-Kyo-Kassner-Magnin-Berger, it also proposes the same philosophical evolution which runs through the novels, that is, a movement from a confrontation with death, always bound to fail, towards a reconciliation between life and death which certain characters in *L'Espoir* and *Les Noyers* discover.[25]

In his later years, as he approached his own death, Malraux retained a sense of wonder at the surprises of life, at the tremendous changes that he had witnessed in his own lifetime—he had seen horse-drawn taxis in Paris and men walking on the moon. But the marvels of technology did not erase the real questions: "Why bother going to the moon, if it's only to commit suicide there?"[26] As always, he remained interrogative, the inveterate agnostic in the world's first agnostic civilization, the first civilization without a supreme value.[27] Yet it, too, is subject to metamorphosis and Malraux was convinced that the twenty-first century would be religious—or simply not exist.

During a rich and varied life, Malraux underwent a number of metamorphoses himself. He never stopped growing, searching, asking the questions that needed to be asked. In the essays assembled here we will follow some of the traces he has left, approach him and his work in several of his many guises: novelist, adventurer, political activist, military leader, art theorist, memorialist, dreamer. We have not attempted a global, definitive study that would in some way enshrine him under glass—appropriately labeled, classified, and relegated to the realm of dead writers suitable for dissertations; rather we present a series of encounters with Malraux and his works, with differing points of departure and using differing critical methodologies, undertaken by writers and readers who have been and are still touched in one way or another by Malraux, by his life, and by his works.

In the opening essay, "Malraux Criticism: Two Exemplary Modes," Norman Rudich compares and contrasts the methods and results of two very different critical approaches to Malraux's fiction as exemplified by two of their foremost practitioners. Lucien Goldmann's Marxist sociological approach looks at the novels from a genetic structuralist perspective, in which formal analysis serves as a prolegomenon to a sociological and historical understanding of Malraux's fiction. For Goldmann, works of art are structured elaborations of more or less coherent currents of ideas or images produced by certain social groups or classes under given historical, political, and economic conditions. W. M. Frohock, on the other hand, analyzes, interprets, and evaluates Malraux's novels primarily as poetic expressions of an individual artist and intellectual whose central preoccupation is essentially metaphysical rather than political: What is man? What is it to be human in the twentieth century? Professor Rudich's study demonstrates the extent to which Frohock's careful, largely formalist literary analysis overlaps in many of its conclusions with Goldmann's sociological approach. Differing methodologies, at least in the hands of such sensitive and sensible critics, can thus lead to complementary and mutually enriching insights.

In "Asia Out of Focus: Decoding Malraux's Orient," Mary M. Rowan probes beneath the immediacy and apparent accuracy of Malraux's Far Eastern settings in *Les Conquérants, La Voie royale,* and *La Condition humaine,* which have led some readers and critics to take these early novels for fictionalized reportage of firsthand experience. While the careful biographical work of Langlois and Lacouture has established the limits of Malraux's early experience in China, Professor Rowan here analyzes the internal evidence in the novels themselves and shows how Malraux's depictions of the Orient depend less on firsthand knowledge than on innovative narrative techniques drawn from the cinema and expressed in elliptical language. Malraux's "filmic sleight of hand" helps create the compelling backdrop against which his heroes work out their political and metaphysical struggles.

Exploring an entirely different avenue of approach, Sergio Villani's essay, "Malraux's Saint-Just," traces Malraux's lasting fascination with this complex figure of the French Revolution. Intellectual idealist, political pragmatist, shaped by and shaping his times, his life (and death) unfolding at the very juncture of history and legend, Saint-Just has left his mark on the impassioned adventurers of Malraux's early novels—especially Garine, with whom he has much in common—and has been a source of inspiration for Malraux himself, as commander of the Alsace-Lorraine Brigade, as statesman under de Gaulle, as artist. Saint-Just symbolizes for Malraux the regenerative power of man to renew and recreate himself and his world.

The world of Malraux's novels is in many ways a tragic one, reflecting Malraux's sense of the world in which he himself lived. In fact, Malraux considered the novel the modern equivalent of classical tragedy. In his seminal essay, "Malraux and Tragedy: The Structure of *La Condition humaine,*" the late Bert M-P. Leefmans disengages from the "profusion of matter and energy" of Malraux's masterpiece an underlying structure which is as rigorous as it is inconspicuous.

The action of the novel is seen to fall into two parallel phases, each moving from preparation to action to recapitulation. Patterns of time, place, action, and relative immediacy or universality of the action at hand all serve to structure the narrative profusion. The juxtaposition of individual elements between the two phases clarifies the novel's internal meanings, highlighting contrasts imbedded in these similarities. The novel as a whole, too, corresponds to the pattern of tragedy, moving "from purpose to passion to perception." The power of the novel is due in part, at least, to this hidden but meaning-filled structure.

Haskell Block approaches the theme of Malraux and tragedy through a comparative study of Malraux and Faulkner as tragic novelists. "Malraux, Faulkner, and the Problem of Tragedy" takes as its starting point Malraux's revealing preface to the 1933 translation of Faulkner's *Sanctuary*. As was often the case when he was speaking or writing of others, Malraux here reveals a great deal as well about his own preoccupation with destiny. His notion of the absurd and the irremediable, akin to Faulkner's, later gave way to a quest for a tragic humanism attesting man's grandeur as well as his misery. Faulkner's novels, on the other hand, leave very little room for tragic heroes; man is utterly destroyed, his defeat is not, like that of Malraux's heroes, ennobled by destiny. It is Malraux's tragic humanism that offers, for Professor Block, some hope in the face of human suffering, degradation, and death.

Within this context of man's plight in a world marked by suffering and death, Mary Jean Green, in her essay, "Malraux and Sartre: Dialogue on the Far Side of Despair," charts the significant personal and literary encounters between Malraux and Sartre in 1937 and again in 1941—years that marked decisive points in the evolution of each writer's view of human action in history. Personally convinced of the futility of active political involvement, Sartre responded to Malraux's participation in the Spanish civil war with his short story "Le Mur": imminent death robs life of all meaning; action is devalued and made meaningless by the arbitrariness of fate. Malraux seems to take up the challenge in *L'Espoir*: the initial isolation and alienation of Hernandez's execution scene are redeemed by the assertion of human will and solidarity, by a fraternity discovered on the far side of death. In 1941, however, following the defeat of the Spanish Republicans and the fall of France, Malraux and Sartre reversed roles, as it were: a discouraged Malraux declined an active part in the Resistance, while Sartre, having discovered the power of the pen, became one of its leading spokesmen. Orestes' call for action and individual commitment in *Les Mouches* seems to echo Moreno's words in *L'Espoir*.

Malraux answered the call and once again entered the fray as commander of the Alsace-Lorraine Brigade.

In "Malraux and Camus 1935–1960: Master and Disciple?" Carl Viggiani probes Malraux's complex and intriguing relationship with another major figure of twentieth-century French literature. Analyzing both published and unpublished materials, he establishes the historical and biographical data that indicate the decisive role Malraux played in Camus's career and the tremendous impact he had on Camus's thought, especially in the late thirties. Camus publicly acknowledged his debts, yet often remained strangely silent, perhaps rejecting his former "master" in his search for his own authentic voice. Malraux, on the other hand, despite his strong support for Gallimard's publication of Camus's early works, often spoke disparagingly of Camus's novels and rejected out of hand any master-disciple relationship with his younger colleague. Professor Viggiani has provided Malraux and Camus scholars with some fascinating questions as well as a solid point of departure for setting out to answer them.

Walter G. Langlois has once again done a tremendous amount of painstaking historical research in order to reconstitute the background and precise chronology of Malraux's early involvement in the struggle in Spain. "Before *L'Espoir*: Malraux's Pilots for Republican Spain" charts the rapidly evolving political, diplomatic, and military situation in the early days of the Spanish conflict. It also depicts the numerous obstacles of all kinds that Malraux and his colleagues had to overcome in order to obtain the aircraft and recruit the pilots destined to constitute, under Malraux's personal leadership, the Escadrille España and thus provide the raw material for major portions of *L'Espoir*.

Malraux's portrayal of the air squadron is one of the components of the narrative structure of this novel, which Nicholas Hewitt finds highly ambiguous and more complex than generally assumed. In "Authoritarianism and Esthetics: The Paradox of *L'Espoir*" he shows how this novel, often thought to mark the disappearance of the adventurer-hero—or at least his integration into a broader democratic fraternity—retains powerful links with the earlier, politically and ethically ambiguous novels. The authoritarian quality of *L'Espoir* is masked by the *apparent* alignment with the struggle of the Spanish people against fascism, and by the *apparent* subordination of metaphysical and heroic preoccupations to a collective political aim. Yet this reading is possible only because of a gross oversimplification of the political reality of the war and a denigration of the spontaneous revolution that characterized its early phases. The prominent esthetic component of the novel, far from safeguarding the values of

European humanism, moves the center of gravity away from the concrete reality of the Spain of the thirties toward a general meditation on art. Esthetics thus serves as yet another means of masking Malraux's persistent authoritarian viewpoint.

Robert Sayre, too, in *"L'Espoir* and Stalinism" finds that an entire dimension of the conflict in Spain is occulted. The silences of the novel include the political dimension of the war, its revolutionary starting point, and the *counter*revolutionary actions of the Comintern, including the Moscow trials and the Stalinist repression of all non-Stalinist groups in Spain. The POUM, which represented a telling critique of the Stalinist position from within the Communist perspective, is also absent. The structure of the novel, patterned on the military evolution, serves to hide another, symmetrically opposed, structure—the dismantling of the revolutionary gains of the people in the name of military efficiency. Those individual characters who offer critiques of the Stalinist position are largely undermined or devalued; the most telling criticism, in the name of the revolutionary collectivity, remains unspoken. For Professor Sayre, then, *L'Espoir* embodies the perspective of the Stalinist fellow traveler and reveals in Malraux a hidden (and effectively repressed) affinity with the fascist ideology that he so persistently combated.

Susan Rubin Suleiman also deals with silence and absence in "Malraux's Women: A Re-vision"; women characters are almost totally absent from Malraux's fiction. Most of the women mentioned in the novels are less than characters, they are reduced to mere *figurantes*; the few with speaking parts are rarely spoken to, even by Malraux's revolutionary heroes. The three women important enough to be fully named—May and Valérie in *La Condition humaine* and Anna in *Le Temps du mépris*—are also problematic, for the episodes in which they appear valorize the masculine and repeat in different modes the themes of separation and alienation between the sexes. For Professor Suleiman such an analysis raises essential questions not only for women—too often co-opted into reading within a perspective that excludes them *as women*—but also for men. The critical blindness that leaves such questions unasked must be overcome if we are all to reach a real understanding of the history of human consciousness.

My own essay deals with blindness of another sort, that present, either literally or figuratively, throughout the entire corpus of Malraux's fiction. "From Fascination to Poetry: Blindness in Malraux's Novels" not only charts the pervasiveness and depth of Malraux's preoccupation with blindness and with injury to the eyes, but also shows how blindness functions in the novels as a powerful image of what Malraux calls "destiny." It makes tangibly present to the reader one or another of the darker sides of the human condition as Malraux sees (or better, *feels*) it: man's vulnerability, his dependence on forces beyond his control, his essential solitude, the difficulty he experiences in attempting to communicate with others. Through the process of artistic creation, Malraux's personal fascination has become an integral part of the poetry of his novels.

Inner experience and its artistic expression are also central to Mary Ann Witt's essay, "Malraux's Shamanism: Initiatory Death and Rebirth," which traces the persistent presence in Malraux's life and works of the experience of the shaman, integrating visionary experience into consciousness and reconciling the mystical, visionary knowledge of the East with the rational knowledge and power of the West. A number of Malraux's characters undergo a kind of ritual death and rebirth akin to shamanic rites of initiation, involving either a ritual climbing of the World Tree or Cosmic Tree, or a ritual death by burial or enclosure followed by reemergence experienced as a ritual rebirth. These experiences, which in some way reflect Malraux's own, lead to an intuition of a fundamental, cosmic, mystical order, "a sacred and simple secret," and to Malraux's conviction of the dual powers of life and art to combat the temptation to nihilism.

Malraux's continuing need over the years to probe this enigma, the mystery of man, is the *fil conducteur* of Ralph Tarica's study, "On Dreams and the Human Mystery in Malraux's *Miroir des limbes*." The elusive nature of this enigma accounts in part for the allusive, interrogative, poetic style of Malraux's memoirs as well as for the privileged role of dream, which seems to represent for him an irreality containing a truth that far transcends that of ordinary, ephemeral reality. Malraux encountered the supernatural in his life; as an avowed agnostic, he attempted to brush it aside; he was led again and again into a dialogue with the transcendent, the absolute, which is alone capable of ordering civilization. The profound goal of all of the texts that make up *Le Miroir des limbes* is to distinguish between appearances—what we call "life"—and the deeper truths of the "unreal," which gives life its meaning and reveals itself to those who are receptive to it in dream. Malraux himself is something of a shaman. He sees his dreams and the interplay between his dreams and his life as means of probing the secret meaning of man's existence in the world. It is perhaps in large measure the persistence of this search— in his life, in his fiction, in his reflections on artistic creation, in his memoirs—that make his life and his works exemplary in so many ways.

Here, then, are fourteen essays, fourteen reflections sparked by and illuminating diverse aspects of Malraux's life, thought, and works. The viewpoints vary, as do the approaches and methodologies. Some of the essays present fresh and refreshing looks at Malraux and his works from a new critical perspective; hence "visions and re-visions" (see Susan Suleiman's opening paragraphs). All of the essays testify to Malraux's lasting impact as a man, as a thinker, as an artist. The volume as a whole seeks to *witness* Malraux as Malraux witnessed twentieth-century man; incompletely, to be sure; imperfectly, no doubt; but with the conviction that there is something in man and his quest, in this man and his quest, that demands such a witness.

Norman Rudich

MALRAUX CRITICISM: TWO

EXEMPLARY MODES

In this essay we shall compare two critical approaches to the early novels of André Malraux: the formalist and the sociological. The formalist approach is well exemplified by the pioneering work of Wilbur M. Frohock,[1] whose close and thorough explication of each text attends mainly to the literary problems of the internal relations between part and whole, plot, character, action, and theme. The sociological approach is represented by Lucien Goldmann,[2] who analyzes the same works from a genetic structuralist perspective in which formal analysis serves as prolegomenon to a sociological and historical understanding of Malraux's fiction. Although this broader framework is only suggested by reference to the further researches that would be necessary to complete the project, Goldmann's extended essay is permeated by considerations of Malraux's relationships to the social, political, and ideological situation in which he wrote his major works. Needless to say, my subject is not the personalities of Malraux's critics but their methods and the resultant influence of the methods upon the overall picture the critics convey of an important twentieth-century novelist and thinker. Interestingly enough, Frohock's straightforward literary study, largely positivist and formal in approach, overlaps significantly in some of its results with Goldmann's theoretical and sociological point of view. What emerges to a considerable degree is that opposition of methods does not exclude complementarity of insights and results.

Goldmann's point of departure is genetic structuralism, his general theory of cultural production, which interprets works of art, philosophy, political theory, and so on, as structured elaborations of more or less coherent currents of ideas or images produced spontaneously by different social classes or groups in the course of practical life under varying historical conditions. In his theoretical introduction to *Towards a Sociology of the Novel* he proposes a definition of the novel that points the way to his treatment of Malraux:

The novel form seems to me, in effect, to be the transposition on the literary plane of everyday life in the individualistic society created by market production. There is a rigorous homology between the literary form of the novel . . . and the everyday relation between man and commodities in general, and by extension between men and other men, in a market society. (G 6)

Why, then, should the novel instead of some other literary form be the genre par excellence of the market society? It is because the exchange value of commodities degrades their use value—their concrete qualities and human purposes—to a mere means to another end, that of market exchange which accumulates capital. The resulting relationships between men and things and among men produce a reified consciousness in which quality is subordinated to quantity and the creative individual is reduced to social marginality.

In view of this, there is nothing surprising about the creation of the novel as literary genre. Its apparently extremely complex form is the one in which men live every day, when they are obligated to seek all quality, all use value in a mode degraded by the mediation of quantity, of exchange value—and this in a society in which any effort to orient oneself *directly* towards use value can only produce individuals who are themselves degraded, but in a different mode, that of *the problematic individual*.

Thus the two structures, that of an important fictional genre and that of exchange proved to be strictly homologous, to the point at which one might speak of one and the same structure manifesting itself on two different planes. (G 8)

Goldmann derives the idea of the problematic individual from Lukác's *Theory of the Novel* (1920). The term refers to an entire gallery of nineteenth-century novelistic characters (for example, Julien Sorel, Lucien de Rubempré, Emma Bovary, Anna Karenina) who are (*a*) irremediably cut off from the societies in which they live, (*b*) faced with insoluble problems of self-realization, and (*c*) trapped in a situation which prevents them from achieving an exact consciousness of the nature of their plight. If they could achieve such an awareness they would become tragic characters. If they could realize themselves in the social life of their time and place they would approach the status of epic characters, although in a true epic the alienation of the individual is never as dismally complete as it is in the novel.

Goldmann perceives three states in the development of the novel, each corresponding to a stage in the economic development of capitalism. The problematic individual corresponds to the nineteenth-century free-market, liberal economy. The second period, monopoly capital, is one of transition in which the individual becomes more and more abstract, a helpless product of social forces, as in Zola, or a spokesman for alienated values, like the characters of Gide. The final stage sees the dissolution of the individual personality in a world of things, the *nouveau roman* of Robbe-Grillet being a prime example. In Goldmann's view Malraux is an author of the transition who combines problematic individuals and collective heroes, to whom we shall return in the body of this essay. Almost invariably Malraux is dealing with the relationship of an individual to the great revolutions of the twentieth century, in China, in Spain, and always on the horizon directly or indirectly is the shadow of the Soviet Union.

This does not mean that Goldmann is interested exclusively in the documentary function of the novel. He denounces Trotsky's critique of *Les Conquérants*, which "deals with the book as if it were a political tract" (*G* 36). He insists upon the "imaginary world" of the novel whose coherence is distinct from that of rational discourse, "for the sociologist of literature knows that very often formal requirements predominate over the conceptual convictions of the author" (*G* 36). Nevertheless, there are analogies between the imaginative and the philosophical productions of a given period which cannot be ignored if one wishes to understand the relationship of an author to his or her time. The crisis of individualist values which characterizes the twentieth century leads to a revival of reflection on the themes of death and action, individual and community, and the meaning of being human. These Pascalian themes are rediscovered by such thinkers as Lukács and Heidegger in philosophy, and Malraux in the novel (*G*

34)—themes that become basic structure of Malraux's political consciousness.

In Frohock's approach social and cultural theory remains largely implicit. He neither affirms nor denies the possibility of a sociology of literature. *André Malraux and the Tragic Imagination* is a systematic study of all the major works of his author from *Lunes en papier* (*Paper Moons*, 1921) to *Les Voix du silence* (*The Voices of Silence*, 1951). Frohock analyzes, interprets, and evaluates these works as the poetic expression of an individual artist and intellectual whose central preoccupation is the ultimate metaphysical question, What is man? and its corollary, What does it mean to be human in the twentieth century? This does not mean that Frohock intentionally slights the importance of politics to Malraux as a person or as an artist. On the contrary, he writes in his introduction: "We all subscribe, and Malraux more firmly than most, to the belief that the political problem is the crucial problem of our lives. The importance of politics in the work is precisely that the crucial nature of the political problem makes their poetry possible" (F xii).

An even more telling statement of this idea appears in Frohock's refutation of Harry Levin's complaint that Malraux's characters go about trying to be tragic heroes: "For precisely because politics is the central problem of our lives, they [Malraux's characters] become our surrogates" (F xii).

Frohock's application of this emphasis on politics in Malraux's novels shows that literary quality is at stake. The esthetic effectiveness of a work is related to the reader's sense of his or her own place in historical time. Both Conrad and Malraux deal with imperialism, but setting and character are altered by the twenty- to thirty-year interval that separates the two writers, as well as by their different approaches to the subject.

If Garine . . . moves us more deeply than does Perken, the reason is that the situation in *The Conquerors* is political and of general import, whereas the hero of *The Royal Way*, who is in no sense a political figure, seems involved in a more private and personal situation. (F xiii)

Nevertheless, Frohock subordinates politics to Malraux's broader philosophical themes: violence, suffering, death, solitude, fraternity, and so on. These are the structures of the human condition revealed by politics but not identical with it. Frohock aims to treat Malraux's work "primarily as the work of a poet," which means that its documentary value may show us "how he felt" at a particular time of his development. Politics must not prevent us from seeing that his works are essentially "dramatic poetry by an intellectual, for whom ideas become themes" (F xii).

In the following pages we shall sample this comparison more concretely by examining the ways in which various works of Malraux are analyzed and interpreted in terms of these two critical approaches. For the respectable reasons of space and time we shall in the main concentrate our efforts on *Lunes en papier*, *Royaume farfelu*, *Les Conquérants* (*The Conquerors*), and *La Condition humaine* (*Man's Fate*). Other works will be referred to when appropriate for illustrating interesting parallels or oppositions in the thinking of Frohock and Goldmann. The most fundamental job of a literary critic is, after all—no matter what else he or she may do—to provide stimulating, instructive, revealing readings of particular literary texts. From such readings there may emerge a sense of what Malraux is up to in the ensemble of his work; a literary personality takes shape. Finally, we shall reflect briefly upon the tensions between literary criticism and political ideology which are particularly unavoidable for Malraux's critics.

Malraux began his literary career in the early 1920s with two puzzling surrealistic works: *Lunes en papier* and *Royaume farfelu*. Frohock's first stated judgment is that Malraux "began his career writing stuff which is playful to the point of frivolity" (F 21); three pages later in his book he admits that Malraux showed talent but denies that he had yet found "a subject": "He has not yet had the experience which will give him something to say nor found a style of his own in which he can say it" (F 24). He attributes more seriousness to *Royaume farfelu* than to *Lunes en papier*. It foreshadows Malraux's later work: "*Royaume farfelu* is again dream stuff, but this time a dream populated by human beings and involving human adventure" (F 24). The critic, for good enough reasons, would like to hurry on to more serious matters.

But these works, surrealistic, bizarre, and apparently pointless as they are, say something significant to Goldmann whether they want to or not. Of *Royaume farfelu* he writes, "The essential content of this work seems to me to be both a consciousness of the vanity and universal death of values and the romantic aspiration to an unknown and unknowable value" (G 19). Fantasy is no escape from meaning. If dream is recountable at all it is because it, too, displays "signifying structures" which have roots in the social reality that produces "mental structures," language, and finally literary expression. What differentiates literature from the social matrix that generates it is its internal coherence, which reveals a qualitatively higher level of consciousness, "possible consciousness." As we have seen, literature is differentiated from the conceptual languages of theory by its creation of an "imaginary universe," the structures of which stand in strict homology to those of social life. This is true for fantasy as well as for realism.

Goldmann agrees with Frohock that *Royaume farfelu* taken by itself is not very good literature. In the light of Malraux's later work, however, Goldmann is prepared to take it quite seriously: "It possesses, among other things, an acute sensitivity to the intellectual and moral crisis of the western world, as felt by one of the most restless and most powerful intellects of the period" (*G* 22).

Frohock reads *Lunes en papier* as "a waking fantasy on a dream pattern" (*F* 23). His entire exposition is devoted to an excellent analysis of the fantastic imagery that attaches the young Malraux to the surrealist movement. He is struck by the fact that all the crazy virtuosities of form can no longer impress a modern reader.

Goldmann reads the fantasy as symbolic and allegorical: "The piece relates in effect the struggles of nonconformist writers against the *Royaume farfelu*, the Empire of Death, the bourgeois society of the period. However, Malraux does not believe in this struggle" (*G* 22).

Goldmann views the balloons that turn into funny little men, named after the deadly sins, as avant-garde artists who go on an adventurous expedition against a château guarded by a genie and an army of nondescript monsters. Although the artists are easily corrupted by a barrel of old brandy, they succeed in killing Death by dissolving his aluminum bones in a bath of acid. Finally, the full futility of this victory is made clear when the artists realize that they have forgotten why they wanted to kill death in the first place. Goldmann classifies *Lunes en papier* as a satire which turns to derision the pretensions of the avant-garde, the surrealists, to storm the bastions of bourgeois conformity and thus win immortality.

Before we comment upon the discussion of Malraux's two notable early novels, we must briefly explain the angle of vision from which Frohock's and Goldmann's approaches will be interpreted. *Les Conquérants* and *La Condition humaine* are both political novels in the most obvious sense of the term: they deal with political situations. (The same may be said of *Le Temps du mépris* [*Days of Wrath*] and of *L'Espoir* [*Man's Hope*].) *Les Noyers de l'Altenburg* (*The Walnut Trees of Altenburg*) is also a political novel, but for more complex reasons: it is grounded in stories of war upon which Malraux develops a complex philosophical debate concerning opposing theories of human history, culture, and civilization. The novel is constructed as a counterpoint between action and thought. The overwhelming question of

Malraux criticism would therefore seem to be: What is there in the
nature of revolution and war which makes them the subjects par excellence for Malraux, the artist and the intellectual? The points of
view of Frohock and Goldmann will be examined in the light of this
question.

Frohock elicits the tensions among the various levels of meaning
in *Les Conquérants* with great accuracy when he writes that Malraux
"conceived *The Conquerors* as political by its setting and action,
tragic by its tone, and metaphysical by its implications" (*F* 37). But
how are these different levels articulated? Malraux reveals his artistic
intention in his reply to Trotsky's critique. Garine, a man tortured by
angst and an acute sense of the absurdity of society, any society, and
of life itself, is meant to be a tragic hero: "Trotsky is looking for a
revolutionary, and Malraux is giving him a tragic hero who happens
to be involved in a revolution" (*F* 44). Now, if Garine's important political role in Canton is as fortuitous as Frohock seems here to suggest, he is implying that some other adventure or situation or style of
life could replace politics as the major setting or action of Garine's
life. One can just as well be haunted by angst and by the absurd if one
is an unknown functionary in some obscure bureau in North Africa
as one can if in a position of high authority in China. But neither Frohock nor Malraux believes that politics merely happens to Garine.
Politics is "the only situation in life which he finds tolerable"
(*F* 44). Why?

Goldmann invokes the same rubrics but reverses the emphasis.
Garine has chosen "historical action" on the side of "freedom, to
leave a mark of his existence in the world of men."

> The structure of his condition is complex for it cannot be defined, as can
> that of authentic revolutionaries, Borodin for example, solely, or even pri-
> marily, by his commitment in the struggle and his hopes for victory. The
> meaning of his participation in the conflict is mediatized and results
> from his desire to give meaning to his own existence. Garine is above all
> an individualist; it is, in effect, the desire to affirm himself *qua* individ-
> ual in opposition to the permanent and in the last resort inevitable
> threat—that of annihilation in the *Royaume farfelu*, in the Empire of
> Death. (*G* 46)

Thus Garine has chosen "a valid cause" despite the fact that action as
such and not value is his real goal. One might ask, then, could he just
as easily have joined the British and the Chinese bourgeoisie in putting down the Canton rebellion? Perhaps. At the end of the novel,
when death is imminent, Garine is asked where he would like to go.
He replies, "'To England, now I know what Empire is—one tena-

cious act of violence. To determine, to compel, that's life.'"[3] But the meaning of the novel would then be radically changed, not only politically but in its tragic and metaphysical dimensions as well. Garine had plenty of opportunity for action in the Foreign Legion or in World War I but rejected it in order to join a revolution. He is in the first place a refugee from the bourgeoisie and cannot escape the modicum of meaning which consists in standing against it. Both Frohock and Goldmann define Garine as an anarchist at heart, a man for whom action is a struggle against death; but neither answers the question of why he joins the revolution. In our view this is not a failing of our critics but of Malraux's novel, which makes the relationship of the individual to historical movements into a mystery. It will remain a mystery as long as the problem is envisaged only from the standpoint of the isolated individual. Starting with *La Condition humaine*, Malraux seriously raises the same problem explicitly in terms of the individual and the community of men. (Women play a small and minor role in Malraux's novels.)[4]

Goldmann is struck by Nikolaïeff's judgment, which he takes also to be Malraux's, that "Garine in power would run the risk of becoming a 'Mussolinist'" (*G* 45). Garine turns out to be in the last analysis an adventurer rather than a conqueror. For Frohock the most important point is not this hypothetical political future of Garine but his status as a symbol of the human condition: "He is meant to have the general significance of a tragic hero" (*F* 44). The tragic and the metaphysical axes rather than the political are decisive for understanding Malraux's art. The image of Garine sick unto death replaces that of the man of action who was seeking the meaning of his life in a revolution. Here is an example of how two very different conclusions supplement rather than negate one another, for by dying when he does Garine may be said to achieve a tragic victory despite the political ambiguities of his individualism, whereas Garine the Mussolinian adventurer would require another novel, one in which tragedy and metaphysics would simply have to go by the board.

In regard to *La Condition humaine* Goldmann and Frohock overlap and diverge significantly concerning the problem of the privileged position occupied by politics in the works of Malraux. Goldmann states:

But however important an element the "chronicle of the revolution" is (and it is much more important in *La Condition humaine* than in *Les Conquérants*) it remains, in the final resort, of secondary importance for a structuralist or even a merely literary analysis. The true novelty of the book lies in the fact that, in relation to the worlds of *La Voie royale* and

Les Conquérants, which were governed by the problem of the hero's individual realization, the world of *La Condition humaine* is governed by quite other laws and above all by a different value: *that of the revolutionary community.* (G 65)

This "revolutionary community" is more than a collection of individuals. Kyo, May, Katow, their friends, and the anonymous thousands of Shanghai militants who surround them, constitute a "collective problematic character" (G 65) which defines itself as being one with, but also opposed to, the International at Hangkow and as being against the Kuomintang. The position of this character is tragic because what Frohock calls "the logic of events" creates an unlivable conflict of values between two necessities: that of deepening the Shanghai revolution and that of maintaining party discipline.

Thus, Kyo's and May's total devotion to revolutionary action is also a total commitment to a tragic destiny. Goldmann points out that their private lives do not constitute a separate sphere, "for May and Kyo are characterized by the organic synthesis of their public and private lives, or, to use Lukács's expression, by the total synthesis of the individual and the citizen" (G 70).

This point reveals a basic strategy of Goldmann's genetic structuralism in action. The imaginary world of *La Condition humaine* reproduces by homology the dialectic of individual and society at a moment of revolutionary crisis. Chiang Kai-shek's betrayal of the Kuomintang's alliance with the Communists, on the one hand, and the orders issued by the International to disarm, on the other, isolate the militants of Shanghai. This situation supplies the totalizing infrastructure of the action. The organization of the isolated Communists of Shanghai is put to a supreme test, is forced into a tragic impasse. *La Condition humaine* recounts through the lives of exemplary individuals, such as Tchen, Kyo, May, and Gisors, the various significant ways in which the tragedy may be played out. They are exemplary but not in the manner of allegory; they are not mere emblems or symbols. They are exemplary because the consciousness of each is structurally related to the social complex that provides the space for their positions. They represent the highest, the most developed "possible consciousness" of the collective tragedy.

Thus Goldmann's concept of a "collective problematic character" provides a framework for relating individual and society at one level and major and minor characters at another. Frohock approaches the problem from a different direction. As always, he is sensitively aware of the technical complexities of novelistic construction. In a sense Tchen, Ferral, and Clappique are minor characters, "but with respect to the exposition of the book's essential subject they loom large and one hesitates to affirm that they are any less important than Katow and Kyo" (F 68). Any one of them could be the protagonist of a separate novel. How, then, should one define the position of these characters vis-à-vis the towering figures of Kyo and Katow? Frohock solves the problem in terms of a juxtaposition of "a number of individual human destinies with the destinies of the heroes of his central tragedy" (F 82). Thus the task of the critic is to relate the main story and the ancillary stories in a manner that will bring out the full meaning of their juxtaposition. A failure to account for both will lead to dire results: "Too exclusive interrogation of the ancillary gives . . . chaos. Too exclusive attention to the fate of Kyo and Katow gives back an answer too simplistic because too exclusively political" (F 82).

At this point the most basic difference between Frohock and Goldmann becomes visible. The political reading is not "simplistic" for Goldmann, since it encloses and entails in his view all the other major themes of the novel: love and death, action, dignity and humiliation, and so on. For Frohock La Condition humaine is a tragedy that is centrally focused on Kyo and Katow, but that "has intentions additional to the tragic ones" (F 68). For Goldmann the "collective character," the "revolutionary community," define the work in the first place as a political tragedy.

This contrast stands out in their different treatments of the death of Katow. The comparison is instructive enough to justify a juxtaposition of the pertinent passages:

This picture is what turns defeat into tragic victory and in a sense orients and orders all the values in the book. The destiny of the man whom the International has abandoned is so much more brilliant than the destinies of those who survive the insurrection that the political import of the novel pales before the more broadly human import. Revolution now seems to be not the subject but the setting in which the qualities and defects, the strengths and weaknesses of human character stand clearly out. (F 89)

In Les Conquérants and La Voie royale, death was the inevitable reality that rendered precarious and provisional all social values bound up with action, which annihilated them retroactively and brought the hero back to the formless, to absolute solitude, whereas in La Condition humaine it is, on the contrary, the moment that realizes in its entirety an organic union with action and a community with the other comrades. In the preceding novels death broke all links between the individual and the community. In La Condition humaine it ensures the final supersession of solitude. . . . That is why his [Kyo's] death is not an end: his life and his struggle will be taken up again by all those who continue the action after him . . . . Similarly, Katow's death is the moment at which he is reunited in the most intense way with the revolutionary community. (G 79–80)

The critics' argument is in no way a disagreement about the heroic nobility of Katow as an individual; the opposition lies rather in the concept of what constitutes individuality. Frohock understands individual character as originating from an immanent source in the human heart. Goldmann conceives individual character as the product of the social relations within which it develops. Katow's heroic self-sacrifice and death are the tragic victory of a defeated revolution. His entire life as a militant revolutionist on the side of the proletariat prepared him for that supreme moment. Of course, this contraposition of views invites a dialectical synthesis, but we shall leave that to the reader.

If time and space permitted, we could usefully extend this comparison to the other novels of Malraux. A number of similarities and contrasts of methods, interpretations, and conclusions attract the attention of the critic interested in literary theory. For example, Frohock sees Malraux's problem in *Le Temps du mépris* and in *L'Espoir* as the need to reconcile the requirements of art with those of propaganda. Goldmann recognizes that in those novels Malraux drew closer to the ideological and political positions of the Communist party, but does not use "propaganda" as a distinct category. At the same time, despite all their divergences, both critics agree (as we see from Frohock's skillful formal analysis and Goldmann's ideological point of view) that *L'Espoir* is a faultily constructed novel. Once more *Les Noyers de l'Altenburg* affords them the opportunity to differ, but this time Goldmann's political reading is opposed to Frohock's provocatively original and controversial anthropological interpretation—in which shamanism is generalized to an explanatory principle for Malraux's mythical personae and mythical characters (F 147).[5]

By limiting our study to *Les Conquérants* and *La Condition humaine*, however, we have eschewed global conclusions. Frohock keeps his promise to concentrate on Malraux primarily as a poet whose works display the creative power of the tragic imagination. And *tragic* here means "grim."

Our world is one of violence. We are here as on a darkling plain, certainly. But there is no good in appealing to love . . . not love but suffering is the rule. And the suffering is irremediable. Cruelty is everywhere; all men experience it, and all men are capable of inflicting it. Each is tortured by his private anxieties and obsessions. And at the end is death and nothing more. This is man's destiny. (F 148)

But it is the refusal to bow to this fate, to accept the absurd ingrained in the human condition, which bestows upon the species "the power and the glory" of being human. Invariably, Malraux's characters discover this power and glory in purposeful action, which is almost invariably political action, even when their avowed purpose is to quiet a private torment. Besides, politics means more than any particular party can confer, since it always means more than itself:

One way to put it would be to say that Malraux's politics seems always to have been a politics of refusal. He has chosen his shifting political colors with reference to what, at any particular time he could *not* accept. The focus of his "fidelities" has not lain in the parties themselves, but in a set of values which—according to the moment—one party or another has appeared best able to protect. What those values are is implicit in all of his work, explicit in his writings upon art. (F 164)

Malraux's politics are therefore fought out on the field of human values. What remains permanent throughout his fiction and his theory of art, according to Frohock, is a broad humanism which he defended first against nazism and then against Stalinist communism. And so, to answer our own original question of why politics hold such a privileged place in Malraux's works, it is because our century more than any other has realized the conjunction of the problematics of political and ethical action. This is why Malraux's characters can be our surrogates, despite the distance that separates most of us from their direct involvement in the struggle for power. We can identify with them in terms of our humanity.

Now, as may be expected, Goldmann to a large extent agrees with this judgment while imparting to it a characteristic change of emphasis.

It seems to me that Malraux is the only writer, apart from Victor Serge, to make the proletarian revolution an important structural element in his novels. Indeed, between 1927 and 1939, Malraux was the only great novelist of this revolution in France. (G 35)

Thus it is not the political as such that makes the difference. It is specifically the proletarian revolution, the revolution of the twentieth century, which Malraux transforms into the imaginary structures and substance of his fiction. That change of angle has its consequences for Goldmann's formulation of what constitutes Malraux's broader humanism:

Would it be too daring to remind ourselves here of our initial hypothesis that the properly literary work of the writer, the possibility of his creating concrete imaginary worlds in a realistic way, was closely bound up with a faith in human values that were universally accessible to all men, the conceptual writings corresponding on the contrary to the *absence* of such a faith that this absence took the form either of the earlier disillusion or of the theory of creative élites that appears first in *Les Noyers de l'Altenburg* and is developed from *Le Musée imaginaire* onwards. (*G* 28–29)

Goldmann is here basing himself on a theory of literary genre derived from Lukács (*G* 106). The imaginary concrete of the novel is contrasted with the conceptual abstract of philosophy. Between them falls the essay, a literary form sui generis, ironic by its very nature because it raises problems that elude philosophical solutions. *Les Noyers* is, properly speaking, neither an essay nor a novel, but an intermediate form which uses fictional situations to raise conceptual issues. By its very structure it reveals an ideological crisis. Malraux, like many other intellectuals of the late thirties, suffered a disenchantment with communism which profoundly changed his political and artistic orientations. He ceased to be an artist.

In terms of this theory, art is the locus par excellence of positive human values. Malraux's shift to anthropology and art history implies the abandonment of the basic faith in the proletarian revolution and mankind which lies at the foundation of his artistic powers. In his discussions of *Les Noyers*, as of *Les Voix du silence*, Goldmann, who does not deal directly with Malraux's nonfiction, retains as most significant the theory of "creative élites."

On this important point we agree wholeheartedly with Frohock. Despite all the ambiguities of Malraux's politics after World War II, despite his adherence to the Gaullist right wing, his later conceptual writings continue to express the broad humanism that all of us must recognize in his novels. The theory of "creative élites" is less important than the refutation of the reactionary Spengler. It is less important than the affirmation of the continuity of human culture, which is a renewal, although on a different level, of faith in man's fate.

What then emerges from this comparison of two modes of criticism? Frohock's examination of Malraux's tragic vision locates its center in the metaphysical experience of the absurd. The lucid acknowledgment of this universal condition of human existence is the prerequisite of the heroism that consists in refusing it. Malraux's main characters try to live in awareness of the absurd while acting as if it did not exist. The meaning of life must be created by the alienated individual through a significant action in the world. This action is most frequently political in nature and affords the experience of "virile fraternity," which overcomes the solitude of man's fate. The art of civilization is the highest expression of this "anti-destiny."

Goldmann, the Marxist sociologist, has a different key term: values. Over the past 150 years, as capitalist society has evolved from a liberal market economy to monopoly and then to technocratic state control, these changes have been registered in the novel of the problematic individual, in the novel of the victimized individual, and finally, in the *nouveau roman*, of the disappearance of the individual. These successive stages reflect a crisis of western individualism. Malraux emerges as one of the great interpreters of this crisis.

In his major fictional works, Malraux examines the dialectic of the alienated individual who discovers in the politics of revolution the collective purpose, human solidarity, and community which give meaning to his life and death. In this dialectic the individual is not negated, does not simply fuse indistinguishably into the community. On the contrary, he discovers and affirms himself as a historical individual whose life has a sense beyond the immediate limits of his own biography. In Malraux's work, individual characters like Garine, Kyo, Katow, and Vincent Berger represent some aspect of a collective character with whom their fates are bound. In this sense, Malraux is a great realist whose creations reproduce imaginatively and by homology the most profound drama of our century. His work will live as esthetic realization, documentary witness, and ideological current of the highest significance for readers of the future.

Mary M. Rowan

ASIA OUT OF FOCUS: DECODING

MALRAUX'S ORIENT

During his stay in the Far East of the twenties, André Malraux first encountered the turbulent atmosphere that inspired his career as an intellectual man of action. Not only the author's two-year stay in French colonial Indochina but also the immediacy of his oriental settings have been adduced as evidence of the realism of the backgrounds of *Les Conquérants*, *La Voie royale*, and *La Condition humaine*. Some critics have cited these three Asian novels as evidence of Malraux's personal involvement in the scenes presented—a type of fictionalized reportage.[1] This has led to the use of tenuous biographical data as a key to the texts. Walter Langlois examined the details of Malraux's Indochinese adventures of 1923,[2] while Jean Lacouture evaluated the biographical data in *André Malraux: Une vie*

dans le siècle.[3] The former work details Malraux's stay in Angkor, Phnom Penh, and Saigon in the 1920s and his lack of firsthand knowledge of China until after 1931. The latter work establishes the amateurish quality of the young man's training, at the Ecole des Langues Orientales (School of Oriental Languages) and as an archeologist, before his departure for Indochina in 1923.

I contend here that Malraux's portrait of the Orient depends on technical innovations drawn from the cinema and expressed in elliptical language. The cinematic techniques of cross-cutting and fadeouts with rapid changes of focus allow him to circumvent specific descriptions. He introduces each exotic locale in a wide-angle panoramic shot, then cuts to a series of closeup frames that fill in foreign details. Painterly touches sometimes soften this stark interplay of perspectives, through which Malraux creates a convincing illusion of the Orient.

Wilbur M. Frohock early noted that Malraux's craft relied upon ellipsis. He also underscored the visual acuity of the author's "basically cinematographic imagination,"[4] an approach developed later by Jean Carduner and Franz J. Albersmeier.[5] Malraux himself first signaled the impact on the novel of the birth of film: "Each great art, through its birth alone, modifies those of the past . . . the cinema corrodes all art of illusion, perspective, movement, tomorrow relief."[6] So Malraux's illusion of Asia owes its authenticity more to the author's mastery of filmic sleight of hand than to his profound knowledge of place. The authorial eye becomes the zoom lens of the camera.

In addition to a language of ellipsis and negation, a network of sensory images sustains each Asian locale. *Les Conquérants* appeals to hearing through the alternation of noise and silence, which combine to depict Saigon, Hong Kong, and Canton. The Cambodian jungle of *La Voie royale* is evoked through the sense of smell—the external stench of rotting vines and leaves internalized in Grabot's syphilitic sores and in Perken's festering knee wound. The sense of smell contrasts with the sense of sight, extinguished in Grabot, who is deprived of his eyes, and beclouded in Perken and the narrator, who are unable to see clearly enough to judge their own and others' behavior correctly. Nature becomes a blind, external force, a putrefying jungle against which man builds flimsy shelters like the Bangkok brothel, the convoy's tents, and the Moï huts. In *La Condition humaine*, all five senses combine to evoke the international city of Shanghai in 1927, a place Malraux did not visit until after the book's publication in 1933.

These techniques of cutting and blurring, together with the underlying sense imagery, will be analyzed in each novel to discover the secret of Malraux's mythic Asia, less true but more compelling than any precise geographic location.

Les Conquérants

Malraux pictures Saigon's French colonial quarters in a panoramic shot: "A desolate city, deserted, provincial, with long avenues and straight boulevards where the grass grows under huge tropical trees" (*C* 5). Although the description is faithful, only the word *tropical* evokes a specific sense of place. Otherwise, the description could apply to any French town. Malraux never names the trees. He opposes to the panorama of the French colonial section a closeup of Cholon, the Chinese quarter, which is distinguished by an atmosphere where "life is nothing more than light and noises; profusion of reflectors, mirrors, globes and bulbs, noises of Mah-Jongg, phonographs, cries of singers, sharp flutes, cymbals, gongs . . ." (*C* 11). The book's prevailing sense image, noise, already has been attached to the Vietnamese ("noise of clogs" [*C* 6]). Here in the opium den restaurant of Cholon, noise becomes more abstract, as it becomes more clearly an image of the Chinese: "A din that is drowned out by the salvos of firecrackers, the crackling of dominoes, the striking of gongs, and from time to time, the miaowing of the single-string violin . . ." (*C* 12).

Malraux refuses the common colonial practice of using native terms to describe local objects, such as *fan-tan* for dominoes. The narrator and Gérard close the Cholon scene by leaving the quarter which has degenerated into "the racket of the Chinese restaurants" (*C* 12).

The narrator neglects to name the Pearl River, which he navigates en route to Hong Kong. There, the panoramic view focuses first on the distant Peak, "the powerful mass of the famous rock" (*C* 23) and then on the surrounding port, "in the bay, very numerous, great steamships sleep, illuminated" (*C* 24). Both of these trademark features of the Crown Colony are familiar from postcards, posters, and documentary films. As the narrator enjoys the view, a junk's vertical sail suddenly obscures his line of vision, eliminating the need for closer description. The details of Hong Kong appear when the narrator walks through its streets, marked by Chinese signs, which he looks at like artifacts, noting only their design and color. Although he is supposed to read and speak Chinese, he ignores the content of the signs. When he approaches the Chinese merchants without speaking to them, they look away and stare up at the ceilings, from which hang "dried cuttlefish, squid, fish, black sausages, lacquered ducks the color of ham" (*C* 25). Critics cite these and similar lists as evidence of Malraux's firsthand knowledge of daily life in China, ignoring the fact that these lists contain objects found in Chinatowns all over the world—in San Francisco and Singapore as well as in Cholon.

The lack of normal noise in Hong Kong adds to the menace of the strike: "silence, without the itinerant merchants' sing-song cries, without Chinese firecrackers, without birds, without cicadas" (C 30). The silence of Klein and the narrator on the second lap of the voyage to Canton is broken by the cries, shrieks, and disputes at dockside upon their arrival. The noise, however, prevents them from observing the activity in the European factory of Shameen, the prize of the Canton strike. Instead, the narrator defines the strikebound city by the absence of men on the sampans, where he observes old women cooking as children play, "lighter and more animated than cats, despite their pear-shaped, rice-eaters' bellies" (C 50). First compared to animals, later the women and children shrink to spots of colors, "the smocks and trousers of the women, blue spots, and the children, climbing up the roofs, yellow spots" (C 50). Seen from the same long distance, the masses in the streets become only a blue-and-white multitude (C 51).

The Chinese are often compared to animals in a series of metaphors, such as: "the mastiff who is the owner" (C 12); "Tang and the second-class pigs" (C 56); or "all Chinese cities are squishy as jellyfish" (C 57). Elsewhere, women on bound feet scurry like penguins, while during a strike meeting the workers vote by moving their necks forward like "dogs that bark without their body moving" (C 104). Before his conversion to Marxism, the terrorist, Hong, had been one of those "whom a diet of fodder kept in a kind of stupidity and constant weakness" (C 97). Thus the beastly state of the masses is contrasted to the rarefied culture of the intellectual mandarin Tcheng-Daï.

Central to all three novels, illness remains the most powerful metaphor for Asia. The narrator of Les Conquérants observes the hero, Garine, and notes: "The most ancient power of Asia reappeared: the hospitals of Hong Kong . . . are full of sick people, and, on this paper yellowed by the light, it is once again a sick man who writes to another sick man" (C 97). Garine assumes the burden of his own illness when he recognizes that "'sickness is oneself'" (C 102), and even the cynical torturer Nicolaïeff muses that, with their way of living, "'one never escapes the tropics completely'" (C 111), thus arriving at the final conflation of illness and Asia.

The contrasts between European and native quarters in the cities of Saigon, Hong Kong, and Canton serve only as a backdrop against which the characters' conflicts demonstrate the philosophic polarities between East and West. Prior to his departure for Cambodia in 1923, Malraux had read widely on the subject of oriental art, one of his early passions. After failing to leave Cambodia with the carvings from Banteay-Srei, he spent several months imprisoned and on trial in Phnom Penh. Then he moved to Saigon, where he spent two years as editor of the newspapers *Indochine* and *Indochine enchaînée*, interrupted only by a brief visit to Hong Kong. Malraux did not have to visit Canton to create the setting for this novel, as he had the raw materials to hand in Cholon, Saigon's Chinese quarter, which his judicious enlarging transformed into the South China port city.

La Voie royale

The captain of the steamer on which Claude Vannec and Perken sail to Singapore shows how the conception of the exploit precedes its execution when he tells Claude that " 'Every adventurer is born from a mythomaniac' " (*VR* 182). The adventurers' destination is evoked in painterly terms as Claude consults his archeological inventory of Siam and Cambodia during the voyage.

From the lines marked on his map, he conjures up a dream palace of Angkor in the technicolor of his youthful imagination. He visualizes the coordinates of the map as the lost cities which await him "the great blue spots with which he had surrounded the dead cities, by the dots of the old Royal Way" (*VR* 178). As if to butt his head against a wall, or project an image on a screen, he throws his imagination "against these capitals of dust, of lianas and of towers with faces, crushed under the blue spots of dead cities" (*VR* 180). Claude builds his palace from data gathered from old travel narrative descriptions and his mind's eye sees "the temples, the stone gods tarnished by mosses, a frog on one shoulder and, their eaten-away [rongée] heads on the ground beside them" (*VR* 181). Before ever having seen them, Claude describes the temples with greater precision than he does once on the spot.

In shipboard conversations, the primacy of the senses of smell and sight are established as well. At Singapore the adventurers part company, as Claude heads for Saigon and Perken goes to Bangkok to prepare the expedition, planning to meet again in Phnom Penh, from where they will depart for the jungle. First, Claude encounters Albert Ramèges in the offices of the French Institute in Saigon, a city which he feels means "colony" as Ramèges himself personifies "bureaucrat." Although Claude insists to Ramèges upon his standing as an orientalist and linguist, " 'I didn't fall from the heavens, but from the

School of Oriental Languages'" (*VR* 193), he never displays his talents. Once in the field, Perken, the mentor who has learned native languages through trial and error, does all the interpreting essential to the plot. Only Perken, the man of experience, knows Siamese well enough to make the natives reveal their secrets.

After Claude's confrontation with Ramèges in Saigon, the scene fades to Siem-Reap, a small town near Angkor, thus obviating any reason to describe Singapore, Bangkok, or Phnom Penh. Claude and Perken arrive on a motorboat and strain to glimpse the towers of Angkor Wat through the foliage. But they see only the beginning of the rain forest, "the odor of mud stretching itself slowly in the sun, of the stale foam drying, of the beasts decomposing . . . the slimy appearance of mud-colored amphibians stuck to the branches" (*VR* 206).

Once on land, they rush to the Residence and never see Angkor, since when the driver points it out to them, "Claude could not see more than twenty meters ahead" (*VR* 207). Even when Claude and Perken talk on the great stone causeway leading to the monument, Angkor escapes them in the darkness, which is relieved only the glow of joss sticks: ". . . half of the stars hidden by the colossal mass spread out before them and which imposed itself, without their seeing it, by its simple presence in the shadow" (*VR* 217).

The adventurers set off from Siem Reap to Banteay-Srei, a temple now easily reached in a few hours by car. They lead a procession of clumsy oxcarts into a slimy, sticky, fetid rain forest, crawling with spiders, leeches, flies, and red ants which resume the theme of illness aways implicit in Asia, "the stifling gangrene of the forest" (*VR* 238).

The travelers glimpse clusters of straw huts on stilts which form the towns of the rare jungle clearings in the flickering light of joss sticks burning before savage Buddhas. After the failure of their attempts to seize the statues of the temples of the Royal Way, they decide to seek out other temples in dissident territory. After half of the carts and all of the drivers have deserted them, Claude and Perken set off for the country of the Steings and Moï, using a Cambodian guide who also resembles a statue: "The stocky Cambodian, his nose curved like those of the Buddhas, had just left the horse and, his hands crossed, was waiting" (*VR* 244). The dissidents' territory, vaguely located in the west, displays none of the voluptuous nonchalance of Laos and lower Cambodia, but only "savagery with its stench of meat" (*VR* 247).

In a conversation aboard the ship with the forester—a twenty-seven-year veteran of the colonies—the degenerate character of the natives of the frontier villages had been predicted. He had described the natives as "'malarial, their eyelids blue as though one had been striking them for a week, capable of nothing'" (*VR* 189). Here reality proves worse than imagination and the inhabitants of the dissident territories in their filthy sarongs seem less than human. Indeed, their Moï guide is on the borderline of savagery, "neither completely animal nor completely human" (*VR* 248). They encounter three Moïs on the path who stare at them, fixed in an inhuman immobility.

Absence and negation define the land of the Montagnards: "No palms; Asia was present only through its heat, the colossal dimensions of a few trees with red trunks and the density of the silence" (*VR* 249). The earlier descriptions of the lowland tropics are negated to describe the hill-country villages and their inhabitants, savage denizens of the menacing tropics.

Described through an accumulation of detailed closeups, the Cambodian jungle is the most believable of Malraux's Asian settings, revealing his familiarity with the Angkor area. Even this description is exaggerated, however, to seem more isolated and wild than this relatively civilized section of Cambodia was even sixty years ago.

La Condition humaine

The process of abstraction culminates in the masterpiece, *La Condition humaine*, from which local color has been eliminated. The city where the various characters with different beliefs meet in the hours of the uprising is described in the most general terms. Shanghai itself becomes a map for the hero Kyo: "He walked no longer in the mud but on a map" (*CH* 326). Place names like the factory quarters of Pootung and Tchapéï or the suburban railroad station Tcheng-Tchéou are added for authenticity. These names could have been drawn from any account of the strike.

Here, the painterly device of chiaroscuro supplements the filmic technique of cross-cutting to produce an impression of China. Clouds, rain, and fog—the alternation of light and dark—flicker over the novel, obscuring Shanghai, which is important only as a stage setting for revolution: "Some very low clouds, heavily massed, torn apart in places, no longer allowed the last stars to appear except in the depths of their tears" (*CH* 326). The city dissolves into a rosy glow under the steady rain: "The troops advanced, guns shining with rain, toward Shanghai, reddish in the depths of the night" (*CH* 340). Shrouded by fog, the workers themselves become shadows as they prepare the revolt: "On the roofs some shadows were already at their post" (*CH* 353). The most important events of the revolt occur at night and in the midst of "dense fog and thick night" (*CH* 501). Kyo is captured upon leaving the Black Cat with May. The fates of all the other characters after Kyo's death are resolved in the glare of daylight.

European and Asian characters blend to form a human chiaroscuro in the central figure of the *métis*, or half-breed. A marginal man, the half-breed must master the world views of both East and West. He is balanced on the knife edge of the future. He stands between the anonymous Chinese masses laboring in poverty, illness, and despair and the effete Mandarins studying the past. The Europeans, each one obsessed by his unique mania—power for Ferral, politics for Katow, esthetics for Gisors, and fantasy for Clappique—are accessories only. The half-breed seeks through exercise of individual liberty to arrive at a new solution to the problem of absurdity, a solution neither of the Orient nor the Occident.

The hero, Kyo, who encourages the struggles of the Chinese workers, has been educated between the ages of eight and seventeen in Japan, his mother's homeland. He bears no resemblance to Gisors, his French father; he displays his mother's blood in his samurai features. Only after his capture do we learn that his Chinese name, Kyo, is an abbreviation of his true Japanese name, Kyoshi. His mixed blood has attracted Kyo to the workers' struggle because he too has been excluded from mainstream society: "Half-breed, without caste, disdained by white men and even more by white women, Kyo hadn't even tried to seduce them: he had looked for his own [the oppressed] and he had found them" (*CH* 361).

Tchen, the logical development of Hong, the terrorist of *Les Conquérants*, may be termed a spiritual half-breed; under the tutelage of his mentor, Gisors, he has even come to hate his own Chinese good sense. Converted early to Christianity and then separated from it through Gisors's influence, Tchen has been divorced from the culture of his ancestors; because of his total liberty he has dedicated himself completely to ideas.

Orientals display European qualities, while Europeans absorb the traits of their Asian surroundings. Gisors, a European connoisseur of Chinese painting, smokes opium, a practice in which Ferral joins him. Old China appears only as a vision in Gisors's drugged daydream as he remembers a day near a lakeside temple where a monk on a curved bridge watched peasants gathering water lily seeds. A commonplace of Chinese landscape scrolls, the idyllic scene of Gisors projects the image of the world the revolution will destroy. In contrast, the banners of the strikers in the streets carry the international slogans of revolution imported from Russia.

The Chinese are again compared to animals. Tchen is called a hawk. Surrounded by corpses after the carnage at the police station, the Chinese coachman weeps for his horses, not his countrymen. Liou-Ti-Uy, leader of the Shanghai bankers, is like an old frog; but the wrinkled eyes of the old usurer are like those of money lenders anywhere on earth. The midnight crowds seem to Kyo like millions of fish making their way through trembling black waters. The terms of comparison remind one of *Les Conquérants*, but the manner of expression has been much refined.

Malraux's image of Asia in each novel thus owes more to the author's interior vision than to his firsthand knowledge of his settings. Neither the individual city nor the looming jungle ever acquires a uniquely identifiable exotic character. Generations of writers of Asian travel narratives achieved the "local color" dear to the genre through an accumulation of detailed descriptions of the everyday life in foreign places. Malraux banishes local color from his novels, which avoid picturesque details of the daily round. He relies on an art of negation and ellipsis, opposed to the conventional reportorial craft, to summon up a foreign atmosphere. The author refers often to maps, travel narratives, and banners that portray the Word (*Logos*) as the foundation stone of his own vision of Asia. Upon this series of abstract signs, he builds up a pattern of life in the Far East by creating a synthesis of words and symbols drawn from literature and painting, both European and Oriental.

Through constant use of the cinematographic devices of cross-cutting and blurring, Malraux distances himself from his setting, glimpsed through veils of rapidly shifting perspectives. He maintains this distance from his characters also. His heroes are either expatriate Europeans or displaced half-breeds, neither of whom evidence much sympathy for the native masses, usually compared to animals.

And yet, these very processes of abstraction serve to create a foreign locale and to evoke a world that is truly "Other" and thus, truly strange. This imaginary Asia becomes more powerful than any meticulous description of real places might have been. It is the antipode of Europe, a backdrop against which the struggles of twentieth century man are fought out. The remoteness of these abstract settings highlights the problems of the protagonists, which attain an urgency on the unfamiliar Asian stage unobtainable in a contemporary European theater. The common themes of the three novels—the rebellion of the individual and the revolution of the group—assume pressing intensity in this imaginary territory, which remains remote from the direct concerns of the European reader, left free to intellectualize about explosive subjects at a safe distance. These novels' essential subjects are those ideological struggles that would erupt in Europe only in the mid-thirties. Malraux's mythic Asia attests to the predictive value of his narratives and the solidity of their philosophical commitment.

Sergio Villani

MALRAUX'S SAINT-JUST

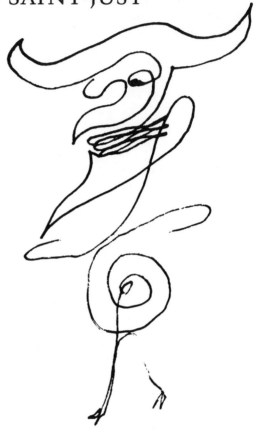

And your friend Saint-Just," de Gaulle adds, as he gives Malraux examples of fiery, intense lives that momentarily brighten history and are then quickly and mysteriously snuffed out, replaced on the road to greatness by other favorites of Lady Fortune.[1] The general's phrase arrests and, perhaps, even startles the reader who may not be aware of Malraux's lifelong interest in Louis Antoine de Saint-Just (1767–94), the Robespierrist commonly remembered as the "archangel of the Terror."[2] The reader more familiar with Malraux is almost equally intrigued to recall some of the novelist's many allusions to Saint-Just, especially in his political addresses. What was the nature of the "friendship" between Malraux and Saint-Just? Inevitably one makes an effort to clarify this rather strange relationship;

and, indeed, upon reflection, it becomes clear that the influence on Malraux of the historical and legendary Saint-Just was considerable and fascinating. Saint-Just was not only a model for the impassioned adventurers of Malraux the novelist but also a source of inspiration for the commander who marched to liberate Alsace-Lorraine and for the statesman who helped shape a new republic in the wake of World War II. For Malraux, Saint-Just, a man obsessed with a sense of greatness, incarnated the energy, the potential for those exemplary actions that make history and nurture in men the consciousness and pride to "bear witness" to human grandeur.[3] Saint-Just's brief life manifested the active, anxious intellectualism that characterized Malraux himself.

Although intellectual, "rhetorical," and a type, the Malrucian hero is never an abstraction and is always defined by a gamut of tragic actions in a particularized geographic and historical setting; in other words, he has a concrete dimension and a cultural identity. Invariably this context is "revolutionary"; that is, according to Malraux, a period of youthful, virile exaltation when the "possible" and a deeply felt "hope" of justice reign supreme (*SJ* 11), a period of "universal values" and "universalizable form of action."[4] In this atmosphere of limitless potential, Saint-Just's notion of "the strength of events [*la force des choses*]" foils the schemes of men who counter the swirls of the prevailing current. On the other hand, the individual who is able to ride the movement of the times is filled with its power, with which he conquers and transforms the character of the world. Thus Malraux remarks that during the French Revolution Saint-Just was guillotined and Hoche was poisoned, but Napoleon was able to affirm his will over the French nation (*CA* 104). The "conqueror," whose "principal trait is an inflexible will," does not so much engineer revolutions as he exploits and directs the energies of revolutionary events.[5] Malraux was thus attracted to revolutionary periods because in their arena of intense energy one could best see man's misery and grandeur, his tragic confrontation with the absurd (humiliation, suffering, death), a malaise of negative hypersensitivity. In the case of the French Revolution, he saw this fundamental human struggle epitomized in the life of Saint-Just, a product and a victim of his historical moment but also of his own will and sense of history.

In his 1954 preface to Albert Ollivier's study of Saint-Just,[6] Malraux attempts to portray all the complexity of this historical figure so often adumbrated by his legendary aura. In general he draws a distinction and tries to establish a relationship between the intellectual whose thoughts and actions were commanded by the vision of an ideal social order and the cruel pragmatist who deemed any means appropriate for achieving his goals. For Malraux, the pragmatist in Saint-Just served at all times the visionary. Although in this essay he does not directly refer to Saint-Just's epic poem *Organt*—which, like his own *Condition humaine*, illustrates a desperate view of man's fate—nor to Saint-Just's writings on the Republic and republican institutions, one has the distinct impression that he was very familiar with these works. On the other hand, Malraux often underlines Saint-Just's need to express an "irremediable epic" (*SJ* 22). Saint-Just thus served the Revolution and the Republic with a religious fervor that bordered on fanaticism; for him, the Republic, a "supreme value," was "not only a form of government, but first an Apocalypse, and the hope of an unknown world" (*SJ* 23). Saint-Just's "future city," according to Malraux, is a totalitarian state, governed by a "single and all-powerful party," which would establish a "spartan society" (*SJ* 19–20). To attain this ideal state Saint-Just intended to turn the disorder of the Revolution into an instrument of order. By means of "exemplary actions" he wanted to fill men with the idea of greatness and, thereby, make them participate in a "transfiguring epic" (*SJ* 27), "the greatest adventure of the Revolution." Malraux thus suggests that Saint-Just's strange silence, his "bitter indifference," his loyalty to his friends during his trial and, once condemned, as he marched to the scaffold, comprised a premeditated attitude designed to attract death in order to make his death his greatest exemplary action, an action that witnessed "the truth that possessed him." "He seems to call on death," writes Malraux, "as the necessary and impending end of his life" (*SJ* 24). In this he resembles Malraux's own heroes (Kyo, Katow, Tcheng-Daï, and others) who find it necessary to make their self-sacrifice exemplary and know that this martyrdom will catapult them into legend. In fact, according to Malraux, "the *aura* of Saint-Just," the mythic figure born out of a "legendary time," has become an intrinsic part of history. Michelet's "Shakespearean figure" made up of contrasting, monstrous qualities has affirmed and magnified itself: the handsome youth who radiates an air of innocence is at the same time the archangel of the Terror who inflicts suffering and death everywhere; the "exemplary friend" harbors the ·"terrible," "great accuser"; the brilliant orator whose rhetoric condemns Louis XVI to death is also the proud, disdainful man, the victim of his own sense of justice, which equates guilt with political power ("on ne règne pas innocemment");[7] the leader who silently and fatalistically accepts his condemnation contrasts with the knowledgeable soldier, "echo of Bonaparte" (*SJ* 15).

Malraux's Saint-Just is thus a complex figure who admirably combines the potentials for action, intellectualism, and self-sacrifice. History and legend give rise to a heroic form that becomes for Malraux a model to imitate, a force prompting active social involvement.

This influence first manifested itself during the Resistance. In 1944 Malraux organized a small army and marched to liberate Alsace-Lorraine. One hundred and fifty years earlier, Saint-Just had also led an army to quell the royalist insurrection in the Rhine, Mosel, and Ardennes regions. As colonel of the independent Alsace-Lorraine Brigade, Malraux assumed the name Berger because it was common in the region of the mission, thus providing some security cover, and, as noted by Pierre Galante,[8] in memory of Berger de Reichbach, an Alsatian family prominent before 1870, whose name he had already borrowed in *Les Noyers de l'Altenburg* ("my grandfather Vincent Berger"). However, if one supposes that Malraux with his brigade was following the example of his heroic figure Saint-Just and thus in some way reenacting history, it is also possible that the fictitious name was suggested to him by the agent Berger, follower of Robespierre and one of Saint-Just's chief collaborators in his mission into Alsace.[9]

After the liberation of France, as various political forces fought to give form to a new Republic, Malraux became a leading supporter of de Gaulle. The general atmosphere of disarray and destruction, the punitive trials of the collaborators, and the urgent need to reestablish strong foundations and respect for the country's institutions undoubtedly at this time recalled for Malraux the era of reconstruction preceding and during the First Republic and, necessarily, one of its major artisans, Louis de Saint-Just. In 1945, as Minister of Information in de Gaulle's second cabinet; in 1947, in charge of propaganda during the *rassemblement*; in 1958, when a new constitutional program was presented to the French people; and, indeed, whenever the occasion presented itself to speak a "fraternal language" and equate the names of France and the Republic with courage, pride, freedom, and sacrifice, Malraux almost always evoked the name of Saint-Just. "For the moment," he wrote in 1951, "she [the Republic] sleeps—like France. Let her sleep: if she would awaken, she could recall for you, through the voice of Saint-Just, that she does not dwell deep in the heart of the humblest men of France because she was skillful in political alliances, but because in the past she brought them the fraternal language of courage and pride."[10] He associated Saint-Just not only with a social and spiritual ideal that has immemorially inspired and unified the French people but also with a realistic, pragmatic sense that, in the midst of disorder and rivaling currents, gives one the readiness to exploit the dominating social trend. This consciousness of present realities ("the strength of events") dictates duty, active involvement, and sacrifice. Malraux himself adhered to this principle of action: tragic social conditions demand an energetic, humanistic response, not indifference and passivity. In de Gaulle's and Malraux's words, "Justice is based on hope, on the exaltation of a country, and not on slippers" (CA 24). Thus, quite instinctively responding to these principles, Malraux made his presence felt in numerous noble causes from the Spanish civil war to the plight of the Biafrans. During his early political career he repeatedly supported the "association capital/work," not because he believed in this interaction but, he explains to de Gaulle, because of his adherence to what Saint-Just called "the strength of events" (CA 23). According to Malraux, Saint-Just gained power over the politicians because he defined himself not by means of ideology but with the "eloquence of actions" (CA 38). So, too, his own characters in L'Espoir, after the initial "lyrical illusion," realize that fraternity and justice, like political ideology, must acquire the form of action in order to become effective and meaningful.[11] For Malraux, Saint-Just's life presented a gallery of exemplary actions put at the service of freedom and the Republic, not because of zeal for the proletariat—"nothing is farther from Saint-Just than the idea of proletariat" (SJ 18)—but because of a passion for freedom itself. "During the Resistance," Malraux explained in an interview, "I espoused France. [. . .] I replaced the proletariat with France."[12]

To what extent did such an image of idealism and action, intellectual and physical energy, influence the creation of Malraux's fictional heroes? James Greenlee notes that Malraux's adjective "accusatory" [accusatrice], used to describe the conduct of T. E. Lawrence in the Middle East, can also be applied to his "fictional European adventurers in the Far East."[13] Indeed, many of Malraux's heroes, and not only the European adventurers, denounce and witness "a mode of life" in natural and social injustices. In a similar way the attitude is also proper to the historical Saint-Just, who was used by the Committee of Public Safety to denounce its foes before the Convention; because of his role, the historian Eugene Curtis has named him "the Accusative."[14] The Malrucian hero's attitude may be generally related to Saint-Just; it would perhaps be exaggerated, however, to suggest that because of this common trait Malraux modeled his characters after the fabled leader of the Terror. The exception is Garine; in fact, several indicants link Garine to Saint-Just. First of all, his name: just as Malraux seems to have adopted the name Berger from one of Saint-Just's agents, so too he seems to have returned to the French Revolution and specifically to the circle of Saint-Just's collaborators to find a name for his hero. Pierre Garin ("called Garine")[15] seems to

have been modeled after Jean-Baptiste-Ollivier Gar[ne]rin, who ful-
filled several functions in the Committee of Public Safety and, in particular, was an agent in the police bureau directed by Saint-Just. The
name Pierre may have been suggested by two other friends and agents
of Saint-Just, Pierre Germain Gateau and Pierre-Victor Thuillier. Another of his close friends, Etienne Lambert, may have become the
Lambert of the novel, Garine's predecessor in the Far East.[16]

Admittedly, this argument is somewhat speculative; still, the correspondences cannot be totally dismissed. Moreover, other facts rein-
force the thesis that Garine is a fictional reincarnation of Saint-Just
and, perhaps, as already suggested, of Malraux himself.[17] On two occasions, Malraux specifically relates Garine to Saint-Just. First, in Les
Conquérants, the narrator, summarizing a file of police intelligence
on Garine, refers to young Garine's imagination as being "totally preoccupied with Saint-Just" (C 154). Then, too, in a 1929 debate focused on the character of Garine, Malraux argued that Saint-Just was
not a republican at the beginning of his revolutionary involvement.
Similarly, he suggested that Garine does not become a revolutionist
until he realizes that with such participation he can affirm his will
and identity.[18] In the debate Malraux also stressed the primacy of action over ideology in Garine, stating that Garine's impasses are overcome "through precise preferences felt in the face of precise problems, through actions."[19] Like Saint-Just, who "defined himself
through the guillotine of Strasbourg and through Fleurus" (CA 38),
Garine believes in the "most effective use of one's strength" (C 153),
regardless of morality, as illustrated in the episode of the two Chinese
caught possessing poison: Garine quickly extracts a confession by
shooting one at point-blank range and immediately threatening the
other with similar extinction (C 285–87). Garine's brutal, uncompromising actions are dictated by the knowledge that power is a product of "tenacious, constant violence" (C 292). Like Saint-Just, the
"professor of energy" (SJ 29), Garine "believes only in energy," in a
"persevering energy" (C 165–66, 276), and in the power and consciousness it brings. To maximize the effectiveness of this energy he
exploits the disorder of the revolution, making it "a weapon" (C 163),
an instrument at the service of his ambition (SJ 15). Like Saint-Just,
he perceives the advantages of coordinating the various forces of the
revolution and thus annexes to his propaganda machine the resources of other offices (police, justice, and so on). According to Malraux, revolutionary exaltation "dies with attrition," and what remains is only a hope for the future, consisting mostly of unknowns
(SJ 25). So it was for Saint-Just and so it is also for Garine. In the grip

of death, he realizes that his achievements cannot be easily defined; he does not even know what will become of the men to whom he has given a "soul" (C 265). After the exaltation of the revolution, between his feelings of insignificance and his action, surfaces thus in him the consciousness of what is fundamentally human—the tragic lyricism, the pathetic grandeur of what is proper to man and to nothing else, a "fraternal sadness" (C 294) that ends in silence, like Saint-Just's silent march to the guillotine.

Like Clappique's personality, Garine's character has a "tendency to proliferate";[20] hence the difficulty of distinguishing the "cynical political adventurer"[21] from the man who, according to Malraux, "escapes the absurd by fleeing into the human."[22] However, the mystery of this character is clarified and almost vanishes when he is compared to Malraux's image of Saint-Just. The adventurer, the revolutionist, the "terrorist,"[23] the military officer, and the intellectual are all faces of Saint-Just, Garine and, in some respects, of Malraux himself. The correspondences can be summarized by the following chart:

Malraux	Saint-Just	Garine
French/Chinese revolutions	French Revolution	Russian/Chinese revolutions
Berger, colonel of Alsace-Lorraine Brigade; Alsatian family in *Antimémoires*	Berger, friend and agent, campaign in Alsace, 1793–94	
In charge of propaganda, information	Propaganda, police, army, justice; "the accusative"	Propaganda, police, army; informer, denouncer
"A life of actions"	"Professor of energy"	"Believes only in energy"
Human condition: tragic	"Bitter indifference," silence	Bitterness

Both Saint-Just and Garine are products of a revolutionary period; they both harness and fashion its energy into an instrument of change and achievement. Yet though this energy enlightens and exalts their consciousness, ultimately it also consumes them, as they succumb to "the strength of events," the historical determinant that spares only a few "protected characters" (CA 105) and those only for a limited period of time. Under the influence of this force, historical existence vanishes into an aura of legend.

Malraux's heroes believe in the inspiring and transforming power of exemplary acts, the stuff of which history is made. Art, freedom, justice, everything that makes man's greatness and his pride is the result of an active charity; without this personal involvement and sacrifice, man's life is as vain as the ephemera, victims of a simple stroke of Nicolaïeff's hand. The exemplary figure conquers death and becomes creative in others. Thus the narrator of *Les Conquérants* finds it difficult to resist the existential truths exemplified by the dying Garine (*C* 281). Malraux's Saint-Just also illustrates how history and legend combine to become a stimulant of imitative action which becomes itself creative of history and legend. The historical and legendary Saint-Just exercised an influence on Malraux, who, in turn, with his actions and his creations, also helped to shape in a small way the character and course of history. In Malraux's tragic vision the individual life is extremely vulnerable and, like the ephemera, easily extinguished; however, the energy that gives moment to history is continually renewed in other lives. This regenerative power constitutes for him man's hope. His image of Saint-Just symbolizes this energy—the primordial, universal impulse that impels man to renew and recreate himself and his world. Saint-Just is thus for Malraux a symbol of history.

Bert M-P. Leefmans

MALRAUX AND TRAGEDY:

THE STRUCTURE OF "LA

CONDITION HUMAINE"

La Condition humaine is not a very long novel, but it is a very full one. In it a large number of characters, a good many of them of major importance, are involved in a great many events and actions of a number of different kinds. And yet, despite this profusion of matter and of energy, for it is a novel of violence, it ultimately gives an undeniable impression of clarity and order. If the obvious question as to how it does so leads to a no less obvious answer, which has to do with form, it is not the purpose here to consider the relation of the artist to the form of his work of art. A larger study than this one might undertake to clarify this question, which is a major one, in relation to this book. But here the focus will be upon the text itself, for it is one which may be considerably clarified by analysis of its structure and of the relation between its structure and its action. Whether Malraux's success in the case of *La Condition humaine* derives from his skill in making what turns out to be a very formal novel so immediately convincing that its form is hidden within its action, or whether it is simply so good a book that a certain form essentially appropriate to its content became somehow inevitable, need not matter here.

Quite early in one's experience with this novel, it becomes clear that its action falls into two major phases. As it begins, with preparations for the uprising in Shanghai, the virtue which informs all of its activity is hope. As the revolt begins, and its initial successes become major ones, hope is no longer uppermost. The difficulties attendant upon maintenance of a now improved position become significant and the dependence of those who could win their immediate battles in Shanghai upon those in Hankow whose actions they cannot control becomes more apparent. As yet there have been no real reverses, but forewarnings of disaster become more frequent and more impressive. Next, in the central fourth part of the book, there comes a brief period of stalemate, filled with violence. It begins with hope frustrated by an absurdity as Tchen is prevented from assassinating Chiang by a shopkeeper who is trying to accomplish something quite unrelated. It ends with hope gone as Tchen, throwing his bomb this time, but at Chiang's empty car, blows himself to bits. The remainder of the book, the second major phase, is precisely as violent as the first, but what informs its action is no longer hope. It is despair. Although as the end approaches, in the same way that doom had been foreshadowed amid the hope of the earlier phase, so here there are intimations of hope arising out of the destruction of its past results.

If this outline is vague and general, the text permits a considerably more precise description of the progress which clarifies the novel's action. This simplest of patterns, that of rise and fall, is accompanied, as it often is, by a more special one which implies greater perception and a deeper understanding of events. It is the pattern which in all tragedy, perhaps, relates to the discovery of value in destruction, provided destruction is understood and used as man can occasionally understand and use it. It is the presence of this pattern in it which perhaps as much as anything else may seem to relate Malraux's novel to drama of a kind whose substance and tone are both very evidently similar to those of *La Condition humaine*.

The book has seven numbered parts, the central one being concerned with the tense equilibrium described above. As the novel begins, Part I deals with preparations for the uprising, Part II with its first successes, while Part III, in the course of which little actually happens, looks back over what has gone before and considers what is apparently to come. Preparation, action, recapitulation. Part IV is filled with action but there are no results. It adds to the intimations of doom but in it the descent does not quite begin. It is a kind of static point in the progress of the book, lacking in kinetic but taut with potential energy. Ascent and descent coexist in it and the remnants of the earlier rise by contrast make more vivid the fall which is to come. Tchen's bomb finally does go off, and then the second major phase can start.

Except that the movement is now downward, toward destruction, the last three parts follow the same pattern as the first three. Once again the movement is from preparation to action to recapitulation. Or in terms of the rhythm which Kenneth Burke finds in classic tragedy, "from Purpose, to Passion, to Perception."[1] And if one considers the action of the novel as a whole in the light of hope, the same broad rhythm is repeated also there. The first major phase, itself moving in this rhythm in its three parts, is the "Purpose" component of the whole book, while the last phase makes clear the "Perception." The central section, Part IV, where appropriately "Passion" accomplishes none of its own ends, makes possible the enlightenment which is the end—as in both senses it is of tragedy—of this novel.

More than this tragic rhythm, important as it is, shapes the structure of the book, however, and the analogy between the first and last three-part sections of it results from much more detail than is represented by the repetition of that broad rhythm. With rather more care than in *Les Conquérants*, Malraux uses time, and somewhat secondarily place, to provide the framework within which to construct his narrative. With one exception his chapter headings indicate time, and in the instances where place is not given it is known from what has gone before. If the time scheme of the novel is objectified, if one draws a picture which gives proper value to the elapsed time of the chapters of the book, and to the intervals between them, one finds what one would probably expect. The picture of the first major section, which first presents the tragic rhythm, is identical with the picture of the last, which repeats it. With this difference, that the characteristics of the first picture are somewhat emphasized in the second. One thing that happens within each section is that the passage of time becomes, in general, slower and slower. In the same way, its movement in the final section is an image of its movement in the first, but so slowed down that as the book ends it comes nearly to a stop—in the only chapter for which no time is given.

There are three related factors in the book which also vary in a similar fashion. As time can be made to move fast rather than slowly, so attention and concern can be directed to an immediately present, small area. This, as one would expect, tends to happen when there is violent action going on. A murder in one's presence leaves one with little attention to spare for other places or larger matters. At the other extreme, there are times when the location of what is going on makes little difference. This is when what is taking place is something other than action, something which tends to lift the reader's mind out of the particular locale into a larger and less specific area. As it is natural for time to move fast when there is violent action, slowly when there is little or none, one finds again what one would expect to find and the time scheme turns out to be a mirror of the pattern of the book as it appears also in terms of place, of action, and of the immediacy or universality of the significance of what at any given moment is taking place.

The extreme examples of this, in a book which proceeds from the most intense, enclosed and lonely violence to detached and experienced contemplation of the most general, are found at its beginning and its end. The tale begins in a dark hotel room in Shanghai where the introverted Tchen, in the middle of the night, under great emotional stress, commits a murder. It ends in Kobe, of all places unrelated to the action, where there is no action, but where questions of the most universal significance are discussed, in bright daylight, in the light of what has gone before. In the former the reader is made aware almost exclusively of the immediate surroundings and the immediate action. That action takes place in almost no time at all, according to the "horaire" of the novel, although for the reader as for Tchen it becomes a long ordeal in terms of subjective time. In the later scene, at Kobe, time and its passage have become almost completely unimportant. The highest concentration in the novel has finally, as it ends, given way to the greatest diffusion.

The transition, however, is not a direct one. Just as the tragic rhythm is repeated in the first three and the last three parts in what are smaller images of its operation in the novel as a whole, so in each of these two major sections the movement away from unity in time, place, action and significance is repeated also, with remarkable similarity in the two sections. Part V begins with scenes which are comparable to those which begin Part I. The scene at Kobe is comparable on all the aforementioned counts to the second part of the scene at Hankow which ends Part III. Apart from the central and, in the sense of the repeated rhythm, separate fourth part, there are only two places in the book where time is moving so fast as to cause successive chapters to overlap in time. This occurs at the beginning of each of the major three-part phases. And as each phase proceeds, time becomes more and more stretched out, the area involved becomes larger, the intensity of the action decreases, and concern moves from the particular to the more general.

Having once been led to approach the analogous sections to each other and compare them, one observes that in addition to these similarities, and also as a result of them, there are similarities in the nature of the action, in the kind of thing occurring at corresponding points in the two sections. The partly simultaneous scenes which begin Part I, concerned with "Purpose," correspond in a number of ways to the also partly simultaneous scenes which begin Part V. The scenes of repose and the battle scenes of the two sections occupy corresponding positions. Throughout, this sort of parallelism is maintained in detail.

Once this becomes apparent, it ceases to be only possible and becomes necessary to bring these sections together, for their juxtaposition, once its validity as an operation has been established, results in considerable clarification of the book's internal meanings. Much of this addition to the significance of its action derives from contrasts which are imbedded in similarity. Such things as different reactions in situations which are analogues, both in the pattern and in general, become revealing, when placed side by side. An early instance of this involves the initial scenes of the two phases. The rising, the creative, nature of the first phase is suggested when the motives behind Tchen's crime are made clear. His action contrasts violently with the first action of the final one. Tchen's murder was destruction for a purpose and it is followed by preparations and action of a very positive sort. Clappique's gambling, on the contrary, although his placing of a bet becomes as much an act of violence as Tchen's placing of a knife had been, is the ultimate symbol in the book of destructive purposelessness, and his procedure after the game-room closes is monumentally uncreative.[2]

As the two phases proceed to "Passion," the initial scenes are followed in each instance by the relatively static and portentous ones which immediately precede the two battle scenes of the book. In each case the latter involve attacks upon strongpoints which are doomed and fall. As would be expected, in the earlier scene the strongpoint is captured, in the later it is lost. After these come what are perhaps the most important scenes of the two major phases, at least in so far as the book is taken to be tragic. They are those in which the isolation of man is most directly considered and they prepare the way most significantly for the contrast which will later appear between the final chapters of the two sections, one of which concludes the book.

At the climax of the earlier of them it is the rugged individual, Ferral, who succeeds in achieving a no more than momentary communion with another individual: in the phase of the novel when the hopes of the masses are in the ascendant, the egoist fails. In the later instance, when these hopes are destroyed, Katow, as nearly a classic hero as there is in the book, likewise achieves a communion which, if also only momentary, is significantly different.

It is necessary to recall at this point that in the earlier of these scenes Valérie has gone to sleep and Ferral is watching her and considering himself. Her function at that moment is to remind him that he is, like her, "Un être humain . . . une vie individuelle, isolée, unique" [A human being . . . an individual, isolated, unique life] (CH 402). Having attained his momentary mastery in the preceding scene—for the light by the bed had been turned back on—he is once again alone. And the light, which had enabled him to have his satisfaction and an odd kind of communion by watching her reaction during intercourse, is precisely the thing which insures his not seeing her again after that night. As in the paradox which is a subject of the work as a whole, the thing which makes communion possible is the thing which insures its subsequent destruction.

In the later scene where Katow awaits execution, the basic concern is again human isolation. The scene provides an extraordinarily moving demonstration of the realizing of the hope which is somehow the concern of all tragedy, that "un homme [peut] être plus fort que cette solitude" [a man can be stronger than this solitude] (CH 542), than the solitude which precedes the mass execution in which all are included. It reaches its peak in Katow's exultant victory over his captors when they demand to know where two of his companions had obtained the poison which had enabled them to escape their executioners by suicide. Whether or not one feels justified in equating the turning off and on of the light beside Ferral's bed with the loss and recovery of the phial of cyanide, it is difficult to avoid noting the analogy between Katow's experience and Ferral's—and therefore also the differences between them—partly at least because they occupy corresponding positions in the many ways repeated rhythmic pattern.

Ferral, insisting upon the light—he must see since he cannot feel—achieves a satisfaction perhaps perverted, in any case as self-centered as can be. Katow, the poison again being found, finds his satisfaction in the ability to provide an escape for his friends, who personally were strangers to him. This permits him to be, moreover, in a way familiar in tragic drama, stronger than what is happening to him. One can go too far with this sort of thing, but if, as is often the case, light and life are equal, while poison certainly means death, one may sense the presence here of the paradox about saving one's life and losing it which, though it means many things in many contexts, is apparently essential to writers of tragedy. It is essential because it always carries with it the suspicion, made certain by the tragic mode, that the idea is more important than the man who dies for it—and becomes so because he does. In any case, if the paradox is here, it makes the necessary distinction between Katow and Ferral with singular adequacy.

If Katow, with his gesture of the poison, with his ritual of communion, has achieved a union with man, he, like Ferral, finds himself alone. If he is accompanied by the anguish of the companions who remain behind, and this at least is something he has won, he nevertheless goes to his death as every man must go. His exultation of the spirit—or of "le coeur viril des hommes . . . qui vaut bien l'esprit" [the virile heart of men . . . which is certainly as valuable as the spirit] (CH 540) and which may after all be a synonym for it—and Ferral's physical triumph in his embrace with Valérie, are the two aspects of a dichotomy which here separates, less the spirit from the body, than the egoist from the lover of humanity. Love, in Malraux as in Dante, is what makes the world go round. If the fates of Ferral and Katow are alike, thus providing a necessary setting for tragedy, it is Katow's concern with something other than himself which insures his stature. Over and over again, the way in which saints and heroes are alike appears.

The temporary victory and the ultimate failure in each case end a phase in which time has gradually come nearly to a stop, in which the location and the concern have become man's position in the universe, and the action of the drama, for the moment at least, has given way to sleep and death. What follows we may recall, but in each case what follows looks back over what has passed and considers what is to come. Purpose has been destroyed in passion and what follows makes more explicit the nature of the perception. From the lonely room in which a murder was committed, the first phase has moved past Ferral's scene with Valérie and then on, following the longest lapse of time in the course of it, to a Hankow which represents all China and all communism. It is here that the paradox underlying man's political fate becomes clear as Kyo learns that the men of good will in Shanghai are to be sacrificed to the brutal impersonality of the revolution. In the second phase, movement is from a stuffy gaming room to Paris, where the concern is international, and worldly, and thence to Kobe where the concern is cosmic. Again the time lapses have become longer as the phase progressed. The Paris chapter, after a schedule which has slipped from minutes to hours to days, in each phase, is labeled simply "Paris, juillet." The final chapter heading, for the first time, gives no indication of time at all. From the text one learns that it is Spring but this is significant not in relation to the passage of time, but in so far as Spring has meaning as the time when things start anew. Time has stopped, but it will start again. The concerns which had earlier become general at Hankow, after returning to the particular in the second phase, have become cosmic at Kobe— where a Japanese painter, we have learned, paints his soul.

Malraux's constant control, his success in making analogy and irony arise out of structure to support the irony which his material necessitates and which is created by the substance of his book, both of these are major factors in the impression of clarity and the awareness of power with which the reader is left upon completion of this novel. His greatest technical success, however, may derive from his ability to limit his work to a quite rigidly maintained pattern which is as rigidly kept out of sight by its apparently inevitable relation to the matter with which it is filled out. Or perhaps it is simply that if a work of art is at once true enough to its subject and good enough, such patterns and such correspondences arise of themselves from some inescapable combination of matter, thought and language.

Haskell M. Block

MALRAUX, FAULKNER, AND THE

PROBLEM OF TRAGEDY

Both Malraux and Faulkner have frequently been discussed as tragic novelists. Both writers defined and expressed a notion of tragedy in theoretical and critical statements as well as in their novels. Despite wide artistic differences, Malraux and Faulkner share a deep preoccupation with the nature and function of tragedy in the novel. An examination of their common elements as well as their divergences can contribute to an understanding of their large and continuing claims on our attention.

Malraux's preface to the French translation of Faulkner's *Sanctuary*, published by Gallimard in 1933, remains a landmark of Faulkner criticism. It is also an important early assertion of Malraux's theory of the tragic novel, a concern the French novelist was to pursue throughout his life. Malraux sees the world of *Sanctuary* as one in which man is always crushed. The savage violence of the novel reflects the utter valuelessness of life as Faulkner depicts it. Perhaps his true subject, Malraux contends, is the irremediable. The victims of Faulkner's macabre adventure are dominated by their impotence in the face of "the irremediable absurd," the blind malevolence of fate. In his frequently cited summation Malraux declares: "*Sanctuary* is the intrusion of Greek tragedy into the detective novel."

It is possible that Malraux derived his formulation from the essay on Faulkner by Maurice Coindreau published in *La Nouvelle revue française* in June 1931. Here, in an assessment of *Sanctuary* written almost immediately after the novel's publication, Coindreau insists, "Limited only to the plot, *Sanctuary* is nothing but a detective novel spiced up with perverse eroticism."[1] He hastens to add, however, that the intrigue is far less important than the dominance of events by a sense of mystery: "Thanks to the mystery that results from this enigmatic style, the tragic scenes avoid the banality of a melodrama." Malraux extends as well as qualifies Coindreau's formulation. *Sanctuary*, Malraux asserts, is "a novel with a police atmosphere without policemen." It may be that both Coindreau and Malraux were somewhat wide of the mark in placing *Sanctuary* within the genre of *roman policier*. Despite the fact that Horace Benbow at times assumes the role of a detective investigating what has happened, he is searching for information that the reader already knows. More provocative in Malraux's formulation is his insistence on the presence of Greek tragedy in *Sanctuary* and his view of Faulkner's novel as its modern equivalent. It is noteworthy that almost all subsequent French criticism of *Sanctuary* has drawn on this formulation.[2]

American readers of Malraux's essay on Faulkner may be impressed not only by the French writer's penetrating critique but also by the omissions in his approach. Malraux does not discuss Faulkner in relation to southern history or the culture of his time, nor does he discuss Faulkner's language and style or his manipulation of point of view. Malraux's partial appraisal stresses one main point: Faulkner as a tragic novelist. Despite a degree of vagueness in Malraux's critical vocabulary, his perspective is of crucial importance for the understanding of Faulkner. At the same time it testifies to the main preoccupation of Malraux as novelist as well as critic at a crucial time in his career.

W. M. Frohock has argued persuasively that Malraux's criticism of other novelists is also a revelation of his own fictional values and practice.[3] When writing about others, Malraux is also writing about himself. Clearly, Malraux singles out in Faulkner those elements which mirror his own artistic concerns. The concept of the novel as tragedy, wherein the pattern of events moves toward inexorable catastrophe, dominates Malraux's fiction as well as his theory of fiction. His novels have frequently been interpreted as modern counterparts of classical tragedy. Gaëton Picon in his pioneering study of 1945 declared, "Technically, *La Condition humaine* is a classical masterpiece, in which one finds the complexity and the balances of a tragedy of Aeschylus or Racine."[4] Other readers have similarly argued that in its movement toward catastrophe, Malraux's novel adheres closely to the pattern of classical tragedy.[5]

Malraux's reflections on tragedy and the tragic are scattered throughout his writings. In all his work, from the early fiction to the later essays on art and human experience, he is preoccupied with the meaning of destiny and the elaboration of a tragic sense of life.[6] In the preface to *Le Temps du mépris* Malraux contends that the world of the novel, "the world of tragedy . . . is always the world of antiquity: man, the crowd, the elements, woman, destiny."[7] Tragedy is here defined in broad, general terms as a configuration of constant and archetypal elements, a reflection of the anguish of the human condition. In this sense, tragedy is not only a pattern of events but a tonality, a climate or a dominant mood. It is inherent in human existence. This preoccupation with generalized values is accompanied in Malraux's novels by a reduction of the role of individual psychology. Commenting on Picon's assertion in *Malraux par lui-même* that "man is higher than [*plus haut que*] the individual," Malraux declared, "The modern novel is in my eyes a privileged means of expression of what is tragic in man, not an elucidation of the individual."[8] Twenty years after the preface to *Sanctuary*, the novel remained for Malraux the counterpart of ancient tragedy.

Nevertheless, the concepts of tragedy and the tragic as Malraux came to elaborate them after World War II are somewhat different from his earlier views. The notion of the irremediable and the absurd has given way to a quest for tragic humanism attesting to man's grandeur as well as his suffering.[9] Tragedy is now invested with positive value wherein the victimization or defeat of the individual is of little importance. In an address to UNESCO in 1946 Malraux saw tragedy as the hallmark of an age of war and its aftermath, and he contended that the only humanism possible in the west is "tragic humanism."[10] For Malraux this tragic humanism, a constant in western experience since ancient Greece, is expressed in man's struggle with destiny. The exaltation of tragic humanism constitutes for Malraux a faith for our times, a source of spiritual regeneration without dependence on any church or dogma.

The concept of tragedy as exemplified by the modern novel was restated by Malraux in his preface to Manès Sperber's . . . *qu'une larme dans l'océan* (1952). Here again, he insists that the novel has become the successor to tragic poetry through its power of representing the conflicts between man and the universe. The modern novelist is akin to Aeschylus and Shakespeare in his interrogation of destiny. Indeed, a whole tradition of the modern novel, "from Tolstoi and Dostoevski to Proust, Joyce, and Faulkner . . . consists in interrogations of destiny."[11] Clearly, Faulkner is not out of place among Malraux's examples, but the view of tragedy in the novel here presented has undergone an important modification. The notion of tragic humanism does not occur in the preface to *Sanctuary*.

We may examine Malraux's view of tragedy in Faulkner from the standpoint of the American novelist as well. Malraux's elaboration of tragedy in the novel reveals striking differences between his views and Faulkner's. Both novelists have frequently been described as tragic poets, yet perceptive readers have noted that Malraux and Faulkner do not mean quite the same thing by *tragedy*.[12] Moreover, it must be recognized that for Faulkner as well as for Malraux, theoretical and critical formulations are often a posteriori justifications that may not wholly accord with the novels.

Like Malraux, Faulkner was seriously concerned with the meaning of tragedy, which he also viewed, at least at times, according to the values and patterns of the ancient Greeks.[13] Destiny is implacable and destructive. Both the guilty and the innocent are doomed, sometimes as the result of blind chance, sometimes through their violations of established order. In *Sartoris* (1929) Faulkner alludes to "the blind tragedy of human events" mirrored in the fate of the family.[14] Virtually all his novels are replete with tragic situations and with heroes who are driven and destroyed by their futile assault on external forces.[15] In commenting on *Absalom, Absalom!* at the University of Virginia in 1957, Faulkner described Sutpen as a victim of the Greeks, "the old Greek concept of tragedy."[16] Despite his fierce volition, Sutpen is crushed by an ironic and malign destiny. As Faulkner put it, "Man's free will functions against a Greek background of fate."[17] Tragedy for him entails both aspiration and catastrophe. This concept of tragedy "as Aristotle saw it," he contends, "is the same conception of tragedy that all writers have."[18] Like Malraux, Faulkner embraces the Greek example.

It must be added that Faulkner's views on tragedy and the tragic are not always consistent. In his remarks on *Light in August* he located tragedy for Joe Christmas in his hero's ignorance of his personal identity: "His tragedy was that he didn't know what he was and would never know, and that to me is the most tragic condition that an individual can have—to not know who he was."[19] Clearly, Faulkner is here describing tragic knowledge rather than a pattern of tragic action. In *Light in August* Faulkner seems to imply that a tragic view of life is but one among many and is far from universal.[20] Yet in other contexts he sees tragedy as inherent and pervasive, "the poor tragic human being struggling with its own heart, with others, with its environment, for the simple things which all human beings want."[21] In this sense, for Faulkner life is rooted in tragedy and all human beings are condemned to struggle and defeat.

To what extent does *Sanctuary* conform to the concept of tragedy in the novel? The central characters are all deeply flawed, lacking any sense of tragic grandeur, no matter how acute and painful their suffering may be. Perhaps suffering and catastrophe are in themselves sufficient evidence for Faulkner of the tragic as a climate or tonality, quite apart from any traditional concept of tragedy.[22] After hearing Temple Drake's account of her brutalization, Horace muses: " 'Better for her if she were dead tonight. . . . And I too; thinking how that were the only solution. Removed, cauterised out of the old and tragic flank of the world.' "[23] Life as it is crushes those who are innocent as well as those who are evil. The very fabric of existence is fraught with suffering and disaster.

In the original version of *Sanctuary*, recently published, Horace gives expression to the nobility of tragedy as well as its harshness in musing on "the dignity in tragedy—that one quality which we do not possess in common with the beasts of the field."[24] Here Faulkner seems for a moment to approach Malraux's notion of tragic humanism, but no trace of this dignity can be found in the final version of the novel. There is no relief from "the evil, the injustice, the tears," no mitigation provided by empty suffering or evasion. The novel ends in a dark embrace of "the season of rain and death" that dominates Faulkner's pages from beginning to end. The world of *Sanctuary* is indeed a wasteland.[25] The anarchy of values it expresses places it wholly outside of traditional notions of tragedy. *Sanctuary* may indeed constitute "one of the most uncompromising expressions of total despair in literature."[26] Malraux was surely correct in viewing its subject as the irremediable absurd, but the notion of tragedy implicit in this view precludes any element of tragic humanism. Nihilism and human dignity cannot coexist.

We may conclude that the tragic in Faulkner is at some remove from the tragic in Malraux. In Faulkner man is utterly destroyed. In Malraux his defeat is ennobled by dignity. One may properly speak of tragic heroes in the novels of Malraux, but it would be far more difficult to do so of the novels of Faulkner. Malraux's assessment of *Sanctuary* is challenging in its originality. It expresses a notion of tragedy in the novel which is strikingly close to that of Faulkner but from which Malraux moved markedly away in both his novels and his reflections. Malraux's developed conception of tragedy may offer a measure of hope and consolation in the face of universal devastation and suffering, but it corresponds only partially and imperfectly to the darker view of tragedy of the world of Yoknapatawpha.

Mary Jean Green

MALRAUX AND SARTRE:

DIALOGUE ON THE

FAR SIDE OF DESPAIR

In the spring of 1937 and again in the summer of 1941 the paths of André Malraux and Jean-Paul Sartre had occasion to cross. Each of these encounters marked an important moment in the evolution of each man's view of human action in history, views which were to change radically in the intervening years. The first meeting took place in 1937, by intermediary, when one of Sartre's former philosophy students, to whom he remained particularly close, asked his help in enlisting on the Republican side of the Spanish civil war. Despite some misgivings, Sartre had enough respect for the student's right to choose that he arranged a meeting with Malraux, who had himself recently returned from active service in Spain and was now engaged in writing a book about his experiences to draw support to the Spanish cause.

Even after arranging the meeting, the politically uninvolved Sartre remained troubled, torn between his sympathy for the antifascist struggle in Spain and his concern for the young man's welfare. As he later described his reactions, "I was very disturbed because, on the one hand, I felt he didn't have sufficient military or even biological preparation to survive the bad times and, on the other hand, I couldn't deny a man the right to fight."[1] He feared the student had no real understanding of the fate of suffering and death which almost surely awaited him in Spain, and he seems to have been convinced of the uselessness of the young man's sacrifice.

Sartre had no real reason to worry, although in the end this enterprise had greater consequences for Sartre himself than for the student. Malraux saw the boy and, with characteristic realism, told him to come back after putting in some practice with a submachine gun. While the student seems to have been content to drop the matter at this point, Sartre was not. Attempting to imagine the situation in which the young man might find himself, Sartre envisioned a fascist prison cell in Spain where three men spend a night awaiting their execution. The results of this meditation on death, as Sartre was to call it,[2] were published in the *Nouvelle Revue Française* of July 1937 under the title "Le Mur."

It is not surprising that this short story should have been suggested by an encounter with Malraux and with the ideal of active political engagement he represented. Four years earlier, in *La Condition humaine*, Malraux had described a parallel scene of a group of revolutionaries facing a cruel and humiliating death. But as they await their execution, Malraux's revolutionaries are able to reaffirm the values of human dignity and fraternity for which they have been fighting. Again, *Le Temps du mépris*, the antifascist novella Malraux published in 1935, shows a man imprisoned by the Nazis and anticipating imminent execution. Although this time Malraux's protagonist is isolated from his comrades, he succeeds in using the creative powers of his own mind to reestablish a sense of participation in a human community and to locate his place in the historical development of his revolutionary cause. Unlike the alienated protagonists of his early novels, Malraux's revolutionary heroes of the 1930s are able to find meaning even in a death cell.

Sartre's short story is quite evidently a powerful argument to the contrary; in "Le Mur" the fact of death strips life of all its former meaning, reducing once brave men to trembling masses of obscene flesh. In the course of the night that separates sentencing and execution Sartre's protagonist, Pablo Ibbieta, records the breakdown of all structures that had previously given meaning to his life: his love for his mistress, his friendship with Ramon Gris (to protect whom he is nevertheless ready to sacrifice his life), and even the anarchist ideals that have long motivated his conduct. Far from creating an atmosphere of Malrucian fraternity, the imminence of death increases the effects of alienation; Sartre's anarchist narrator dissociates himself from his comrade-in-arms from the International Brigades and both men refuse to extend their sympathy to Juan Mirbal, the innocent boy who has been condemned only because his brother is an anarchist.

Sartre's characters move in a universe of arbitrary and unpredictable events which resist their attempts to control or even understand them, a situation that is underlined by the strange twist of Pablo's liberation. In *Le Temps du mépris* Malraux's protagonist had also obtained his liberation in the end, when an unknown comrade had unexpectedly turned himself in in his place. As Malraux's conclusion provides concrete evidence of the vision of revolutionary fraternity which had sustained the prisoner throughout his solitary confinement, Sartre's ending reinforces the dominant theme of the meaninglessness of human action. After his two companions have been led off to execution, Pablo is again asked by his captors to reveal the hiding place of his friend. By this point, Pablo is conscious only of the absurdity of his captors' insistence on carrying on purposeful activity in a world that he now sees to be without meaning: "Their little activities seemed shocking and burlesque to me; I couldn't put myself in their place, I thought they were insane."[3] Pablo can only imagine the interrogators as future corpses: "These men dolled up with their riding crops and boots were still going to die. A little later than I, but not too much" (*M* 33). He even tells one of the Phalangists to shave off his mustache: "I thought it funny that he would let hair invade his face while he was still alive" (*M* 35). In order to poke a hole in these men's unwarranted seriousness, Pablo sends them on a wild goose chase to seek his friend in a cemetery—where, because of an unforeseen series of events, Ramon Gris is, in fact, found and killed. The story ends with Pablo laughing uncontrollably in the prison courtyard.

Although "Le Mur" was not intended to convey a political message, it does reflect with some accuracy Sartre's political positions at the moment of its composition, and it also threatens to lead the reader to similar conclusions about political action. While Sartre's opposition to fascism is not as clear in "Le Mur" as in "L'Enfance d'un chef," which concludes the collection in which both stories were finally published, Pablo's fascist captors are shown to be arbitrary, indifferent to human suffering, and even wantonly cruel. The sentencing takes place immediately after a few short and meaningless questions, to which it seems strangely unrelated. Much of the discomfort experienced by the condemned men is due to the presence of a Belgian doctor sent to observe their physical reactions to the fact of impending death, an episode that points uncannily ahead to other even crueler examples of Nazi medical research. Under the doctor's alienating gaze, which sums up the full negative force of the Sartrean *regard*, the condemned men find themselves reduced to helpless blobs of *en-soi*. The salient example of fascist cruelty and injustice is the decision to condemn the young and totally apolitical Juan, who is finally dragged off to his execution in a state of total physical collapse. To the politically militant Sartre of the 1960s, in fact, Juan's role in the story assumed central importance. When a film was made from "Le Mur" in 1967, Sartre saw it as relevant to contemporary political events because of its depiction of "the horror of death inflicted on man by man."[4]

Despite Sartre's later claims for political relevance, however, the argument of the story he actually wrote in 1937 seems to radically devalue political action. While it is true that the drama of Pablo Ibbieta plays itself out against a background of fascist cruelty, the conclusions he draws from this experience do not point in the direction of resistance. At the end of the story he is left paralyzed by laughter at the arbitrary nature of the universe, and, although he apparently survives to become the narrator of his own story, the reader is given no clue as to the direction he has taken. Thus Sartre, in the one piece of fiction he wrote about the Spanish civil war, reaches an apparently pessimistic conclusion; the conclusion, in fact, corresponds exactly to what we know of his own political attitude at the time, one of pessimism about the success of the antifascist struggle in Spain and, particularly, about the efficacy of his own or any individual's contribution to such a cause.

Sartre's conviction that the Spanish civil war was a lost cause is particularly striking. He later attempted to excuse the negative tone of "Le Mur" by explaining that it had been written in the atmosphere of the Republican defeat: "Since at that time we were operating in the context of the Spanish defeat, I found myself much more sensitive to the absurdity of these deaths than to the positive elements that might emerge from a struggle against fascism, etc."[5]

Yet "Le Mur" was clearly written some time in late 1936 or early 1937, most probably between Malraux's return to France in February

1937 and the time of the story's publication in July of that year. In the spring of 1937 the victory of fascism in Spain was far from being a foregone conclusion. Republican forces had just succeeded in the defense of Madrid and had won several major military victories, episodes that Malraux at the same moment was using to justify the title of his own book on the civil war, *L'Espoir*.

Even more negative than Sartre's vision of the historical process, however, was his view of the potential for individual action within it. As recorded by Simone de Beauvoir, both she and Sartre were, in the thirties, convinced of the uselessness of any political action on their part. Although they were in complete sympathy with the wave of Popular Front activity, the two young intellectuals were hesitant to involve themselves in mass movements; they even stayed home from the 1936 Bastille Day parades, pointing out to Sartre's student, who did participate, the futility of his conduct. A few days later, the events of the Spanish civil war were to effect a profound change in their attitude—but not in their actions. Finding themselves, for the first time, directly concerned by political events, they were no longer fully content with the role of spectators: "For the first time in our lives, because we were profoundly concerned over the fate of Spain, indignation was no longer a sufficient outlet for our feelings."[6] But while they cheered the enlistment of their Spanish friend Fernand, they themselves remained firmly convinced of the uselessness of any such action on their part: "Our political impotence, far from furnishing us with an alibi, left us feeling hopeless and desolate. And it was so absolute. . . . There was no question of our going off to Spain ourselves; nothing in our previous background inclined us to such headstrong action" (*FA* 334). It is in the context of this feeling of helplessness that de Beauvoir gives her account of the student's attempt to enlist, and it is clear that such an attitude lies at the origin of "Le Mur."

At the time "Le Mur" appeared, Malraux was hard at work on *L'Espoir*, which was ready for serialization in *Ce Soir* by November 1937 (portions of it also appeared in the December *NRF*). Sartre's powerful argument against political action, appearing in the prestigious *NRF*, cannot have gone unnoticed by Malraux, especially since it was grounded in a vision of human existence not unlike that of his own early novels. It is my contention, as well, that he did not allow it to go unanswered. Whether or not this is true, there does appear in *L'Espoir* an episode that echoes the story of Pablo Ibbieta. It is lived by a character named Moreno, who makes only two fleeting appearances in the book—both of which occur, however, at crucial points in the novelistic structure. It is this minor character who is responsible for one of the novel's most cited passages: "The tragedy of death is that it transforms life into destiny."[7] Moreno's statement is quoted with approval by Sartre himself in his later writings, most notably his major philosophical statement of the period, *L'Etre et le néant* (*Being and Nothingness*).

Moreno's experience is, like Pablo's, that of the man condemned to death. One of the few Marxist officers in the Spanish army, he has been arrested at the beginning of the war and held in a fascist prison, where he is continually exposed to the sound of executions in progress. During the time he spends awaiting his own death, this formerly committed Marxist ceases to believe in anything; after his escape he tells his friend Hernandez, "'I've given up believing in all I once believed in . . . . I believe in nothing now'" (*E* 262).

Moreno's discusson with Hernandez, Malraux's idealistic Republican commander, takes place in Toledo on the eve of the city's collapse before Franco's advancing troops. To the disillusioned eyes of Moreno—who in this, too, reminds us of Sartre's Pablo—the frenzied activity of the Republican soldiers preparing to defend the city is a meaningless "farce [*comédie*]." He has discovered a world in which acts of human will have lost their power, in which matters of life and death seem to hang on events no less arbitrary than the toss of a coin. His fellow prisoners have, in fact, spent the better part of their time flipping coins in an attempt to predict their own fate, and this concretization of chance has come to sum up Moreno's experience: "'Remember, no one on earth can escape what's coming to him, his truth; and it isn't death, no, it isn't even suffering; it's the spin of a coin, of a penny'" (*E* 266). Moreno's prison experience has revealed to him not only the inevitability of death but the ultimate futility of human action.

Surrounded by the fraternal presence of his comrades-in-arms, Hernandez is able to offer a strong argument against Moreno's nihilism. He knows that the fraternal action of the civil war has transformed human lives, like that of the hunchbacked woman whose appearance has elicited Moreno's original mocking comment. In the eyes of Hernandez she represents, on the contrary, the deeper meaning of the revolutionary movement: "Unlike Moreno, all he saw was her fine zest. [. . .] She, who until now most likely had been condemned to loneliness, was at last playing an active part in the world" (*E* 264). In opposition to Moreno's vision of the futility of human effort, Hernandez argues, against the background of the ancient royal city of Toledo, that human action has had the power to change the course of history: "'This street must have looked much like it does now in the days of Charles the Fifth. Yet the world has moved on since then. Because men wanted to move it on, despite the pennies—perhaps even with a full awareness that those pennies were waiting in the background'" (*E* 267–68).

Hernandez is keenly aware that the attitude expressed by Moreno is the dark side of the revolutionary experience, the antithesis of the revolutionary hope which is the subject of Malraux's novel. At the end of the conversation, therefore, he advises Moreno to leave the Republican army: "'If . . . you still can see only the comic-opera side of our milicianos, if nothing in you responds to the hope that animates them, well then, go to France, there's nothing for you to do here'" (*E* 268).

After Moreno's departure, however, his argument returns to haunt Hernandez himself in the form of a piece of paper money with which he is confronted by his fascist interrogators after the fall of Toledo. The bill is the one on which Moreno had distractedly made a pencil mark to illustrate his statement about death and destiny. As Hernandez faces his questioners, he begins to see the world through Moreno's eyes, in a vision of absurdity which echoes Pablo Ibbieta's: "'So, men were taking themselves seriously. . . . How living people waste time over futilities!'" (*E* 294). Like Pablo, Hernandez now sees these men as future corpses: "Hernandez stared at the little head, the long neck which would look still longer when the man was dead. And he'd die just like everyone else. . . ." (*E* 294). And, as in Pablo's case, a noble action—that of forwarding letters from the fascist commander of the besieged Toledo Alcazar to his wife—ironically returns to haunt Hernandez, to grant him privileged treatment when he least wants it and to reveal to him the futility of human action itself. Later, as he watches the beginning of the long series of executions, he reflects: "'If I hadn't had Moscardo's letter sent on, if I hadn't tried to behave decently, would those three men be there? . . . . And, damn it, even if I'd acted otherwise, it would have made no difference. There were plenty of fellows who acted otherwise'" (*E* 300).

The scene of the execution of Hernandez seems, in fact, to be an image in negative of the similar execution scene in *La Condition humaine*. Despite his wish to make his death an affirmation of fraternity—he has been captured while covering the retreat of his comrades—Hernandez finds himself irremediably isolated from others, so much so that he refuses to participate in an effort to escape. His earlier vision of a world made meaningful by human action is replaced by an absurdist vision in which the rows of men about to be executed appear to jump backward into their graves even before the shots are fired.

Malraux has risked allowing the nihilistic philosphy of Moreno to invade and dominate this central scene in *L'Espoir*, a scene that W. M. Frohock and other critics find to be in conflict with the logic of the propagandistic intention of the novel.[8] Even here, however, Malraux does not allow this powerful image of absurdity to stand unquestioned. The next man to be executed is a simple streetcar conductor who has been seen earlier protesting his innocence and lack of political involvement. He claims that the fascists have wrongly interpreted the marks left on his shoulder by the pouch he must carry on his job as evidence that he has been carrying a rifle. His protests, of course, go unheeded, and he now finds himself facing a firing squad. He thus embodies in Malraux's work the figure of innocence condemned which Sartre had portrayed in the young Juan Mirbal. But when confronted with death, the streetcar conductor refuses to collapse in helpless terror, as has Juan. Rather, he expresses his contempt for those who are about to kill him: "The little man gazed at them, stolid in his innocence as a stake rooted in the soil, and gave them a look of undying, elemental hatred that had already something of the other world in its intensity" (*E* 302). Standing before the firing squad, he raises his fist in the salute of the Popular Front, a gesture which, made by the apolitical streetcar conductor, is no longer a mere statement of political allegiance but an expression of human protest against an unjust universe. The one raised fist becomes an inspiration to the other condemned men, and the fascist firing squad finds itself powerless to prevent this last assertion of human dignity. Thus Malraux has taken Sartre's strongest example of human helplessness and turned it into an affirmation of human will.

The image of the raised fist not only provides a response to the absurdist vision of Moreno but also constitutes a link between the scene of the execution of Hernandez, with its pessimistic overtones, and the positive vision of the novel's culminating scene, the "descent from the mountain." In this scene, with which Malraux chose to conclude his film version of *L'Espoir*, the heroic combat of Magnin's group of Republican aviators is identified with the unending struggle for survival of the peasants who rescue them from a mountaintop plane crash. The effort simply to assert human life in this rugged and hostile environment is, in the eyes of the observer Magnin, an "austere triumph," and the gestures of the people who surround the improvised stretchers, the raised fists of the silent watchers seem for him to sum up "the will of the people" (*E* 563). Thus, even in the scene of Hernandez' execution, the moment in *L'Espoir* when hope in human action is most absent, Malraux has placed a contradictory image, an image which he takes up and elaborates in his concluding scene.

The execution scene does not, of course, form the conclusion of
L'Espoir, as it did of *La Condition humaine*. In the earlier novel Malraux was dealing with a failed revolution; he presents the revolutionary struggle in Spain, on the other hand, as one with a strong potential for success. The execution scene in *L'Espoir*, therefore, is merely
the low point on a trajectory that moves from the spontaneous enthusiasm of the early days of the war through catastrophic defeat to
recovery and—what is in the novel, if not in historical fact—a victorious outcome. Malraux thereby gives himself the opportunity of
having Moreno himself provide a response to his own former nihilism. The Spanish officer makes a brief reappearance in the novel during the scenes of the bombardment of Madrid, where he is seen sitting calmly in a cafe in the midst of the explosions. He recalls the
earlier argument with Hernandez as he tries to explain to a disillusioned companion the meaning he has found in joining with others
in a possibly hopeless struggle. In articulating this meaning, he invokes the term used by all major characters in the novel when called
upon to justify their action: "There's a fraternity that is only to be
found beyond the grave" (E 436). Malraux's Moreno thus returns to
answer the question left hanging by Sartre: What source of meaning
can survive the devastating experience of the man condemned to
death?

The dialogue between Sartre and Malraux did not end in 1937, but
its continuation took place under circumstances which would have
been difficult to predict. Both men were made prisoners of war by the
defeat of France in 1940; the French defeat followed hard on the heels
of that of the Spanish Republic, which Malraux, in particular, had observed at close hand. Judging from the biographical evidence available, the sequence of defeats constituted for Malraux a devastating
attack on his optimism about individual action in history, as it destroyed his hopes for the historical vindication of the values he had
defended in word and deed throughout the preceding decade. After
escaping from the German camp, he did begin almost immediately to
work out in fictional form a response to this failure of the historical
process, but his manuscript, finally published as *Les Noyers de l'Altenburg*, can hardly be considered a call to resistance.

The pessimistic and uninvolved Sartre, meanwhile, experienced
the French defeat in totally different fashion. Ironically, for the man
who had mocked the Autodidact of *La Nausée* (*Nausea*) for having
discovered his purported love of humanity in a World War I prison
camp, Sartre himself proceeded to discover human solidarity as a
prisoner in World War II. And by writing a Christmas play for his fellow prisoners, he went on to discover the joys of *littérature engagée*.

Upon his release from the camp (because of his very apparent eye troubles), Sartre energetically set about organizing a Resistance network, optimistically titled Socialisme et liberté. At the first opportunity, he and Simone de Beauvoir traveled through the unoccupied zone seeking the support of the leading French intellectuals who had sought refuge there, including Gide and Malraux. The encounter between Sartre and Malraux has been described by de Beauvoir. According to her account, the earlier roles had been completely reversed; it was now a quiescent and pessimistic Malraux who tried to convince a militant and optimistic Sartre of the futility of individual action: "Malraux heard Sartre out very courteously, but said that, for the time being at any rate, action of any sort would in his opinion be quite useless. He was relying on Russian tanks and American planes to win the war" (FA 570–71).[9]

Malraux's refusal of Sartre's plan of action was evidently not an isolated incident, since, according to Jean Lacouture, he gave similar responses to solicitations received from other Resistance groups far better organized than Sartre's, including the network connected with the Musée de l'Homme (Museum of Man) and the Combat movement.[10] Retreating with his family to a villa in the Midi and later to a village in the Corrèze, Malraux in the years 1940–42 devoted his time to literature, foregoing the role of man of action he had so eagerly and so recently espoused. Not, in fact, until early 1944 and the arrest by the Gestapo of his brother Roland, who had himself been a Resistance leader, did Malraux accept the active role in the Resistance movement which would lead to his postwar prominence. For the greater part of the wartime period, it appears that Malraux had begun to doubt the commitment to action which he had so strongly supported in L'Espoir. In the words of Lacouture, "He had not lost all faith in action, but he was tired of it, disturbed, more conscious of questions than of certainties."[11]

While the defeat had taught Malraux some hard lessons about human action in history, it had brought home to Sartre the consequences of his own failure to act, and it was an experience he was not about to repeat. Although his Resistance network was soon disbanded for reasons of practicality, Sartre as a writer and intellectual became an important spokesman for the Resistance cause. His 1944 play Les Mouches (The Flies), whose use of the Orestes myth allowed it to slip past the German censors, showed that the action of a single individual could have the effect of liberating an entire society.

In the years preceding and during the war the paths of Sartre and Malraux had intersected at two crucial moments as each was moving in an opposite direction on the spectrum of political involvement.

The words spoken by Sartre's Orestes to defy an all-powerful Jupiter in *Les Mouches* seem to sum up the two writers' mutual and contradictory experience and, strangely enough, to echo those which Malraux had much earlier put into the mouth of a regenerated Moreno: "Human life begins on the far side of despair."[12]

Carl A. Viggiani

MALRAUX AND CAMUS

1935–1960:

MASTER AND DISCIPLE?

The relations between André Malraux and Albert Camus have often been described as those of master and disciple, even—and above all—by Camus himself (but emphatically not by Malraux). To the best of my knowledge, this important subject has not received the systematic attention it deserves.[1] We do know that they encountered each other in numerous ways between the early thirties and the time of Camus's death, but no one has traced the encounters fully. I had hoped in this essay to be able to do so, but I discovered almost immediately as I began the investigation that the biographical situation is hazy, to say the least; information exists, to a certain extent, but it is widely scattered and fragmentary. It seemed to me, therefore, that before we could explore Malraux's and Camus's literary and

ideological relations, an attempt had to be made to set down the
basic facts of their personal relations. When and how did they meet?
What did they write, say, think about each other? When did Camus
first read Malraux? Before others he acknowledged as his masters?
Simple questions like these must be answered before we can go on to
more substantial matters. So I should like here to address some of
them and try to draw from the answers some conclusions that will
lead to further study.

Most of the reliable published information about Malraux's and
Camus's contacts can be found in Herbert Lottman's encyclopedic
biography, *Albert Camus*. But, since the information is necessarily
scattered across hundreds of pages of text, we are not left with a clear
picture of the two men's relations over three decades (nor was it Lottman's intention to provide such a picture). We are nevertheless
deeply indebted to Lottman. In these pages I have strung together
Lottman's information, summarized it, added to it from Lacouture's
biography of Malraux and from my own research on Camus and Malraux, and placed it all in the historical context.[2]

In June 1935, the time of their first meeting, Camus was twenty-
one years old (and already a reader of Malraux), a graduate student in
philosophy at the University of Algiers, a militant in the Algerian
Communist party, a leader of young Algiers writers and intellectuals,
and a rising new star on the Algiers literary horizon. (Algiers in the
early thirties witnessed a burst of literary and philosophical activity.)
Deeply influenced by his first master, the philosopher Jean Grenier
(who had already met Malraux), he had decided to become a writer a
few years earlier, but it was 1935 before he began work on the three
masterpieces of his first period (cycle of the absurd); in the next six
years he would write *Caligula*, *L'Etranger (The Stranger)*, and *Le
Mythe de Sisyphe (The Myth of Sisyphus)*. Malraux, by 1935, had already published most of his novels. *La Condition humaine* took the
Goncourt Prize of 1933. He was at the height of his fame. In early
1935 came *Le Temps du mépris*—later disavowed by him—which
was nonetheless a decisive milepost in his career and in many others', including especially Camus's.

In the tense political atmosphere generated by the conflict between Left and Right in Algiers, *Le Temps du mépris* must have
fallen like a small bombshell among the intellectual community. As
the very first French work of fiction about the Nazis and the concentration camps, it invited an energetic response to them. In part to
counteract the activities of French fascists in Algiers, Malraux was
asked in June 1935 by the Algiers section of the Comité de Vigilance
des Intellectuels Antifascistes (Committee of Vigilance of Antifascist

Intellectuals) to address them and their supporters. At this meeting Camus heard Malraux's "Réponse à La Rocque," an answer to Colonel de La Rocque's earlier speech to his Croix de Feu followers. It is hard to believe that Camus did not meet and talk with Malraux, and yet it is true that Camus never said anything about it and Malraux said that they did not meet then. Only Camus's friend Robert Namia recalled that after the speech Camus approached Malraux and talked to him. This seems both natural and consistent with what we know about Camus.

The effect of *Le Temps du mépris* and Malraux's visit and speech can be seen in Camus's decision to open the first season of his Théâtre du Travail (Workers' Theater) with his own adaptation of the novel. Malraux answered Camus's request for permission to adapt the novel with a one-word telegram, "Play [*joue*]" (*L* 95). With considerable fanfare, this first collaboration between Malraux and Camus opened on the evening of January 25, 1936, to an audience of hundreds—if not thousands (the number is variously reported)—who came to celebrate the new company, Camus, Malraux, and the growing power of the leftist forces which five months later became the Popular Front government. Camus wrote a short, powerful transcription of the novel on the Piscator model he would also use in *Révolte dans les Asturies*.[3] According to witnesses, the huge audience burst into the "Internationale" at the climactic moment of the anti-Nazi meeting in Prague. Camus never again enjoyed such a triumph in the theater. Whatever Malraux may have meant to him before January 25, 1936, Malraux must afterward have become that steady presence in his consciousness that Camus called master. The play launched his career with brio; it was his triumphant entrance into the public world as writer and man of the theater, and he owed some of his success to Malraux. The author of *Le Temps du mépris* would intervene just as decisively in Camus's career at least once more later, and he might have changed Camus's life again in 1960, had Camus not been killed before their scheduled meeting.

From 1935 until 1940 their paths did not cross again, as far as it is known, although each in his way was engaged in continuous warfare against what they both called nihilism. Malraux was in Spain, France, and America, fighting and speaking against fascists and Nazis. Camus was in Algiers, militating in the Communist party until 1937; then from 1937 until 1940 he was writing for and directing the left-wing newspapers *Alger Républicain* and *Le Soir Républicain*, first as investigative reporter and eventually as coeditor with Pascal Pia, until his opposition to colonialism and the war forced him to leave Algiers. He left the city in March 1940 for Paris. Although they did not meet between 1935 and 1940, Malraux stayed very much in Camus's mind: some months before he left Algiers for Paris Camus included an adaptation of *La Condition humaine* in the program of his second Algiers theatrical company, Le Théâtre de L'Equipe (Group Theater). The war had other plans for him, however, and the play (had it been written?) never reached the stage.

By 1940 Malraux's close friend Pascal Pia had become a good friend of Camus's. Pia quickly recognized Camus's gifts, hired him as a reporter for *Alger Républicain* in October 1938 and soon offered to share editorial responsibilities with him. In 1940 Pia left Camus in charge of *Le Soir Républicain* and took a job with *Paris Soir*. When military authorities closed down *Le Soir Républicain* he arranged for Camus to be hired by *Paris Soir* as subeditor. It was Pia who in the spring of 1940 took Camus to a screening of Malraux's film *Espoir* for the benefit of the ex-President of Spain, Juan Negrín. He introduced Camus to Malraux but "Malraux scarcely paid attention to the young unknown" (*L* 221). In April 1941, Camus, now back in Oran after the defeat of France, sent the manuscripts of *L'Etranger* and *Caligula* to Pia, who had good connections at Gallimard (including Paulhan and Malraux) in hopes that he could have it read there. Pia forwarded the manuscripts to Malraux and also sent *Le Mythe de Sisyphe* when it arrived. Malraux liked *L'Etranger* especially (and talked about it to everyone who would listen, he said in an interview with Frédéric J. Grover in 1975),[4] and sent all three works to Gaston Gallimard with a firm recommendation to publish. According to Lacouture, Malraux sent a card with the manuscript of *L'Etranger* that said, "Very important." In July 1942 Malraux wrote to Camus from Cap d'Ail to tell him that he had seen copies of the novel in bookshops on the Riviera. Later that year Malraux endorsed Pia's recommendation that Gallimard give Camus a monthly stipend of about 2600 francs. In November 1943 the publisher gave him the office in the Gallimard building on the Rue Sébastien-Bottin that Malraux (and Paulhan) had occupied and that Camus kept, I believe, until his death.

By early 1944 Malraux and Camus were active in the Resistance. They were well known on the literary scene, and if Camus was the lesser light, his star was rising very fast. Camus was living in Paris. He was soon to be the editor of France's best postwar newspaper, a hero of Resistance journalism, a writer with hundreds of thousands of devoted daily readers. He was thirty and no longer merely a protégé of Grenier, Pia, and Malraux. It was nevertheless through them that he entered the circle of the *NRF*, met Gide, Martin du Gard, Groethuysen, and Parain, and became the intimate of the young Gallimards, Pierre and Michel. He dined (date not given by Lottman) at the home of Pierre and Janine Gallimard in the first months of 1944; Malraux was there, too, and after dinner they walked and talked each other home. (Was it during this conversation along the Paris quays that Malraux remarked perspicaciously to Camus that neither of them knew how to write about women?)[5] Perhaps not long after the dinner with the Gallimards, Malraux asked Camus to arrange a hideaway in Paris for Major George Hiller, the British agent who fought with Malraux in the maquis and who later was wounded with him at Gramat. Around the same time (spring 1944), with Michel Gallimard and Francis Ponge, he went to Drieu La Rochelle's office in the Gallimard building, removed cans containing the only print of Malraux's film *Espoir* from a closet, where it had been hidden under files, and took it for safekeeping to the home of Josette Clotis in Neuilly. Thus was the film saved for posterity. An unusual photograph of Camus and Malraux (with two *Combat* writers) records their meeting in an office at *Combat*. An intense, almost fierce stare joins the two obviously undernourished heroes (Malraux is in uniform). It was probably taken in November 1944, a few days after Josette Clotis was "cut in two" (Malraux's phrase) at Saint Chamant (November 11); Malraux passed through Paris before rejoining his brigade in Alsace. Why he went to *Combat* we do not know. Just after the war they met once again at the home of Michel and Janine Gallimard (Michel having replaced Pierre as Janine's husband) in the company of Bernanos and Bruckberger, where subjects of conversation included the purge trials and the punishment of collaborationists. Shortly afterward, in a long interview with Roger Stéphane, Malraux made disparaging remarks about leftist and "Café de Flore intellectuals," meaning especially Camus.[6] Malraux had moved to an anti-Communist position while Camus still believed in the possibility of cooperation with the French Communist party. Their relations remained good enough for Arthur Koestler to bring them together at Malraux's apartment on October 29, 1946 (Lacouture says spring 1947), with Sartre and Manès Sperber (Lacouture adds Simone de Beauvoir) to talk about forming a group of non-Communist intellectuals as an alternative to the Communist-dominated Ligue Française des Droits de l'Homme (French League of Human Rights). It could have been predicted that the meeting would fail. Camus's report of the discussion (see below) made it clear that a coalition of leftist intellectuals aimed at denouncing Russia or supporting the RPF (Rassemblement du Peuple Français) (as Lacouture suggests) was an unlikely eventuality.

After 1946, as Malraux became increasingly involved in the RPF and Camus withdrew from politics, contacts between the two became rare. They must have met between 1946 and January 1959, when Malraux attended the opening of *Les Possédés* (*The Possessed*), but neither Lottman nor Lacouture records a meeting; nor did Camus mention one in his notebooks. In *Le Miroir des limbes* (*The Mirror of Limbo*) Malraux wrote of a talk with Camus around the end of the war, during which Camus wondered—according to Malraux— whether eventually the world would have to choose between Russia and America; Malraux answered that for him the choice was not between Russia and America but between Russia and France. Malraux's nationalist feelings and support of de Gaulle in the forties and fifties, however much he and Camus agreed on the threat Russia represented and other political problems of the times, were bound to keep them apart. In the only relevant mention of Camus in *Le Miroir des limbes*, Malraux said that Camus met with de Gaulle during the latter's "crossing of the desert" (early or mid-fifties?) and that at the end of their talk Camus asked the general what a writer could do to serve France. This was an unlikely question for Camus to ask. De Gaulle's answer, for which purpose Malraux probably told the story, was of course a perfect response to an impossible question: "Anyone who writes (pause), and writes well, serves his country" (*ML* 678). Unlikely as the exchange seems, Malraux reported it as taking place well before May 1958. He probably arranged it. I was told in 1958 that while de Gaulle had invited Camus to his Paris office during his weekly visits before returning to power, Camus refused to see him. Soon after May 13, 1958, when the colonels' putsch ended the Fourth Republic, I saw on Camus's desk a brief handwritten statement that was supposed to go into the prefatory remarks of *Actuelles III* and that declared his intention to fight any move toward dictatorship in France, from Left or Right. It was never published, there or elsewhere, to my knowledge. Camus had already met with de Gaulle, on March 5, 1958, and was assured by the general that he would return to power only by legal means. (Did Malraux arrange this meeting?) Nothing else is known about the meeting, Lottman (who provides the date) says, nor is it known whether they met again. In June 1958 Malraux invited Camus, Mauriac, and Martin du Gard to form a commission to study and report on accusations of torture in Algeria. Camus was the least negative of the three Nobel Prize winners solicited; the commission was aborted. At the height of the Algerian war, in 1958 and 1959, Camus addressed appeals to Malraux and de Gaulle for clemency for Algerian rebels, a number of them condemned to death. Some of the appeals were successful. These were the last of their political contacts.

The next-to-last episode involving Malraux and Camus took place about seven months before de Gaulle came to power. On October 17,

1957, Camus learned that he had received the Nobel Prize. His first reaction was to say that Malraux should have had it. He repeated this often enough during the weeks that followed for it to have been an honest declaration. Camus knew how much he owed to Malraux and he knew he had not written anything that matched *La Condition humaine* and *L'Espoir*. Thus his response to the award was just and generous; Malraux rightly said in a note to Camus that it honored both of them. Malraux, for his part, defended Camus against his detractors, calling them a conspiracy of "failures and homosexuals," and their attacks "ignoble" (*L* 724). On October 17 Camus paid tribute once again to Malraux at the Gallimard reception in his honor; he repeated his belief that Malraux should have had the prize and added that Malraux was one of the masters of his youth. Small comfort for Malraux, who clearly deserved the prize, but proof not only that Camus possessed one of his and Malraux's favorite virtues, admiration, but also that he paid his debts, or at least tried. Malraux was also capable of generosity. He lent his great prestige to the opening of Camus's stage adaptation of *The Possessed* in January 1959, occupying a prominent box with Georges Pompidou. The play was a *succès d'estime* but it lost money, and Malraux's Ministry of Culture helped out by authorizing reimbursement to the theater of about 1.5 million francs in taxes. During this last year of Camus's life, discussions and negotiations were taking place between Camus, his representatives, and Malraux and his Ministry concerning the establishment of a national repertory theater for Camus. Final discussions were planned for the first week of January 1960. Camus was killed on January 4. Malraux sent police escorts to accompany his widow to Villeblevin, scene of the accident, and he dispatched a representative from his ministry to the town in order "to take charge in the name of the government" (*L* 666) and to be sure that no ritual, even a blessing of the body, be allowed, because, he said, Camus would have been opposed.

To the best of my knowledge there are very few published comments by Malraux concerning Camus and his writings, so in what follows our attention will focus on Camus's comments about Malraux. The few published statements by Malraux are of particular interest to Camusians, however.

The best source of information about Camus's attitude toward Malraux is his *Carnets*, notebooks that he kept for twenty-five years and never intended for publication in his lifetime. I shall refer here only to notes that will be recognized as direct or indirect references to Malraux or that are inspired by him. Camus started the *Carnets* in May 1935, by which time (he was twenty-two) he had made a num-

ber of basic decisions about his life and work. He had already published essays and reviews in *Sud,* and he had written fairy tales for
his first wife, Simone Hié, as well as autobiographical essays that
would eventually go into *L'Envers et l'endroit.* All these pieces have
a tentative, adolescent character. But the first entry in the notebooks
reflects a strong life commitment and a firmness and clarity of aims:
he declared what he wanted to say and why. The why is more pertinent here than the what: he had, he said, to "bear witness."[7] Whether
it was the fact of Malraux's visit to Algiers, the *Temps du mépris* triumph in January 1936, his readings of Malraux, or the combined
effect of all three, the notebooks for 1936–38 have more references to
Malraux than all the rest. Early in 1936 he diagrammed his basic
themes and their dynamic relations: at the top, left and right, were
"absurdity" and "lucidity"; close to the base were "the Saint" at one
corner and "socialism" at the other; at the base were "heroic values."
Already, as he would in later life, Camus saw his dilemma as a choice
between contemplation—or a certain state of spiritual being or activity (the "Saint")—and some kind of militant (political or other)
witness ("socialism"). As will become clear later, this was essentially
the choice between his two great masters, Grenier (who advised
Camus to join the Communist party but himself stayed aloof from
politics or "history") and Malraux. Choosing between one and the
other and sticking to the choice remained difficult for Camus all his
life, and until the end he vacillated between—as he put it in his note-
book diagram—"silence" and "action." At this time, the notebooks
show that he was already beginning to think with other bipolar concepts (for example, the choice between Christianity and Communism) and the ideas of the absurd, heroism, and death. In May 1936,
after writing one of the many exhortations to himself to work, re-
build his health, and strengthen his will, he placed among his projects a philosophical essay on "absurdity," an essay on "strength, love,
and death under the sign of conquest" and an "essay on death and
Philosophy—Malraux India." These and other notes written in May
1936 reflect the Grenier–Malraux ties and opposition and pick up or
echo themes found in *La Tentation de l'Occident* (*The Temptation
of the West*) and *Les Conquérants* in particular.

An essay on Malraux was among the half-dozen projects Camus
was thinking about in April 1937. In July, after an anguishing trip
to central Europe that ended in a separation from his young wife,
Camus went into a period of intense creativity. *Caligula* and his first
novels were taking shape in the notebooks. He wanted to write something about the "gambler" and the "adventurer." In September (he

was twenty-three) he reached a turning point in his life and writing, an immense liberation; "revolt" would henceforth be his attitude toward the world, revolt and a no to everything not "tears and sun." In January 1938 a note forged the familiar relation between revolt and revolution; the revolutionary spirit can be found in its entirety in man's protest against the human condition, the only and eternal theme of art and religion. All revolutions, starting with Prometheus', are aimed against the gods. In June 1938 he once again prodded himself to work on "the Absurd" and an "essay on forty hours," both to go into the *Mythe*. As the Spanish civil war moved toward its foregone conclusion and World War II began to loom—and after reading *L'Espoir*, surely—Camus gave voice to a fundamental preoccupation, one that would last until his death, his preoccupation with what Malraux called "virile fraternity." From the beginning, however, Camus's attitude reflected a cleavage between them. As he saw it, the only fraternity possible, with the war rushing toward Europe, was the "sordid and viscous" fraternity of death in combat. At heart a pacifist, Camus always saw the soldier-hero as a potential threat. Kyo and Rieux are incompatible. Camus could not and never did celebrate a warrior society. This helps explain the allegorical mode—so strange to many—of *La Peste* (*The Plague*) and why Malraux found the novel so dull. In Camus's ethic, virile fraternity becomes solidarity (*La Peste*) and finally, a "strange love" (*L'Homme révolté* [*The Rebel*]). He was ridiculed by many for proposing a Salvation Army ethic for the jungle of history. To his credit, Malraux did not, during Camus's lifetime, publicly join the mean-spirited voices of criticism that greeted both *La Peste* and *L'Homme révolté*.

Notes written in December 1938 show that the two books that made Camus's reputation, *L'Etranger* and *Le Mythe de Sisyphe*, both inspired by the experience of the absurd, were fully formed and had only to be written. The Pascalian-Malrucian vision of man as condemned man waiting to be executed, of world as prison, of life as destiny [*l'humaine condition*] of consciousness as lucidity, these familiar themes are there, ready to be integrated into the works of the next two years of writing.

If one judges by the *Carnets*, the decisive encounter of Camus with Malraux was over by 1939. In 1940 Camus finished *L'Etranger*, in 1941, the *Mythe*. "Beginnings of freedom," he wrote. He knew that he was moving into a new stage of his life, thinking and writing. Including independence from his masters? Probably. The references to Malraux thin out and practically disappear from the *Carnets* between 1939 and 1946. In January or February 1942, there is a note about the

interest of certain writers—Gide, Dostoevski, Balzac, Kafka, and
Malraux—in justice and its absurd functioning; he told himself to
find the explanation.[8] There is no further mention of Malraux until
1946, when Camus summarized the discussion with Sartre, Sperber,
Malraux, and Koestler in Malraux's apartment in October, as follows.
Koestler did not get what he (and Malraux?) seemed to want, a commitment to denounce Stalinism. Sartre was opposed to it. Camus had
not yet reached the cold-warrior stage and seemed more concerned
with making public the intellectuals' responsibility for nihilism
in our times. In his summary, Camus curiously ascribes only one
brief intervention to Malraux ("Is the proletariat the only historical
value?"). According to Lacouture, Camus during the discussion made
the mistake of using the word *proletariat*, prompting Malraux to demand a definition; Camus failed in his attempt to define it; Sartre
became angry. The meeting apparently got nowhere, and the discussions were not resumed.

There is only one more clear reference to Malraux in the published
notebooks. Written in June 1947, it is a note about a projected study
of Grenier. Like the one of Malraux, it was never written. In the note
he saw Grenier and Malraux as contraries who were attracted toward
each other. The world, he said, is today a dialogue between the two.
In this formulation what was evident but implicit in his writings of
the thirties and early forties becomes explicit. "The world" is clearly
Camus's consciousness (it may also be the external world, but that is
another matter) and it moved between two poles, which have many
names: East-West, contemplation-action, saint-hero, disaffiliation-
commitment, "*solitaire-solidaire*," etc.—and, above all, Grenier-
Malraux. Camus would remain torn between the two, and, when he
was in the disaffiliated stage, he felt guilty (as evidenced by *La Chute*,
or by "Jonas, ou l'Artiste au travail" in *L'Exil et la royaume*).

A final note, in the still unpublished notebooks for 1951–54,[9]
reached all the way back to *La Tentation de l'Occident*, which had
appeared twenty-eight years before. A "Lettre à M.," it urged "M." to
remain faithful to the West and the western value of intelligence
tempered by feeling. It warned against embracing the East's sacrifice
to the "gods of history." Obviously, if—as I think—the note was directed to Malraux, it was answering the arguments of the *Tentation*
and shows how strong the hold of the book remained. By this time
(1954), both Malraux and Camus had firmly committed themselves
to the war against the "gods of history."

Camus's unpublished notebooks for 1954–60 will probably reveal
more frequent contacts with Malraux toward the end of the decade

because of the discussions and impending decisions concerning the Camus national theater. They will perhaps be—like a lot of the notes of the previous three years—more personal and candid, even about Malraux. They may reveal further reflection on Malraux's works, for during the last years of the fifties Camus, in writing "Le Premier Homme" ("The First Man"), was going back to his roots, to World War I, and he may well have met Malraux once again along that path.

Camus's remarks about Malraux that were intended for publication are very different from the ones found in the *Carnets*. There are two repeated themes in them and little else: Malraux was a great writer; Malraux was one of his masters or one of the masters of his youth. These themes come back with few variations from the beginning to the end of Camus's career. It is a strange fact, however, that Camus never wrote an essay on Malraux or even a review of his books, and never said more than a few words about him in works where discussion seemed necessary, in *Le Mythe de Sisyphe*, or in *L'Homme révolté*, where Malraux is not even mentioned. One can only guess at the reasons for this reticence. A feeling of taboo? Of inadequacy? The reason may be far simpler. In any case, one of his earliest published mentions of Malraux is in his review of Sartre's *La Nausée* (*Nausea*), dated October 20, 1938 (*Alger Républicain*). He said in disappointment that *La Condition humaine* was the model of the "secret fusion" of experience and thought, life and reflection on life, and that Sartre's book did not measure up to the model. That "secret fusion" was the stuff of great novelists. Three weeks later, writing about Nizan's *La Conspiration*, he said flatly, "Malraux . . . is a great writer." (*Alger Républicain*, November 11, 1938). In *Le Mythe de Sisyphe* he paid Malraux the ultimate compliment: all the great novelists are "novelist-philosophers"—Balzac, Sade, Melville, Stendhal, Dostoevski, Proust, and Malraux. This is an extraordinary company, in which Camus never placed another contemporary French writer. Other flattering references can be found scattered among his occasional writings. Twice during the war, like many others still haunted by *Le Temps du mépris*, he used the title of the novel as title of newspaper pieces, first in *Le Soir Républicain* (December 14, 1939) and then in the *Combat* of the liberation (August 30, 1944), to speak of the age the world was passing through. The *Combat* editorial was prompted by the discovery of the bodies of thirty-four tortured and executed members of the Resistance. In it he said 1933 began an age that one of the "greatest among us" has called "le temps du mépris."[10] The deeply deferential tone of these judgments is matched by the public acknowledgments, made in interviews starting in 1951,

of his great debt to Malraux. In his interview with Gabriel d'Auba-
rède in May 1951 he revealed which French writers had shaped his
beginnings: "Grenier was, and has remained, my master . . . [Gide]
reigned over my youth . . . Gide, or rather, the conjunction Malraux-
Gide. . . . At the time Montherlant also affected me deeply" (*Essais*,
1889). Between his receiving the Nobel Prize and his death he repeatedly paid this tribute to Malraux, in informal remarks and in print. In
an interview for *Paris-Théâtre* (1958) he explained why he chose to
adapt *Le Temps du mépris* twenty-two years before: he said he wanted
to do action theater. Besides, he added, he loved the book.[11] In one of
the last of the numerous interviews of Camus's final years, Jean-
Claude Brisville asked him which writers had formed him or helped
him become aware of what he had to say. Camus's answer: among
the moderns, Grenier, Malraux, Montherlant; from the past, Pascal,
Molière, nineteenth-century Russian literature, the Spaniards (*Essais*, 1923). His public opinion of Malraux could not be clearer, nor
the effect Malraux had on him.

On the other hand, Malraux rarely expressed his feelings about
Camus's work for publication; when he did, his comments were de-
nigrating and, in some cases, devastating. Roger Quilliot wrote him
when he was preparing the Pléiade edition of Camus to ask about
Malraux and Camus in Algiers. Malraux answered that he did not
think he had met Camus there, but that he had spent an hour with
him and Pia when the film *Espoir* was shown to Negrín in Paris in
1939 or 1940. He remembered having "talked" about *L'Etranger* to
Gaston Gallimard, but claimed that he had only very confused memories of *Le Mythe de Sisyphe*. The tone of these answers is conde-
scending. His remarks to Frédéric J. Grover in a 1975 interview are
worse. He once again dismissed the *Mythe*. Essentially the book was
"Chestov and [Camus]," he said. He could not keep *Le Mythe de Sisyphe* and *L'Homme révolté* straight and indeed could not say what was
in them. In fact, he told Grover, all he really had in common with
Camus was Gallimard! In praise that utterly damned the book, he
called *L'Etranger* (*The Stranger*) "une réussite artistique" ("an artistic
success"), said it made you think of a Hemingway short story! He
thought Camus was basically a man of the theater. Grover nevertheless persisted in his tacit effort to relate the two writers: *La Peste* was
after all a reprise of the theme of *La Condition humaine*, was it not?
Yes, Malraux, said, but *La Peste* was Camus's "Duhamel side," and
he found the novel so dull that he finished reading it only out of a
feeling of obligation.[12] This dismissal of Camus and the deliberate
and egregious attempt to disassociate himself from him are as pecu-

liar as Camus's silence about Malraux in *L'Homme révolté*. Malraux simply would not have him as his disciple (as he would not have the other great of the generation, Sartre, about whom he also made disparaging remarks).

We can draw a certain number of conclusions from the results of this preliminary exploration of Malraux's and Camus's relations. The first is that Malraux had an extraordinary and a decisive effect on both Camus's life and his career. In 1935-36 Malraux helped launch Camus's career in the theater—always Camus's consolation for the defeats of life and the place where he was happiest—and five years later he started him off on his swift rise to fame by urging Jean Paulhan and Gaston Gallimard to publish *L'Etranger*. Would Grenier's and Pia's support have been enough to sway an editorial committee headed by Paulhan? Perhaps, but I doubt it. The extent to which Malraux was responsible for Camus's very important associations with Gide, Paulhan, Groethuysen, Martin du Gard, Parain, and others in the *NRF* and Gallimard professional and family circles remains to be determined more precisely—once again Grenier and Pia were also involved—but Malraux's sponsorship was probably very helpful. Malraux could very possibly have been the one who suggested that de Gaulle invite Camus to talk with him. This occurred at a critical time, when Camus was not sure of de Gaulle's intentions. De Gaulle's assurance that he would take office only by legal means may have determined Camus's remaining on the sidelines during the turbulent spring and summer of 1958. (He was so unconcerned about France's future in that perilous time that he went on a long boat trip to the Greek isles.) It is clear, furthermore, that Malraux and Camus met on numerous occasions between 1935 and 1960 and that they had good personal relations; but we do not know the precise nature of these relations. Presumably they were amicable. Camus never spoke of them for publication. One would conclude from Malraux's remarks of 1975 that they were quite distant, almost nonexistent. The facts indicate otherwise. We should add here the odd coincidence that two men who had come to know Malraux independently (?) and became friends of his during the twenties, Jean Grenier and Pascal Pia, both played very important roles in Camus's life and career. Pia, soon eclipsed by his protégé, eventually, and probably with justification, turned against Camus. Grenier, also eclipsed by his student, remained the benevolent father figure and mentor until the end. Camus said that from childhood he believed that a star was guiding his destiny. In fact, if there was such a star, it functioned to a great extent through the interventions of Grenier, Pia, and Malraux. It seems clear to me that further study of the personal relations of Malraux and Camus would be very useful. There is obviously more there than meets the eye, and what is there will throw light on both of them, on their works, on their circles, their age. Since there is probably very little written material available, the study will have to be carried out by interviews of family, friends, and associates. Obviously, time is running out.

Turning next to Camus's *Carnets*, those for 1936–38 show how deeply involved Malraux was in the sudden spurt of writing that produced, in the next six years (from 1936 to 1942) *Révolte dans les Asturies*, *L'Envers et l'endroit*, *La Mort heureuse*, *Caligula*, *Noces*, *L'Etranger*, and *Le Mythe de Sisyphe*. Basic themes in Malraux's writings, especially the *Tentation, Les Conquérants, La Condition humaine*, and *Le Temps du mépris* can be found in the notes: the absurd, of course, is the most important of these themes. Others are heroism, the conqueror, revolt and revolution, solidarity, the rectificatory function of art, the writer as witness. It is furthermore evident that from these years onward, it is along the axis Grenier-Malraux that Camus's consciousness and thought and art will move (see one of the best ironic-pathetic statements of the dialectic in "Jonas, ou l'Artiste au travail," which ends with the dilemma *solitaire-solidaire* and the *artiste* almost dying from his inability to choose between them). Essentially the dialectic is saint-hero, contemplation-action, disaffiliation-commitment, and so on. The discourse habitual to Malraux can also be found in the notes: that is, for example, the habit of posing the great questions (the human condition) and oppositions (East-West), of thinking metaphysically. One must obviously be very careful not to leap to a conviction of influence or borrowing. The cast of mind and discourse could just as easily come out of Grenier or other writers Camus was deeply interested in at this time (Dostoevski, Nietzsche). In the case of the absurd, Grenier could, once again, be an equally important factor; furthermore, Camus had probably read *Fear and Trembling* by 1936 and found by then the first modern statement of the absurd. Only a careful study of texts will make clear which of the masters were helping to shape an independently formed experience of the absurd. This I think is true of other basic themes—terrorism, for example—as well. The murder episode in *La Mort heureuse*, so reminiscent of the opening of *La Condition humaine*, the anomalous Conqueror in *Le Mythe de Sisyphe* (I do not think he belongs in Camus's world vision), the title "Le Premier Homme" for the novel he was writing when he was killed, which recalls the beautiful ending of *Les Noyers de l'Altenburg* and its last words, "Ainsi, peut-être, Dieu regarda le premier homme," these and other recalls make it tempting to leap immediately to an idea of servile discipleship or borrowing, but I am afraid the matter is far more complicated than that. That Camus spoke with his own powerfully authentic voice cannot be disputed.

The paucity of references to Malraux in the *Carnets* from 1939 to 1954 show, in conclusion, that the years 1936–39 were the years of greatest impact and that afterward what echoes there are of Malraux are really distant recalls. They also show, however, that Camus never stopped reflecting on Malraux's writing, quite apart from any selfish interest he might have had in Malraux's benevolence.

If we turn, finally, to the public statements that these two figures made about each other, the question of lordship and bondage becomes somewhat of a puzzle. Malraux's outright dismissal of Camus has two prongs: first, Camus is an inferior writer (he is really a "man of the theater"), and second, Camus is not his intellectual heir (*La Peste* reflects Camus's "Duhamel side"). There is an obvious wish to cut off the younger brother/son/disciple. Camus's attitude toward Malraux was more ambivalent, to say the least. Recognizing his indebtedness, he paid him public tribute. But the coin of that tribute seems cheap when seen in the light of Camus's silence about the master; there is no mention of him in *L'Homme révolté*, and he never wrote the essay first projected in the mid-thirties. It is also true that he never wrote the essay, planned around the same time, on Jean Grenier, his other great contemporary master. (In Grenier's case, too, Camus acknowledged his debt and paid perhaps more generous tribute.) Camus's inability or refusal to write these essays (I think he wanted to) reflects complicated feelings. I believe for a long time Camus wished to be like Grenier, the sage, safely out of the violent turbulence of the artist's and militant witness's life, the philosopher-guru meditating and guiding, but discreetly and at a distance. Inevitably, like so many young people of the thirties and forties, he also wanted to emulate Malraux, the adventurer, soldier, conqueror, committed writer, leader, statesman, at the epicenter of history. He tried both ways, and finally had to find and affirm his own authentic self, *ni Grenier, ni Malraux*, to use a favorite rhetorical figure of his. His silence is his tacit disavowal, dismissal, of them, I think, a recantation of his own discipleship. Neither the silentiary saint nor the thundering warrior hero. The creator, perhaps, in his own version of the Nietzschean ideal, which he might have realized in his last years in his last planned cycle of works, "La Création corrigée."

These preliminaries leave the essentials unsaid. The next step is to

fill out the biographical and bibliographical areas, find out more precisely, if possible, when Camus read the works of Malraux, when he
started reading the *NRF*, the existentialists—especially Kierkegaard.
The study of texts can follow. While it is clear that Malraux's impact
was great, it makes little sense to study that impact if we have yet to
determine at which points between 1930 and 1935 Camus encountered his various masters.

Walter G. Langlois

BEFORE "L'ESPOIR": MALRAUX'S

PILOTS FOR REPUBLICAN SPAIN

On August 19, 1936, the *London News-Chronicle* published a dispatch from its correspondent in Republican Spain that has unexpected interest for Malraux scholars. The item noted: "Eighteen French warplanes have reached Barcelona. . . . The majority of the pilots . . . are to remain in Spain as instructors or pilots."[1] The arrival of these planes and airmen at the end of the first month of the Spanish civil war marked the culmination of nearly three weeks of tireless behind-the-scenes efforts by several members of the cabinet of French Socialist Premier Léon Blum; these men were determined to send urgently needed military aid to the Spanish Republic, threatened by a right-wing insurrection. Most historians now agree that this August shipment had some military importance because it helped the Madrid government to slow—if only briefly—the relentless advance of the rebel forces moving against the capital. This, in turn, was a factor in thwarting the disgruntled generals' plans for a rapid coup. However, the arrival of these aircraft and pilots on the peninsula was also a noteworthy event in literary history. For one of those who had been involved from the very beginning in organizing this whole enterprise was the French novelist and political activist, André Malraux; a majority of these men and planes were almost immediately organized into the Escadrille España, an air unit under his leadership. This experience of Malraux's as a squadron commander provided material for major segments of his great novel *L'Espoir*.

In 1952 W. M. Frohock—the first serious scholar to work on Malraux—accurately noted that information was not then available for the writing of a definitive study of this novelist, one that would illuminate the autobiographical and historical elements underlying his principal creative works, particularly *L'Espoir*. Indeed, Frohock summed up virtually all that was then known about Malraux's involvement in the Spanish civil war when he noted that shortly after the conflict broke out the writer had crossed the Pyrenees to help organize some men and materiel for the Republican air force.[2] Now, three decades later, following Frohock's lead, other critics and historians have explored certain aspects of Malraux's Spanish experience.[3] Yet the initial weeks of his commitment—particularly his activities in recruiting the pilots that were soon to fly in his squadron—have remained obscure. It is this element, so important for an understanding of the overtones of his novel, that we hope to clarify here.

I

When French Premier Léon Blum arrived at his office on the morning of Monday, July 20, 1936, he found on his desk a telegram from José Giral, Prime Minister of the Spanish Republic. It read: "Surprised by dangerous military coup. Ask you to reach immediate understanding with us for furnishing arms and airplanes. Fraternally yours, Giral." As Blum later recalled, the news of this insurrection stunned him. To be sure, he was aware that the political situation in Spain had been tense since the February election victories of the Frente Popular (Spanish Popular Front) had brought a coalition of mildly reformist Republicans to power in Madrid. He also knew that two political assassinations during the previous fortnight had greatly increased the ideological polarization between Right and Left that had been taking place for years. However, only two days earlier, Luis Jiminez de Asua— a close personal friend who was high in the Madrid government—had confidently reassured him that the Republic was firmly in control of the situation on the peninsula and that there was nothing to fear.[4]

Upon receiving this telegraphed appeal for arms and aircraft from the Spanish prime minister, Blum did not hesitate. He immediately instructed Edouard Daladier, his Minister for War and Defense, and Pierre Cot, Minister for Air, to see what could be made rapidly available to Madrid. By noon a list of Spain's specific arms requirements had arrived at Blum's office. The list was rather modest under the circumstances: in addition to eight 75 mm cannon, some machine guns, and various types of ammunition, it included twenty-five Potez bombers. By the end of the day Daladier had begun gathering the munitions requested, and—even more important—Cot had located a group of Potez-25s that he felt might fill Spain's immediate aviation needs. These two-seater biplanes, powered by 500 horsepower Farman engines, had originally been designed a few years after World War I to serve as observation and light bombing craft for the French air force, and they had been in service since 1929. By 1936 they were officially classed as obsolescent, and most had been withdrawn from active military units and placed in storage. In reviewing the records at the Air Ministry, Cot had found that about two dozen such recently decommissioned planes were parked at an army depot in northern France. He immediately ordered them moved to the military airport at Mondésir, near Etampes, about fifty kilometers southwest of Paris. He also instructed the personnel at the field to check them thoroughly, fuel them, and paint over the French markings on the fuselage with gray paint in preparation for delivery to the Spanish Republicans.[5] He knew that these old craft were so simple in design that no special training was required to fly them, and he assumed that pilots of the Republican air force would soon come to Paris to ferry them to the peninsula.

The next day, Tuesday, July 21, two Spanish aviation officers—Ismael Warleta de la Quintana and Juan Aboal de Aveal—arrived from Madrid to oversee the purchase of the arms and planes requested by Giral.[6] Not surprisingly, one of the first French officials whom they visited was Pierre Cot. In response to the air minister's questions, the two envoys painted a bleak picture of the Republican air force. As far as could be estimated, a good portion of Spain's military planes and equipment was still in government hands, but virtually without exception this materiel was so obsolete as to be worthless. Most of the aircraft were models from the early 1920s, *built* in the 1920s. Although bombers were urgently needed to stem the mechanized insurgent advance, Warletta and Aboal reported that except for a few old seaplanes the Republic owned no such machines whatever.[7] Upon hearing this, Cot told the envoys that he had located a group of about twenty Potez-25s that could be used as light bombers. If price agreements could be reached and contracts signed, he was sure that this initial consignment could leave within a few days. He was also virtually certain that very shortly he would have some additional, more modern machines to offer Madrid, notably eighteen fast Dewoitine fighters that could easily be altered to carry some light explosives, and about half a dozen multiplace Potez-54 heavy bombers. As far as he was concerned, it was only a question of bringing the necessary Spanish pilots to Paris to man these various craft.

Warleta and Aboal were quick to respond that they themselves were ready to fly two of the Potez-25s to the peninsula and to lead the remaining planes there. However, they pointed out that it would be extremely difficult to provide any additional Spanish pilots. The few competent and unquestionably loyal airmen available to Madrid simply could not be spared to come to Paris; they were too urgently needed for military operations against the advancing rebel forces. Cot was distressed to hear this news because he knew that it would make the task of getting the French planes to the peninsula very difficult. For from the outset Foreign Minister Yvon Delbos had indicated that he would allow only Spanish pilots to be involved in any ferrying operations; he was afraid that the slightest hint of French involvement in the Spanish insurrection would be used as an excuse by certain anti-Republican nations to intervene in support of the rebel generals.

Then Warleta and Aboal proceeded to give Cot some additional discouraging information about the sad state of the Spanish Republican air force as far as personnel were concerned. When the Republic was established in 1931, its leaders took a resolutely antimilitary stance. Largely because of this policy, few new pilots were trained in the early 1930s and none at all in 1934 and 1935. Thus, at the time of the insurrection, many of the air force personnel were physically somewhat beyond their prime. Moreover, because of the lack of new equipment, their flying experience had been limited almost entirely to obsolescent planes. Certainly no one among them had had any training in the kind of skills that would be required to man modern multiplace bombers or to fly fast new pursuit ships. This personnel situation was further complicated by the fact that most pilots were officers who came from the small elite class of Spanish society; when the revolt broke out, a large proportion of them had immediately defected to the insurgents.[8]

In a certain sense, the problem of manpower was even more critical for the Republican air force than that of machines, but Warleta and Aboal hastened to assure Cot that their government was fully aware of the situation and prepared to try to correct it. What Madrid proposed was to hire civilian flyers, not only to convey the Potez-25s to the peninsula but also for subsequent service with the Republican air force. The envoys revealed that they had even brought a considerable sum of money in gold with them to Paris so that this project could be funded immediately.[9] After further discussion Cot told them that he would turn this whole problem of recruiting pilots over to his friend and political associate, Léo Lagrange.

Léo Lagrange, a long-time aviation enthusiast, was Undersecretary for Sports and Leisure, a newly created post in the Blum government. In connection with his efforts to encourage recreational flying in France, he was in touch with a number of flying groups and clubs.[10] He knew that through these organizations he could probably contact enough pilots—individuals who were temporarily out of work or who might be willing to give a day or two of their time, particularly on a weekend—to ferry the Potez-25s to Spain, for pay. However, he was also aware that these recreational flying clubs would not likely be able to provide the skilled professionals required to take the more sophisticated Dewoitines and Potez-54s to the peninsula and to fly them in combat until Spaniards had been properly trained to take them over. Such tasks would require airmen with some kind of fairly recent military experience. Cot had already indicated that he intended to try to obtain some volunteers—not only pilots, but also bombardiers, navigators, and mechanics—from among French air force reservists. However, Lagrange knew that there was another possible source for such technically trained individuals: the various groups of antifascist refugees who had been gathering in Paris for more than a decade, particularly the Italians.

The late 1920s and early 1930s had seen the establishment of a number of authoritarian or fascist governments in Europe, most notably in Italy, Germany, and the USSR. As these regimes had become increasingly oppressive, more and more of those who dared to speak out in opposition were silenced, imprisoned, or forced into exile. These individuals came from a variety of milieux, and many had training in different vocational and professional skills; in their exile all were united by a passionate desire to continue the struggle against dictatorships, wherever they might arise. A large proportion of these exiles had taken refuge in France, where they had set up a number of semipolitical organizations to further their cause. Of the national groups the Italians were by far the oldest and the largest. Mussolini had assumed power in Italy in October of 1922, and as his regime grew more dictatorial, successive waves of Italian socialists, republicans, and liberals fled to safety in France.[11] To help him contact any of these people who might have training useful to the Spanish Republican air force, Lagrange decided to turn to his close friend, André Malraux.

By the mid-1930s Malraux had become recognized as a leader in the worldwide antifascist movement. During his two-year stay in Indochina in the mid-1920s he had experienced firsthand some of the injustices of French colonial authoritarianism, and after his return to the metropolis in 1926 he had gradually become an increasingly outspoken opponent of such political systems.[12] The subsequent rise of oppressive right-wing governments in Italy and Germany led him to become directly involved in numerous antifascist organizations and in leftist politics in general. Between 1933 and 1936 he appeared at dozens of rallies and meetings and he became friends with certain political leaders—Cot and Lagrange, among others—who were appointed to high positions in Blum's government following the Popular Front victories of June 1936. Thanks to his antifascist activism, Malraux had also established contacts with the heads of many of the refugee organizations in Paris. However, there was one association of antifascists for whom he felt a special ideological and personal affinity. It was the Italian Giustizia e Libertà (GL; Justice and Liberty) group, founded in Paris in the late summer of 1929 by a dynamic Florentine intellectual named Carlo Rosselli.

Historically, GL is probably the most significant and interesting of all the non-Communist organizations of this kind that arose during this period. It was a movement led by people of high principles who were committed to the overthrow of the dictatorship and the establishment of a free, democratic, and republican regime in Italy.[13] While the initial purpose was primarily political, the GL leaders soon saw that something more profound than a social revolution was required to defeat authoritarianism, and they began to push for a metaphysical renaissance that would provide the base for a total liberation of man and the beginning of a new kind of life. Although strongly influenced by some of Marx's theories, GL was resolutely anti-Communist, and Rosselli—a kind of modern-day *condottiere*—is credited by scholars with having done more than anyone else among Italian exiles to prepare a new class of intellectual leaders who were not bound by traditional ideologies.[14] Since GL's fundamental commitment was to a libertarian "religion of man" that was very similar to Malraux's humanism, it is not surprising that in the years just before 1936 the writer formed friendships with several leaders of this organization, notably Rosselli and one of his chief lieutenants, the author Nicola Chiaromonte.

But Justice and Liberty was not just a group of armchair philosophers; it was also a movement deeply commited to action, particularly to nonviolent gestures that would call attention to the antifascist cause and embarrass the regime of Il Duce, while at the same time fostering a spirit of resistance to fascism among those living under its shadow. In the early 1930s GL gained a certain notoriety by organizing a series of audacious propaganda flights over Italian cities in imitation of the 1918 feat of Gabriele D'Annunzio above Vienna. An initial leaflet-dropping incursion over Milan in the summer of 1930 was followed by plans for half a dozen others over various population centers of the peninsula. At one point several GL leaders even went to Madrid to confer with Manuel Azaña, Indalecio Prieto, and the Spanish flying ace Ramón Franco about a possible base on Spanish territory. One project that aroused particular interest abroad (even though it was thwarted by Mussolini's secret police) was scheduled for October 1930, to mark the anniversary of the 1922 march on the capital that had originally brought the dictator to power. The pilot involved was a courageous and idealistic young Republican named Giordano Viezzoli, a flyer in the Italian air force. Viezzoli's trial, imprisonment, and subsequent escape to France sparked worldwide interest, and Lagrange must certainly have been aware of his presence—and that of several other Italian airmen—in the ranks of the GL in Paris.[15]

Very shortly after learning of the information brought by Warleta and Aboal, Lagrange contacted Malraux. He wanted his friend to set up a conference with representatives of GL to discuss what help the Italian antifascists could give to the Spanish Republicans, particularly to their air force. Lagrange probably even knew that the leadership of GL had already decided to take action in support of Madrid. Indeed, very soon after the outbreak of hostilities Rosselli had received a firsthand report of the situation from a close friend who had been visiting the peninsula, and he immediately sensed that the struggle in Spain represented something more than just a nationalist military coup. As he pointed out in an editorial he wrote for the GL newspaper at the time: "The Spanish revolution is our revolution . . . [and] the civil war of the proletariat in Spain is the war of all antifascism. . . . The place for revolutionaries capable of bringing an effective technical aid to Spanish comrades—for technicians are needed above all—is in Spain."[16] Rosselli believed that all antifascist groups, irrespective of doctrinal differences, ought to make a commitment to provide such help, but when he approached socialist and Communist exile groups in Paris he was rebuffed. These ideological purists had not yet formulated their official position on the conflict and were unwilling to do anything until such a policy had been set. Undaunted,

Rosselli and other GL leaders decided to begin organizing things on their own. At this point Malraux's request for them to meet with Lagrange was received.

According to one of Mussolini's secret agents who had infiltrated GL, the gathering took place in Malraux's Rue du Bac apartment on the evening of Wednesday, July 22, the day following the arrival of Warleta and Aboal in the French capital. Those present—in addition to Lagrange, Malraux, and Malraux's friend the Russian writer Ehrenburg—included Rosselli, Viezzoli, Chiaromonte, Alberto Cianca (one of the founders of GL), and several other, unnamed Italians. There had been a recent ideological disagreement between Rosselli and Chiaromonte, but at the outset of the meeting Malraux was able to effect a reconciliation between the two men. Then Lagrange outlined the critical state of the Spanish Republican air force, particularly as far as its personnel were concerned. Obviously, it was necessary to recruit some qualified technical people as rapidly as possible, and Malraux asked Rosselli if GL would be willing to help. Rosselli indicated that he had already begun such an effort and that one pilot, Viezzoli, was immediately available from GL. He promised shortly to provide the names of additional personnel whose technical skills would be useful to the Madrid air force. He hoped to begin sending these volunteers to the peninsula in the very near future, paying their travel expenses from his own resources if necessary, and he agreed to keep Lagrange informed.[17]

Following the meeting with Rosselli, Malraux himself prepared to leave for a week's stay in Spain. He was going there as the representative of the prestigious Comité mondial contre la guerre et le fascisme (World Committee Against War and Fascism), of which he was co-president, to bring the Republic assurances of support from antifascists all over the world. He had also been asked by his friends in the Blum cabinet to make a survey of Madrid's military requirements so that the government could make some informed decisions about providing supplies, particularly aircraft, to Madrid. As he left Paris Malraux must have been fairly optimistic. He knew that Cot and Daladier were gathering the necessary materiel and planes, and that a certain number of antifascist volunteers—in majority Italians— would shortly reach the peninsula to place themselves at the orders of Republican officials. He could not have foreseen that some rather serious complications would soon radically alter this whole situation.

As we have said, following Giral's appeal Cot and Daladier had rapidly set about locating war materiel for Madrid. They had not been able to make any final commitments, however, because top officials at the Spanish embassy, more sympathetic to the rebels than to the

Republicans, had refused to sign the necessary financial documents. Fortunately Madrid had foreseen such a possibility and had asked a trusted former cabinet minister, the socialist leader Fernando de los Ríos, to interrupt his vacation in Switzerland and come to Paris to take charge of these negotiations.[18] De los Ríos arrived in the French capital early on the morning of Thursday, July 23, and within hours he had consulted with Cot and Lagrange. He assured them that Madrid fully intended to honor any financial commitments made in fulfillment of the Giral request and asked that appropriate contracts be drawn up immediately, under his authority. This was the go-ahead that Lagrange had been waiting for. He had already made preliminary contacts with a number of pilots for the Potez-25s, and following the meeting with de los Ríos he began telephoning and wiring these individuals. Since the recreational aviation clubs had produced few volunteers, the Spanish government was obliged to offer generous remunerations to obtain most of the personnel required for the ferry operation. Each pilot was to be paid a basic stipend of 20,000 francs for the flight to the peninsula, in addition to 10,000 francs for "travel expenses" and an insurance policy of 200,000 francs.[19]

Lagrange instructed these mercenaries to begin assembling at the Villacoublay military field on the next day, Friday, July 24, so that they would be ready to fly the Potez-25s to Spain during the weekend. It was planned that the planes would leave in two squadrons of ten craft each, led respectively by Warleta and Aboal. The destination was to be the privately owned Air France airport of Prat de Llobregat on the outskirts of Barcelona. Those pilots wishing to return to France immediately would be flown back aboard one of the regular Air France flights from North Africa that made an intermediate stop at Barcelona. The trip to Spain was an unusually demanding one for planes of this vintage, but in view of the generous rate of pay most of the hired airmen felt that it was worth the risk.[20] Then, only a few hours before it was to begin, this whole convoy operation was abruptly canceled.

Political circles in Paris had been very agitated since the first confirmed news of the Spanish uprising was received on Monday morning. France was ideologically polarized in much the same manner that Spain was, and public opinion in the country was sharply divided between those who wished to send help to the Madrid Republicans, and those who wanted the generals' coup against the "reds" to succeed. French newspapers at both ends of the political spectrum sought to involve their readers on one side or the other of the Spanish cause, and to link it to the French political scene. The conservative press in particular—fearful that aid from the Popular Front government of the socialist Léon Blum would help defeat the conservative rebels—decried any action that might give an advantage to Madrid. From the very outset, these papers featured stories about Giral's request for arms and the arrival of the two Spanish air officers, as well as all kinds of rumors about the suspicious activities of Daladier, Cot, and other Blum officials. Their purpose was to arouse opposition, both in the parliament and among the general population, to any pro-Madrid activities. On Thursday, July 23, while Léon Blum and Yvon Delbos were away in London for a high-level diplomatic meeting, two conservative morning newspapers published full details about the materiel that Blum was planning to send to Giral.[21] This information, leaked by prorebel officials at the Spanish embassy, made a *cause célèbre* of the Potez-25s waiting at Villacoublay. On learning of the furor, Premier Blum telephoned Paris and instructed Cot and Daladier to delay any further action until after his return to the capital the following day. He was determined to honor his initial commitment to Giral, but he now felt that it would be advisable to use greater circumspection in the whole matter.[22]

Shortly after landing in Paris late that Friday, July 24, Blum arranged a meeting between himself, Cot, Delbos, Daladier, and the unofficial Spanish envoy, de los Ríos. At that meeting (subsequently outlined in a report that de los Ríos sent to Giral), it was decided— after much discussion—to move ahead as originally planned, but very prudently. The matter of the pilots was troublesome because Foreign Minister Delbos was still adamantly opposed to any suggestion that French flyers be used to ferry the Potez-25 planes to Spain. None of the ministers present favored using French military personnel for this task, but Cot argued that there would be very little risk involved if civilians were hired. De los Ríos reiterated that it would be virtually impossible for his government to provide any personnel from its woefully undermanned air force, and he reemphasized Madrid's eagerness to recruit such mercenaries. In spite of very grave reservations, Delbos finally agreed to a compromise: civilians could be employed to fly the Potez-25s as far as Perpignan or some other airfield in southern France. Once there, however, the planes would have to be turned over to Spaniards for the rest of the journey to the peninsula. De los Ríos said that he would contact his government to see what could be done to implement this decision.[23]

Then, unexpectedly, early the next morning a group of what might be called conservative ministers in Blum's coalition government informed the premier that they were unalterably opposed to any effort, however circumspect, to help Madrid; indeed, they were prepared to resign if their objections were not heeded. Faced with a crisis that might shake his government, Blum called an emergency meeting of all his ministers late that afternoon to try to reach a compromise. After heated discussion, Blum and the few pro-Republicans who supported him were forced to abandon their original plan of providing arms and planes to Madrid directly, on a government-to-government basis, as Giral had originally requested. Henceforth Paris would officially commit itself to a neutralist position. As was noted in a bulletin issued shortly after the meeting, in the interests of preventing international complications and even though it was a question of the legal government of a friendly nation, the Council of Ministers had decided "that no export of war materiel to Spain would be permitted."[24]

In reality, however, France's position was a bit less restrictive than this statement might suggest. For during the meeting it had been revealed that a secret clause in the 1935 commercial treaty with Spain obliged Madrid to purchase a considerable quantity of war materiel each year from France, and even the conservative ministers did not wish to set aside this provision. It was finally agreed that in spite of the officially proclaimed embargo, the possible sale to Spain of certain items—most notably unarmed aircraft—might be allowed. However, it was to be clearly understood that such sales were not to pass through any government channels; rather they were to take place, at least nominally, between representatives of the Madrid government and various private individuals or business firms in France. By this stratagem, the appearance if not the reality of the neutrality policy would be honored. As far as pilots were concerned, there was a tacit agreement that, as de los Ríos put it in his report to Giral, authorization would be given "for private industry to turn over to us and *to move* the materiel that we shall buy."[25] Obviously, what the Council had in mind was a kind of nongovernmental or private entity that would be responsible for recruiting civilian flyers to ferry the Potez-25s, and presumably any other aircraft purchased from France, to fields near the southern border. There Spanish pilots would take them over. It is very doubtful that the ministers foresaw that a broad interpretation of this policy would lead to the formation of a separate unit, led by Malraux, of foreign mercenary and volunteer airmen in the service of the Spanish Republican air force. However, within a fortnight that was precisely what happened.

II

At the time that the crucial Saturday, July 25, meeting of the Council of Ministers took place, Malraux was already in Spain. He had left on his semiofficial fact-finding mission the previous afternoon in a government aircraft provided by Pierre Cot. He planned to stay in Madrid and Barcelona for a week, conferring with various leaders, making some public statements on behalf of the antifascist groups with whom he was associated, and establishing contacts with certain officials—most notably at the Air Ministry. When he learned that the French government had changed its original policy, however, and was now officially prohibiting arms shipments to Spain (this news reached Madrid on Sunday afternoon), he decided to go back to France as soon as possible. He felt that it was imperative that he do something to conteract this heavy blow struck against the Republic in the name of neutrality. On the Monday morning return flight to Paris in the official plane, his traveling companion was Alvarez de Albornoz, the new Spanish ambassador to France; the latter's presence in the French capital had been urgently requested in order to solve certain problems created by anti-Republican bureaucrats. Having read de los Ríos' report, de Albornoz was aware that the Council's embargo was not absolute—for unarmed aircraft could still be sold, after appropriate authorizations had been obtained—and that the establishing of some kind of private aviation group was envisaged to move such materiel. During the long flight back to the metropolis, the ambassador and his companion doubtless discussed this whole matter at some length.[26]

When Malraux landed in Paris that evening, he was wholeheartedly resolved to do everything in his power to help Madrid solve the severe personnel and equipment problems it faced, particularly in its air force. Shortly after his return he gave a newspaper interview in which he made this commitment clear. After giving details about some of the general needs of the Republic as he had observed them during his brief visit to the peninsula, he emphasized that the situation there had suddenly become critical because the insurgents had started to receive shipments of military equipment, including aircraft, from the fascist powers. "There is not a day, not an hour to lose," he affirmed; France must organize itself as soon as possible and exert "its greatest efforts to obtain for the Spanish government and its troops the materiel that they need." In his opinion, a decisive military confrontation between Republicans and rebels would take place in the very near future, and to fight effectively "the soldiers of freedom need weapons, aircraft, pilots, and military technicians." It was clearly in France's self-interest to respond to these needs, for otherwise the rebels would be victorious and would install an authoritarian government south of the Pyrenees. This would mean that France would be confronting right-wing regimes across three of her borders![27]

Suiting his actions to his words, in the next few days Malraux renewed his efforts to obtain men and equipment for Spain. As far as pilots were concerned, most of those needed to ferry the Potez-25s had been recruited. (Unfortunately, adverse publicity had again postponed the dispatch of this contingent of planes to Madrid, and some of the pilots had already begun to leave Mondésir to return to their regular jobs.) However, the more modern Dewoitines and Potez-54s that Cot had located presented a much more complex problem. Upon making some inquiries, Malraux learned that the first leg of the flight of these new planes to the peninsula was provided for. The French aircraft firms involved had reluctantly agreed to permit a few of their company pilots to fly them as far as Toulouse, and several off-duty Air France personnel had also promised a bit of additional help. Since these men were aviation professionals, they were familiar with recent-model planes and quite capable of handling the Dewoitines and Potez-54s. Several of them indicated their willingness to make more than one trip if necessary, to move all the machines to the Toulouse staging area. Unfortunately, because of various restrictions and professional commitments, these pilots could not agree to fly the planes all the way to Spain, much less take them into combat, however sympathetic to the Republican cause they might have been.

Thus the real personnel problem began at Toulouse. To be sure, Cot was still hoping to get some skilled volunteers from the French air force reserve and from among recently discharged airmen, but on such short notice it was unlikely that this source would be very fruitful. At this juncture Malraux again turned to Carlo Rosselli to see what GL could do. According to a confidential report to Rome from the Italian embassy in Paris, the two men apparently met again on Tuesday evening, July 28, just twenty-four hours after Malraux's return from Spain with de Albornoz and a week after his previous conversation with representatives from GL.[28] At this session Rosselli was able to report a certain amount of success in his recruiting efforts. The pilot Giordano Viezzoli had already left for the peninsula, as had an experienced machine gunner named Veniero Spinelli. A number of additional GL members or sympathizers—including Giuseppe Zuddas, Aldo Garosci, Camillo Berneri, Pietro Nenni, Nicola Chiaromonte, Zanella, Piatti, and a skilled mechanic from the Talbot plant named Angelo de Simone—would be leaving soon as well. As Rosselli explained it, a system of triage had been organized at a Rue Lafayette recruiting center to identify and classify the skills of any Italians who volunteered for Spain. Those, like himself, with experience as officers in World War I were particularly prized because they could be assigned to lead groups of foreign volunteers or to act as advisors for units of the Spanish People's Militia. However, all individ-

uals with specific aviation experience, of whatever kind, were ear-
marked for possible service with the Republican air force, as were
those whose civilian occupations lent themselves to such duty.[29] To
attract as little attention as possible, most of these volunteers were
planning to go to the peninsula individually. Once in Spain they were
to report to air officials at Barcelona or Madrid for further instructions and assignments.

Malraux then told Rosselli that he had been asked to "serve as a
liaison agent between the French government and the Popular Front
of Madrid." After explaining the subtleties of the Council's new position on aid to Spain, he confirmed that he was one of the private individuals who was to be responsible for organizing the dispatch of volunteers and war materiel to the peninsula. Since he had no official
links to the government, he could pretend to act on his own initiative, thus conforming to the new Council policy. After discussing
further plans for the rapid sending of as many volunteer skilled Italian workers and airmen as GL could recruit, Rosselli told Malraux
that he himself was very eager to get to Spain. He particularly wanted
to go to Barcelona, where the idealists of the anarchist movement were
most active. Malraux promised to help, but arrangements proved to
be very difficult and Rosselli finally had to leave for Barcelona on his
own.[30]

In spite of such recruiting efforts by Malraux and others, the number of volunteers who possessed the vocational and technical skills
needed for modern warfare—and which were so tragically lacking
among the Republican forces—remained very small. To publicize
this personnel need and to arouse support for Madrid generally, the
major groups within the French Popular Front decided to sponsor a
mammoth public rally at the Salle Wagram on Thursday evening,
July 30. Malraux, widely known as an unusually effective orator, was
the featured speaker. Since he had just returned from Spain, his remarks carried great weight. From the accounts of those present, it is
clear that one of his primary purposes was to highlight Madrid's need
for technical specialists and to put pressure on reluctant French political leaders to support the recruitment of such individuals.[31]

After giving some general impressions of what was happening on
the peninsula, illustrated by vivid anecdotes, Malraux brought up the
problem of Madrid's arms requests. Those who were ideologically opposed to the French and Spanish Popular Fronts maintained that the
Republic ought not to be permitted to purchase materiel abroad, but
Malraux pointed out that by international law and custom the legal
government of any country was fully entitled to acquire on world
markets whatever it needed to maintain its internal security. He ad-

mitted, however, that such sales to Madrid by a foreign government could be dangerous because they might serve as a pretext for intervention by several nations openly sympathic to the rebels. Therefore he was in favor of "no international intervention in Spain," a position entirely consonant with the policy officially adopted by the Blum government on July 25. He hoped that this kind of restraint might prevent Hitler and Mussolini from giving arms to the insurgent generals, an action that would inevitably enlarge and prolong the tragic conflict.

In his Wagram speech Malraux also emphasized that such a restriction ought to apply only to aid that was official, or from government to government. There was no reason, he said, for preventing friends of the Spanish Republic from sending technical aid and volunteers to strengthen various elements of the People's Militia of the Republic. On the contrary, "the French people demand that their hands be untied," he asserted. "For example, the Spaniards need drivers for their vehicles, instructors for the different branches of their defense forces, doctors, engineers." If qualified volunteers could be found, they ought to be permitted to go to Spain without difficulty. In addition, some kind of "commercial assistance" ought to be organized so that Madrid could purchase materiel from private business firms in various parts of the world. Such a system would involve few international risks because no governments would be directly involved, and it was clearly justified on legal as well as humanitarian grounds. In any case, he concluded, the channeling of help through such private groups was one of the best ways for antifascists abroad to help Spain in her fight to remain free.

By a strange coincidence, on the very day that Malraux spoke at the Wagram rally, an event took place that had a major impact on French policy toward Spain. As has been suggested, one of the main reasons for the reluctance of many French officials to help the Spanish Republicans was a fear that such action might be used to justify similar moves by Italy and Germany, the two fascist states that were openly sympathetic to the rebel generals' cause. Although Malraux and others had already reported that such aid was being sent to the insurgents, there had never been any concrete proof of the charge, and pro-rebels in France dismissed it as a propaganda lie. Then, late in the afternoon of Thursday, July 30, Pierre Cot unexpectedly received word that three foreign aircraft had made forced landings on French territory in North Africa. Preliminary information indicated that they were Italian warplanes on their way to one of the insurgent headquarters in Spanish Morocco. Cot immediately realized that if this indeed proved to be the case it would establish beyond any doubt that Mussolini was sending aid to the rebel generals. Such a confirmation would, in turn, justify French supporters of the Republic, like himself, who wanted to take similar action. In view of the importance of this incident, Cot decided to dispatch an unimpeachable witness to investigate and report back to him. The man he chose for this task, a widely respected conservative army officer named General Denain, left for North Africa that very evening. For the next twenty-four hours Paris was abuzz with rumors about these foreign machines, and the incident even came up during parliamentary debate on the government's Spanish policy. Foreign Minister Delbos took the occasion to reiterate that as yet France had authorized no such war materiel whatsoever to be shipped to the Spanish Republic, but he emphasized that the government would not commit itself to "continue in this attitude [of restraint] if certain foreign governments decide to furnish arms to the belligerents."[32]

Early on Saturday, August 1, just before the regular ministers' meeting, Cot received absolute confirmation by telephone from General Denain that the three planes in North Africa were part of a contingent of twelve Savoia bombers that had been hastily withdrawn from Italian military units in Sardinia and dispatched on Mussolini's orders to the Spanish insurgents. They were manned by regular personnel of the Italian air force. Not surprisingly, this information played an important role in the Council's discussions that morning. All the ministers were incensed at this proof of Italy's involvement in the Spanish conflict, but the conservatives were still strongly opposed to France's taking any comparable action. Several knowledgeable members of the Council then pointed out that in such a direct contest to supply arms, France could not win; after several years of minimal funding and reduced production, the French aircraft and munitions firms were simply unable to match the manufacturing capacities of the two most bellicose nations in Europe: Italy and Germany. In view of this situation, some of the ministers supporting Madrid felt that it might be in the ultimate best interests of the Republic to institute a complete, multination embargo and stop *all* arms shipments to Spain. For in this way the superior production of the fascist countries would not be made available to the insurgents, and the balance of power would not be tipped in their favor. The conservative ministers also favored this suggestion—albeit for different reasons—and the Council directed Foreign Minister Delbos to make appropriate overtures to Italy and Great Britain. If they were favorably received, he was immediately to contact the other nations in Europe about a general nonintervention agreement. As a concession to the pro-Republicans, the Council agreed that until responses had been received and "because of the war shipments now received by the insurgents," the July 25 export restrictions on materiel for Spain would be removed. This would permit Cot and Daladier to send to the peninsula all the planes and other war supplies that they had gathered in response to Giral's July 20 appeal.[33] As Blum later revealed, these shipments would virtually exhaust the reserve stocks that France then had available.[34]

Fortunately, the sending of personnel to the peninsula was much less complicated. In the ten days since the outbreak of the right-wing rebellion, a number of dedicated—albeit largely unskilled—volunteers had come forward to offer their services to the Republican embassy in Paris. However, the status of this recruitment operation was somewhat ambiguous, and at its August 1 meeting the Council decided to clarify the matter. Doubtless goaded in large part by the knowledge that the planes sent to the rebels in North Africa had been manned by Italian military personnel, the ministers decreed that volunteers of any nationality—whether mercenaries or not—were to be permitted to go freely from France to Spain, provided only that they not carry arms while on French soil and that they travel on individual passports, not collective ones.

As has been suggested, specific appeals by antifascist leaders such as Malraux had produced few of the skilled technicians that the Republic so urgently needed, particularly for its air force. Fortunately the new Spanish ambassador, Alvarez de Albornoz, had been quick to take measures to improve this situation. Experience in obtaining pilots for the Potez-25s had proved that money was a powerful incentive, and the Spanish Republic had at its disposal the enormous gold reserves of the Bank of Spain, the third largest in Europe. In its fight for life, Madrid was prepared to be generous. Albornoz authorized the drawing up of recruitment agreements for aviation personnel, valid for a period of one month. Renewable by mutual consent, these contracts granted pilots a basic stipend of 25,000 francs, payable in French money. Of this sum, 10,000 francs was paid in cash upon departure from Paris, with the remainder deposited in a bank account and available after thirty days. In addition, during the period of service the Spanish government agreed to provide the pilots with a life and accident insurance policy for 200,000 francs, valid for all risks, including risks of war, and to guarantee transportation back to the French capital.

But just what did the "recruit" agree to provide in return for such generous financial rewards? The model contract specified unequivocally that "for the total period of one month" the signer was to place himself "at the entire disposal of the Spanish government for any aeronautical tasks that will be required of him." It was further noted that the airman was to render the required services "on French or Spanish territory," a qualification evidently intended to cover possible ferrying operations from France to the peninsula or the bringing of damaged planes to workshops at fields in southern France for repair.[35]

When the generous terms offered by the Spanish government became known, the few original volunteers for the Republican air force who had come forward out of idealism, antifascism, or simple love of adventure were rapidly joined by a number of less admirable individuals of various nationalities whose motivation was entirely financial. These people were glib in claiming all kinds of technical expertise, particularly as pilots. However, there was no question of entrusting them with a valuable late-model aircraft, either for ferrying or for combat, until their professional skills had been thoroughly checked out. Since this obviously could not be done in France, de Albornoz made arrangements for most of these mercenaries to join men from GL and other groups going overland to the Prat de Llobregat field in Barcelona or to Barajas in Madrid.

As de Albornoz, de los Ríos, Cot, and Lagrange began planning for the establishment of this mixed group of mercenary and volunteer aviators, it quickly became evident that someone was needed to act as overall head of the unit. André Malraux was the obvious choice. To be sure, he was not a flyer himself. However, he had long had a considerable interest in flying, and his daring airborne expedition of archeological exploration to Yemen in early 1934 had gained him worldwide attention.[36] In addition, he was known to be resourceful and imaginative, a dynamic organizer and natural leader who did not hesitate to make decisions and to act forcefully when occasion required. (Indeed, de Albornoz knew that he had begun recruiting cadre for the Republican forces—via his contacts with Rosselli and GL— even before his initial trip to Spain.) In his personal relationships, Malraux was fair-minded and unpretentious, if a bit impatient on occasion, and his whole philosophy of life was rooted in a profoundly democratic respect for man as man that was fully in agreement with the basic position of the Spanish Popular Front. Finally, he enjoyed the respect and confidence of a number of top officials in both the French and Spanish governments, a very necessary element if he was to be fully effective.

When Malraux was approached about this project, he pointed out that he had no technical expertise, either as an airman or as an administrator, but de Albornoz hastened to reassure him. Although the arrangement he had in mind would make Malraux the "responsible leader of the pilots" and officially recognized as such by the Spanish government, for purely technical matters he would be assisted by two specialists who would be fully qualified aviation professionals. These individuals would also be responsible—under his direction— for certain bureaucratic tasks, including maintaining liaison with the Spanish military leadership.[37] As de Albornoz envisaged it, Malraux's prime responsibility would be the recruiting and administering of the personnel of this unit and, ultimately, the procurement of its equipment. This task was a challenge that appealed both to Malraux's sense of adventure and to his antifascist ideological commitment, and he did not hesitate long before accepting it.

The Council's decision on 1 August to relax export restrictions and to authorize volunteers to leave for Spain allowed this whole project to move into high gear at last. On Monday and Tuesday, August 3 and 4, a certain number of necessary administrative steps were taken to implement the ministers' decision. First, Finance Minister Vincent Auriol advised the customs posts under his jurisdiction that the July 25 embargo on arms and aircraft was lifted. Until further notice, such exports would require only the normal permits and visas. Then the Spanish ambassador and the French manufacturers involved submitted formal applications to the Ministry of Foreign Affairs for permission to sell certain war materiel—including fourteen Dewoitine pursuit planes and six unarmed Potez-54 bombers—to the Madrid Republic. Most of the necessary exit documents were ready within twenty-four hours. At the same time Pierre Cot ordered the twenty planes to be moved as rapidly as possible to the Toulouse-Francazals airport, the partly civilian-partly military field in southern France chosen as the staging area for the whole operation.[38]

To ferry the fourteen Dewoitine fighters to Toulouse, arrangements were made to use three company pilots named Doumerc, Lepreux, and Roulland. Three additional civilian airmen, Bois, Hallotier, and Guidez, were also recruited for the task.[39] Guidez was a former military flyer, and it is likely that the other two men had a similar background or were from among Air France personnel. An initial convoy of six of these planes left the military base at Villacoublay on the morning of Tuesday, August 4, for Toulouse. Five arrived at Francazals without incident, but a mechanical or navigational problem obliged the sixth craft to make a forced landing that extensively damaged it. The pilots of this first group immediately returned to Paris on an Air France flight. The next day, four more Dewoitines were ferried to Toulouse by Roulland, Guidez, Bressor, and Idmée, followed on Thursday, August 6, by the remaining four, pilots unknown.[40]

The arrival of the Dewoitines at Toulouse must have made Commander Quédru—the representative of the Air Ministry waiting to receive them—a bit uneasy, for these pursuit ships were hard to manage, even for pilots who had had experience with modern military craft, and their high speed made landings particularly tricky. Once they were on the ground, it was discovered that "the wheel housings of certain planes were scraping the tires" and so the whole squadron was taken to the nearby Ateliers Dewoitine to be thoroughly checked by mechanics of the company.[41] Unfortunately, little further information has been uncovered about these fighters or the pilots who flew twelve of them to Spain on Saturday, August 8, but it appears that most of the airmen involved were mercenaries.

The ferrying of the six bombers to Toulouse began on Thursday morning, August 6, after hurried air trials of their brand new engines had been completed. The Potez firm assigned regular company flyers Decamp, Nicolle, and Destrés to be the principal pilots of the initial group of three planes. However, it is virtually certain that the co-pilots on these multiplace craft were volunteers or mercenaries from Malraux's group who needed to become familiar with the workings of these machines. As a precaution—and so that it could later be claimed that the bombers were "unarmed," as stated in the export permit—at the last moment the three machine guns on each craft were removed from their mountings, hurriedly "tied up and wrapped in rags" and stored inside the cabin, along with some cases of ammunition and a certain number of bombs.

The first two planes arrived at Toulouse without mishap on Thursday afternoon, but Destrés (who experienced some mechanical problems and had to make an emergency stop at Bordeaux) did not arrive until somewhat later. As has been indicated, Francazals was partly a civilian field, and the presence of these big machines—obviously warplanes—aroused considerable interest. Seeing this, Commander Quédru ordered the pilots to move the craft to Montaudran where they were immediately rolled into hangars and secured from curious eyes. All three of these pilots returned to Paris the next morning, to be ready to ferry the remaining three Potezes southward.[42]

During this period, some important developments were also taking place on the diplomatic front. On Wednesday, August 5, England replied favorably to France's nonintervention initiative, followed the next day by a similar, but more qualified, reaction from Italy. Although Delbos immediately extended his proposal to most of the other countries in Europe, in an official statement he was careful to point out that until answers had been received France herself would make no firm embargo commitment; too many arms shipments were being sent to the rebels by foreign powers.[43]

The Blum government hoped to keep its preparation of men and materiel for Spain fairly confidential, but conservative newspapers were soon featuring rather detailed accounts of the movements of supplies and personnel toward France's southern border. When alert observers in Toulouse telephoned contacts in Paris with information about the arrival of a score of new fighters and bombers at Francazals, the news was promptly conveyed to the British ambassador, Sir George Clerk. On Friday afternoon, Clerk paid a hurried visit to the Quai d'Orsay to tell Delbos in forceful terms that such activity was not at all consonant with France's sponsorship of a nonintervention proposal. He even issued what was virtually an ultimatum: if these activities did not cease at once, Britain would withdraw its support of the entire initiative.[44] Very upset at this possibility, Delbos convinced Blum to call an immediate emergency session of his closest ministerial collaborators. There, after lengthy and often bitter debate, it was decided to impose a strict embargo on *all* shipments of materiel, including warplanes, to Spain. However, as a conciliatory gesture to the pro-Republican ministers—and in consideration of what foreign supporters of the rebels had been doing—it was agreed to delay the official announcement and imposition of restrictions until the following evening. At that time the full Council would ratify the action and issue a formal statement about the new policy. In the interim, Daladier, Cot, and Lagrange were to have a free hand in sending to the peninsula whatever they had gathered.

Earlier that Friday, Cot had been alerted about the impending embargo decision, and he had quickly informed Malraux. Obviously it was urgent to get the planes at Francazals out of the country before the ministers closed the frontiers, so Malraux took immediate action. He rented a plane and flew to Toulouse to try to convince the pilots waiting there to begin ferrying the craft to Spain immediately. (Twelve of the Dewoitines and three of the Potez-54s were ready to go, with the remaining three bombers to arrive from Paris the following morning.) When he got to the field, he found that the airmen— almost all of them mercenaries—had made other plans for the evening: they intended to go into the metropolis to enjoy the cinemas and other attractions of the city. Moreover, as far as they were concerned, there was no question of "risking a night landing in such rapid machines, on airfields that were unknown," and they categorically refused to begin leaving before 5 A.M. the next day. As a rather malicious account in *Action Française* noted, the so-called commissar who had come "with supplications and threats" to try to get these airmen to leave for Spain was the same person "who had directed the whole operation, arranged the contracts with the pilots [. . .] and had bought them new equipment at great expense." This individual was identified by the conservative paper as "a writer at *L'Humanité* who, although not an aviator, had nevertheless once distinguished himself by a series of 'vols' [flights, thefts] in Indochina!"[45]

Unsuccessful in this attempt to get the convoy off to Spain, Malraux returned to Paris in order to be ready to leave for Francazals the next morning with the remaining three Potez-54s. The embargo would not be officially declared until evening, and he was determined to get the planes and men gathered at Toulouse to the peninsula before the deadline. Although some of the details of this final episode in the story are missing, it appears that these three bombers—the last of the group of new aircraft that Cot had located—left the Paris area for Toulouse early on Saturday morning, August 8. The planes were probably again piloted by the Potez company men Decamp, Nicolle, and Destrés, with Guidez, Corniglion-Molinier, and an unnamed third volunteer (possibly Jean Dary) serving as copilots. Several passengers, including Malraux, were also aboard.

When this little convoy landed at Toulouse-Francazals in midmorning, it was met by the duty officer for the military portion of the field, a certain Captain Jean Esparre. By a remarkable coincidence, this officer had been stationed at Djibouti, French Somaliland, in February 1934, when Malraux and Corniglion-Molinier made a refueling stop there on their flight to Yemen. After greetings were exchanged, the flyers asked Esparre to have the mechanics at the military center check over the machines that were being convoyed to Republican Spain. However, the captain felt that he could not provide such assistance because he had heard news that "the Blum government had just decided upon a nonintervention policy." Thereupon Malraux and his companions left for Montaudran, to have the work done by company mechanics there.[46]

While the Potezes were being given a final inspection, Malraux went to the airport canteen that served as unofficial headquarters for the field to learn the status of the departures to Barcelona. He was told that the twelve undamaged Dewoitines had already begun leaving for the peninsula, but that there were problems with three of the five bomber pilots (Corniglion-Molinier was evidently to be the sixth). These three men had been paid a sizable advance to take the Potezes to Spain, but they came to Malraux and told him that they were no longer willing to honor this commitment. They even made a pretense of being clever, saying that the money they had received had "upset" them so much that they didn't want to risk anything more! Of course, there was no question of their returning these funds. Malraux was furious, but as he told a friend, the Russian correspondent Koltzov, at a meeting in Toulouse shortly afterward, there was nothing that he could do. In view of the unusual circumstances, he certainly could not go to the police and denounce these men for fraud!

Koltzov, eager to leave for Spain in Malraux's convoy, tried to placate him by suggesting that perhaps these three pilots had simply become frightened by the international complications of the situation that had just arisen. At least, he said, they had not accepted the money and taken off in the planes with the intention of turning them over to the rebels and being paid a second time. Malraux replied that he still found such a lack of probity in his countrymen to be deeply disturbing. However, he was somewhat encouraged that two of the original five pilots were keeping their agreement and were preparing to take the Potez planes to the peninsula before nightfall. Indeed, one of these individuals, a young man named Abel Guidez, had not taken any money, nor even spoken of payment for the flight. Two out of five was 40 percent, admitted Malraux, and if 40 percent of French pilots were prepared to fight fascism then there was still some hope. But he pointed out realistically that "the problem is [to know] if that 40 percent is really 40 percent, and not 20 percent or zero."[47]

When Malraux returned to the airport with Koltzov later that Saturday afternoon, everything seemed calm and normal. The two men had no trouble getting onto the field because the guard who was supposed to verify entry passes was dozing at his post. Private sport planes were taking off or landing as usual, and in the canteen some mechanics were arguing over glasses of wine. Malraux casually strolled toward the hangars with Koltzov nervously following him. They approached a large twin-motor Potez whose propellers were turning slowly, and Malraux began speaking to a young man stretched out on the grass nearby. When Koltzov hesitated, Malraux muttered out of the corner of his mouth: "What are you waiting for?" Thereupon the Russian hopped into the cabin, followed by the young man—it was Guidez—who took his seat at the pilot's controls. A mechanic pulled the chocks from under the wheels, and the big plane took off immediately. As it gained altitude, Koltzov looked back to see Malraux standing on the runway, "legs spread, hands in his pockets, a cigarette in his mouth—like a music-hall owner during a dress rehearsal." Malraux followed with the two other bombers shortly afterward and by early evening had joined the rest of the contingent of

men and planes waiting at the Barcelona airport. A few days later the
unit was in Madrid.[48]

On August 14, 1936, the United States Department of State in
Washington received a confidential report about the arrival of these
French aircraft in Spain that was considerably more detailed than the
similar item published by the *London News-Chronicle* a few days
later. This uncensored radio message came from the destroyer USS
Quincy, en route from Barcelona to Marseilles with a group of Americans fleeing the civil disturbances in Spain. Evidently based on information received from an eyewitness, it read:

12 airplanes, Dewoitine, land planes up to date in every way arrived from
France landing at local Government aerodrome [in Barcelona]. These are
pursuit planes 850 horsepower engines. Three planes were cracked up on
landing; they carried places for machine guns, 2 on fuselage and 2 on up-
per wings. Planes came with French pilots some or all of these believed
intending to stay in Spain. Two pilots are Italian, 1 or 2 German and 3 or
4 [other] foreigners, no Americans. Reported to be rough crowd and soldiers of fortune. It is stated that they intend to take planes to Madrid. Six
Botet [Potez] planes also arrived making 18 in all that started for Barcelona. Botet planes carried gun turrets one in nose, one on top of fuselage
behind the pilot and one below the fuselage, all had bomb racks, gun
mountings but no guns. Planes believed to require expert handling and
Spaniards not believed capable handling.[49]

This report not only marks the modestly successful end of three hec-
tic weeks of effort of Republican sympathizers in France. Even more
important, it records the first moments of life of the unit of French
and foreign airmen that was to become the major vehicle for Malraux's personal—and literary—crusade in Spain.

Nicholas Hewitt

AUTHORITARIANISM AND ESTHETICS: THE PARADOX OF "L'ESPOIR"

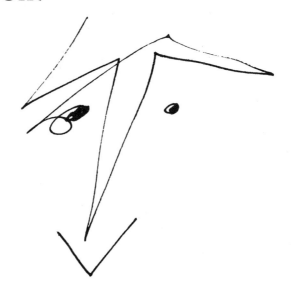

In the canon of Malraux's fiction *L'Espoir* has traditionally been seen as an important stage in the integration of the problematic hero into an acceptable moral and social context. Thus, critics who emphasize the humanist properties of Malraux's work, like Charles D. Blend and Joseph Hoffmann,[1] note the disappearance, or at least relegation, in the novel of the morally disturbing adventurer-heroes of *La Voie royale* and *Les Conquérants*, with a corresponding accentuation of essentialist ethical preoccupations centered on the concept of fraternity. Similarly, political studies of the novel have concentrated on the assimilation of the earlier anarchic and authoritarian heroes into a broader and more satisfying democratic field of action. For David Wilkinson *L'Espoir* announces the advent in Malraux's work of the "liberal hero,"[2] while for Lucien Goldmann it constitutes the highest point of Malraux's commitment to Communist organization and discipline, a commitment that eradicates automatically the problematic elements of the earlier novels: "The subject of *L'Espoir* is the *nonproblematic* relationship between the Spanish people and the international proletariat and a disciplined Communist party opposed to revolutionary spontaneity."[3] Thus, the novel is seen to build upon the positive elements of human dignity and revolutionary comradeship explored in *La Condition humaine* and the celebration of "virile fraternity" within the German Communist party contained in *Le Temps du mépris*, while looking forward to the edenic vision of *Les Noyers de l'Altenburg*.

Yet *L'Espoir* and its position in Malraux's work present problems which are more complex and which do not coincide with an optimistic interpretation of the fiction as following a smooth transition from authoritarianism to liberalism. In the first place, the two predominant elements of the narrative, Manuel's *Bildungsroman* and the chronicle of Magnin's air squadron, contain powerful links with the earlier politically and morally ambiguous novels. At the same time, while Malraux's depiction of the political relationships during the Spanish civil war may be viewed by Goldmann as "nonproblematic," it is only so because he offers a partial and partisan view of the war itself. Finally, the liberal-humanist interpretation of the novel derives considerable support from the powerful presence of esthetic preoccupations within the text, whereas that presence and those preoccupations may be seen as highly problematic.

The evolution of Manuel from the frivolity of the young cinema technician to the seriousness of the battle-weary commander is an experience of initiation. As he admits, "'I believe that another life began for me when I started fighting'" (*E* 848).[4] Yet that initiation is not merely, or even mainly, concerned with the practice of realistic politics; that role in the novel is left to Garcia, Pradas, and Vargas. Rather, it is an initiation into the problems of command, the metaphysical significance of the leader, and it is for this reason that Manuel's mentor is Ximénès, the professional soldier and an essentially nonpolitical character.[5] Thus, with the couple Ximénès-Manuel, Malraux continues his exploitation of the philosophical relationship, directed toward action, between master and neophyte, begun with Perken and Claude Vannec and continued with Garine and the anonymous narrator of *Les Conquérants*.[6]

The nature of Manuel's role is precisely indicated by the colonel's remark, "'It is more noble to be a leader than an individual . . . it's more difficult'" (*E* 579), which is based upon an entire past history of Malraux's speculations on the hero. The contrast between leader and individual looks back to the indictment of Western individualism in *La Tentation de l'Occident (The Temptation of the West)* and "D'une Jeunesse européenne" ("On a European Youth") and the search for an antidote in the person of a Nietzschean aristocratic leader. It is a dichotomy that builds also on the distinction in Hegel and Nietzsche between master and slave, by which the master can attain heights of nobility permanently denied the inferior individual, a nobility directly proportional to the difficulty of the enterprise.[7] With Manuel's mission as leader, Malraux remains in the mainstream of his considerations on action, and the necessarily elitist properties of the leader do not totally coincide with the waging of a democratic war.

This inbuilt elitism of his role serves to isolate Manuel from the democratic fraternity that is one of the novel's major innovations. Already he exhibits a certain distrust of the static, essentialist individual, with his humane values. As he claims to the fascist aviator, Alba, "'I am not interested in what people *are*, I am interested in what they *do*'" (*E* 573). His fraternity is a fraternity of action; when a delegation of workers come to see him Malraux comments, "For the first time he was confronted by a fraternity in the shape of action" (*E* 662). Yet, because Manuel's action cannot be *with* his comrades, but is, rather, *on* his comrades, it leads to a departure from fraternity and to an inevitable isolation, crystallized in the episode of the execution of the deserters. Of this scene, Malraux notes, "He had never felt so acutely that it was necessary to choose between victory and pity" (*E* 759), and Ximénès adds, "'You want to act without losing any sense of fraternity'" (*E* 774). The importance of the execution is twofold: it highlights the continuing impossibility of the total assimilation of the man of action into a collective enterprise, and it shows the primacy of the values of command over the essentialist values of humanity and pity. Apart from an absence of melodrama, Manuel's execution of the deserters is no different from Garine's shooting of the well-poisoner: in both cases, humane values are subordinated to *Realpolitik*; in both cases, the distastefulness of the action serves to increase the prestige of the perpetrator; in both cases, an acute sense of isolation is the result.

The rise to prominence of Manuel, therefore, testifies to Malraux's continued preoccupation in *L'Espoir* with the metaphysical—rather than political or ethical—significance of action and authority. The disturbing ambiguities in Perken and, more strikingly, in Garine, are muted in the portrayal of Manuel but are nevertheless present and serve to impede a smooth transition to an authentic liberal and democratic viewpoint.

A further obstacle to this transition is constituted by Magnin's air squadron which, like Manuel, appears initially as unambiguously at the service of democratic ideals. Nevertheless, apart from the intrigues surrounding the dismissal of Steiner, the group remains remarkably removed from political concerns and is devoted to an almost abstract exercise of collective heroism. There are certain obvious reasons for this: the air war is described by Malraux as "the most romantic form of warfare" (E 837); it inherits the glamour of the aviators of World War I;[8] in addition, the pilot, alone in his machine, is a ready symbol of man in a heroic, purely metaphysical context—a symbol that was used already by Malraux in Le Temps du mépris and that is particularly associated with the novels of Saint-Exupéry. When the air squadron begins night flights, Malraux notes, "Destiny had taken the place of battle" (E 615), and he goes on to describe the emotions of the pilot, Leclerc: "Leclerc, with his cloak over his head, felt free— a divine freedom, above sleep and war, above pains and passions" (E 615). In addition, Malraux is careful to give to the squadron a timeless quality in the way in which they conform to a well-established narrative pattern of the epic—the arrival of an elite group of warriors from a far country, or from many countries, come to save a place in danger; he makes consistent use of this pattern from "Ecrit pour un ours en peluche" onward. In this context of a deliberate displacement from the present, the description of Magnin, whose "blond-gray walrus moustache made him look like a bemused Viking under his helmet" (E 479), places the entire narrative in the heroic lineage of Claude Vannec's mythical grandfather.

The ambiguity of the squadron, which is both fighting a specific political battle for the Republic and engaged in an eternal mythical combat, is symbolized by the way in which it is split between the political volunteers—Magnin, Scali, Jaime Alvear, and Attignies— and the mercenaries—Leclerc, Sibirsky, and Karlitch, who have a long heroic past and are disparagingly referred to as "warriors [guerriers]" (E 674). Yet the term warrior has important connotations in the intellectual history of France in the interwar years and serves to denote a resurgence of barbarism which threatens the humanist position. In the squadron the warrior is an archetypal manifestation of the adventurer-hero, distinct from the political volunteer and the professional soldier, who obeys principles of self-definition irrespective of social or ethical concerns.[9] Not only is he morally disturbing, he is also politically unreliable. Hence, Karlitch, who has previously fought for Wrangel and the White Russians, finds himself by accident fighting for the Left for the first time; a worried Scali, interrogating a fascist aviator, notices a similarity between him and House: "He didn't look like House, but they belonged to the same family" (E 549). Later, Malraux writes of Scali: "Scali liked the volunteers, distrusted the soldiers, and hated the warriors. Karlitch was a simple case, but what about the others? . . . And there were thousands like that with Franco" (E 789).

The air squadron, therefore, which constitutes an isolated, archaic world, permits the survival in the novel of the authoritarian personality of the hero figure. The mercenaries, who present strong affinities with the fascists, are resurrected warriors whose barbarism challenges the moral concerns and political sophistication of the Republican cause. Nor do the political volunteers, in spite of their commitment, escape totally the ambiguities of their mercenary comrades: by their very role as airmen, they are distanced from, above, the more complex concerns of the war on the land, and they come to assume a medieval chivalric image. For all its bitterness, Leclerc's jibe to Jaime Alvear, " 'You're a knight of the International'" (E 682), has profound meaning.

Both of the major components of the narrative structure of L'Espoir, therefore, present the ambiguities contained in the air squadron itself: an advance toward integration in a democratic movement but, at the same time, a persistence of the amoral and apolitical metaphysical concerns of the adventurer-hero. Manuel and Magnin have not yet satisfactorily shaken off the ghosts of Perken, Garine, and Ferral.[10]

What has continued to mask the authoritarian qualities of L'Espoir is the fact that, as Goldmann implies, it appears to align itself unproblematically with the Spanish people in their democratic struggle against the fascist insurgents. By espousing the cause of the defense of the Azaña Republic, Malraux may be seen to avoid the political ambiguities of his earlier novels, notably Les Conquérants, and to progress to a subordination of the metaphysical and heroic preoccupations of his protagonists to a collective political aim. Such an interpretation, however, is only possible if the Spanish civil war is viewed as a simple conflict between a legitimate liberal Republic and its Communist allies and a fascist rebellion supported by the Italian and German governments. In such a situation, the conflict must be viewed as a war, and the dominant issue becomes that of attaining the same efficiency in warfare, with a resulting temporary loss of humanity, as that achieved by the fascists: hence the Communists' hostility to "spontaneity," noted by Goldmann.

As Noam Chomsky has pointed out, however, this analysis of the war, conveyed particularly in the standard Anglo-Saxon studies of the subject, those by Hugh Thomas and Gabriel Jackson,[11] is already partisan. In an essay in *American Power and the New Mandarins* he devotes considerable space to a demonstration of how Jackson's work, which he praises as an outstanding contribution to liberal scholarship, nevertheless has a false objectivity which consistently tries to minimize the importance of one crucial factor in the Spanish conflict: the popular revolution that occurred behind the Republican lines in 1936 and 1937. He writes:

During the months following the Franco insurrection in July 1936 a social revolution of unprecedented scope took place throughout much of Spain. It had no "revolutionary vanguard" and appears to have been largely spontaneous, involving masses of rural and urban laborers in a radical transformation of social and economic conditions that persisted, with remarkable success, until it was crushed by force.[12]

For Jackson this popular revolution, carried out by non-Stalinist Marxists or by anarchists, was either a sideshow—of minimal significance compared with the struggle against Franco—or, more important, a dangerous force that actually impeded that struggle. For Chomsky, on the other hand, and for his sources,[13] this revolution, far from being a dangerous diversion, constituted the very motive force of the Republic's fighting power, and the final defeat of the Republic found its cause not in the inefficiency of the Spanish workers, but in the failure of the government and the dominant Spanish Communist party (Partido Socialista Unificado de Cataluña; PSUC) to give the revolutionary potential of the rural and urban masses full reign.

It is in this context that the central political debate of wartime Spain must be seen: the conflict between the partisans of a strongly centralized government and military command and those who saw in spontaneous action the only means of winning the war. The former argued that only a strongly controlled, disciplined force could resist Franco's army. Their efforts were concentrated therefore on limiting the revolution by the suppression of land collectivization and by the reintroduction of a professional army to replace the revolutionary militias. If the notion of revolution was accepted at all, it was in a subordinate position to the all-consuming demands of the war. Thus, Largo Caballero stated to the London *Daily Express*: "Win the war first. Then we can talk about revolution,"[14] a comment echoed by José Diaz, for the Spanish Communist party: "We can't have a revolution if we don't win the war. . . . We must win the war first."[15]

The non-Stalinist Left, however, and the anarchists refused to accept the incompatibility between victory and revolution. For them, far from being destructive and diversionary, the revolution is central to the Republic's power to wage war. Thus, Broué and Thémime sum up the position of the POUM (Partido Obrero de Unificación Marxista) and the JCI (Juventud Comunista Ibérica): "The war and the revolution are inseparable. In no way could we accept the postponement of the revolution until the end of hostilities."[16] They quote the Italian Marxist Berneri: "There is only one choice: either victory over Franco by means of a revolutionary war, or defeat."[17] Finally, the conflict between the PSUC and the POUM is crisply summed up by Orwell, who described the "PSUC line":

At present nothing matters except winning the war; without victory in the war all else is meaningless. Therefore this is not the moment to talk of pressing forward with the revolution.[18]

and that of the POUM:

It is nonsense to talk of opposing fascism by bourgeois "democracy" . . . The only real alternative to fascism is workers' control. If you set up any less goal than this, you will either hand the victory to Franco, or, at best, let in fascism by the back door. . . . The war and the revolution are inseparable.[19]

The conflict was therefore between two diametrically opposed policies. The "centralizers" could conceive of opposition to Franco only on Franco's terms: the organization of a highly mechanized army. They saw the élan of the masses as inadequate to the task and as a danger to the enterprise. The aim of the government and the PSUC, therefore, became that of disciplining, forming, and directing that élan. The left-wing opposition and the anarchists, however, continued to maintain that it was in that very undisciplined nature of the masses' fervor that the strength of the Republic lay, and that attempts to restrain it would be disastrous.

There is considerable evidence to show that this was, at least partially, the case. So great was the government's fear of revolution behind its own lines, and the Communists' of spontaneity, that they conducted a battle on two fronts, against Franco *and* against the left-wing opposition. As Orwell remarked, after his experience in Barcelona: "A government which sends boys of fifteen to the front with rifles forty years old and keeps its biggest men and its newest weapons in the rear is manifestly more afraid of the revolution than of the fascists."[20]

Similarly, the absorption of the irregular militias into a regular army, with uniforms, pay, and military discipline (announced by Manuel's execution of the deserting volunteers), seems to have produced, not the expected increase in efficiency, but a general disillusionment, illuminated by the Italian commentator Bertoni, who wrote: "The Spanish civil war, stripped of any new faith, of any notion of social change or revolutionary grandeur . . . remains a terrible question of life or death, but is no longer a war that affirms a new regime or a new humanity."[21]

In spite of the fact, however, that this vast revolution is a well-attested fact, it is apparent that in *L'Espoir* Malraux has chosen to depict it superficially and to denigrate it in favor of the centralizing position. The role of the POUM is never mentioned, not even in those sections dealing with Barcelona, where the party was a powerful force. The popular revolution in the novel is undertaken uniquely by the anarchists and is harshly, if nostalgically, criticized. The novel becomes the story of the attempts of Garcia, Vargas, Manuel, and others to curb the excesses of the anarchists and weld the Spanish people into an efficient fighting unit. The positive potential of the revolution, the arguments of Berneri and the POUM that only with a spontaneous revolution could the Republic defeat Franco, are ignored.

Yet even though the ideological conflict is reduced to that between Communists and anarchists, the latter receive only superficial analysis. Malraux's interest in them is restricted to his admiration for them as picturesque fighters, as esthetic elements in the struggle. His description of Puig and, particularly, of Le Négus, is exactly similar in tone to Robert Brasillach's evocation of the death of Durutti in November 1936: "That superb beast lying on white silk, its head encased in a white turban."[22] At the same time, however impressive the appearance of the anarchist combatants, they constitute an undisciplined and unreliable element in the Republican ranks which proves inadequate to the technological nature of modern warfare. Thus, the growing disillusionment of the revolution as the failure to grasp what Jackson terms "the unsuspected complexity of modern society."[23]

The way in which *L'Espoir* dismisses the notion of an effective popular revolution in Spain in favor of a highly controlled, mechanized war is crystallized in the conversation between Garcia and Vargas, on one side, and Magnin, on the other, in the War Ministry. It is this crucial debate which concludes with Garcia's reluctant pronouncement, "'Our modest role, Monsieur Magnin, is to organize the Apocalypse'" (*E* 532), and which centers on the emotional demands of the apocalyptic vision and the necessity of organization and control, a conflict introduced at the very beginning of the debate by the Republican songs wafting into the Ministry.

It is to Magnin, significantly a "revolutionary socialist" and therefore close in ideology to the POUM, that the role of defender of this Republican lyricism is given, while Garcia and Vargas have the reluctant role of propounding an unpalatable but, for Malraux, incontrovertible fact that "a *popular movement*, like this one, or a revolution, or an uprising, preserves its victory only by a technique *contrary* to the means that produced that victory" (E 532). Thus the bulk of the dialogue is given to Garcia and Vargas; Magnin, for his part, is reduced to short, often unfinished interventions which attempt to defend the popular, emotional element in the war but which serve merely to permit Garcia to underline the untenable nature of the revolutionary position. The structuring of the episode, therefore, is designed to show the inevitability of the centralizing approach to the war. This is supported by historical arguments in the course of the debate: to emphasize the need for the formation of an army, with the consequent abolition of the militias, Vargas states, "'Wrangel's army was beaten by the Red Army, not by the partisans'" (E 530). Similarly, Garcia dismisses the notion of the people, as used in the context of the French and Russian revolutions, pointing to its inadequacy in twentieth-century warfare (E 529). Finally, although Garcia examines at length the Spanish situation in terms of two successive coups d'état—Franco's failed pronunciamiento, followed by the intervention of the fascist powers—he finds no place in his analysis for the revolution on the Republican side.

It seems clear, therefore, that Malraux has chosen to depict the Spanish civil war solely as a struggle against Franco, a struggle that necessitates the suppression of the popular revolutionary forces in Republican Spain and their replacement by a technocratic, disciplined army. That Garcia should accept this conclusion only with regret adds pathos and dignity to his situation, but it does not alter his position. For if political integration of the earlier adventurer-hero is possible, it is possible only in an egalitarian, popular movement of the sort represented by the POUM and the anarchists and to which Orwell gravitated automatically in 1936. The elitist bias that Chomsky detects in the refusal to deal seriously with such a movement allows him to categorize Jackson's history as establishment liberal scholarship.[24] In the case of Malraux, this bias, this rejection of spontaneity in favor of discipline, obedience to commanders, and order, reinforces the authoritarian characteristics of the novel, seen already in Manuel and the air squadron, and constitutes little progression from the earlier works. Manuel's execution of the deserters serves as a metonymic image of the philosophy of the Republican high command; and Garcia's function and lonely responsibility are not, after all, any different from those of Garine.

At this point, it is traditional for humanist criticism of Malraux's work to invoke the surprisingly large esthetic component in *L'Espoir* to guarantee its liberal and democratic credentials, on the basis of assumptions like George Santayana's, "that art is *prima facie* and in itself a good cannot be doubted."[25] Quite apart from traditions of twentieth-century esthetic thought which have concluded that art is neither automatically ethically good (Thomas Mann) nor politically democratic (Walter Benjamin), however, the presence of artistic preoccupations in *L'Espoir* cannot be easily interpreted as a natural safeguard for the values of European humanism.

Clearly, for an ostensibly political war novel, *L'Espoir* is unusually concerned with artistic and professional intellectual preoccupations. Malraux has taken care to fill his cast of characters with artists and writers: Manuel is a cinema technician, Scali and Alvear are art historians, Garcia is an ethnologist, Lopez a painter given the task of saving works of art from destruction, Guernico is a Catholic writer, and Shade is a journalist. In addition, Malraux invokes the tragedy of Unamuno's last days and—in the person of the peasant who narrates the nativity of the Christ in an unjust Spain—introduces a popular storyteller of a high level. At the same time, these artist-heroes act in a Spain whose esthetic history is always present (the constant presence of Cervantes, Alvear's reading of *Don Quixote*, Toledo's associations with El Greco) and which Malraux is at pains to transform into a metaphysical battleground in an eternal struggle. It is significant in this contest that the final episode of the novel, which supposedly celebrates the specific military victory of Guadalajara and looks forward to an eventual Republican success in the war, should contain the comments of the guide to the palace who situates the action in a vast historical spectrum and announces the pessimism of Möllberg in *Les Noyers de l'Altenburg*: "'The principal enemy of man, gentlemen, is the forest. The forest is stronger than we, stronger than the Republic, stronger than the revolution, stronger than the war. . . . If man ceased to struggle, the forest would cover Europe within sixty years'" (*E* 855). The center of gravity of the novel, therefore, moves firmly away from the concerns of Spain in the 1930s toward a general meditation on the artistic possibilities of man as the sole guarantee of his survival. In this way there is complete continuity in Malraux's thought from the early novels to the postwar art philosophy. Ultimately, Malraux is aiming at an antidote to humiliation: for Kyo Gisors, that solution is found in "dignity"; for Barca, in *L'Espoir*, it lies in "fraternity"; and in the postwar artistic writing, it becomes quite explicitly the preserve of a narrow group of artists who have avenged their humiliating past by their immortality. On two occasions Malraux uses the example of Gorki's funeral as a symbol of the artist's revenge on the human condition: "In the immense national funeral of the vagabond Gorki, I believed I saw the revenge for the anonymous and miserable death of the vagabond Villon."[26] The problem is that the concern of Malraux's artists is ultimately with their metaphysical self-justification, which they achieve only through the practice of their art, rather than with political or ethical issues; the artist-heroes of *L'Espoir* view and undertake their political action in metaphysical and esthetic terms. In this sense they form part of the "culture de Grands Navigateurs,"—explored in *Les Voix du silence (The Voices of Silence)*[27]—whose aim is the rectification of the human condition by the creation of a controlled and ordered autonomous world. Thus, Garcia's imposition of order in the conduct of the war is indissociable from his profession as an intellectual.

It is for this reason that the protagonists of *L'Espoir* are not immune from the charges leveled at *La Condition humaine* by such diverse political critics as Ilya Ehrenburg and Robert Brasillach, that the portrayal of the characters has less to do with the concrete situation than with the transcendental esthetic philosophy of the author.[28] At the same time, critics of Malraux's art philosophy have argued that this body of writing (which spans the entire period of his literary production) is hardly humanist in itself. Maurice Merleau-Ponty, in an essay on Malraux's position among Western cold war intellectuals such as Koestler and James Burnham, objects that "in spite of everything, they have not attempted to find the way to a humanism for all men,"[29] and sees the roots of this failure, which applies to the art philosophy *and* the fiction, in a particular interpretation on Malraux's part of the nature of history itself:

There are two views of history, one of which is ironic and meaningless and made up of absurdities, because each age struggles against the others as if against strangers, imposing on them its anxieties and its visions. It consists of oblivion, rather than memory; it is made up of fragmentation, ignorance, and exteriority. But the other view, without which the first would not exist, is constituted and reconstituted gradually by the interest that carries us toward what is different from us. . . .[30]

Undoubtedly, it is this first sense of history which informs Malraux's work, against which the only solution may be sought in a struggle for transcendance through form. For Merleau-Ponty, however, such a view is barren and at best can lead to a grandiose fossilization: the dead painters of Malraux's imaginary museum, like the combatants in the Spanish civil war, may achieve a sense of fraternity, but it is "a fraternity of painters in death."[31] Finally, the view of history as battleground precludes the accession to a true humanism, based upon assimilation into collective activity and respect for the other person, for "true history is derived entirely from us. It is in the present that it finds the strength to give back to the present all other values. The other person whom I respect draws strength from me as I do from him."[32] This authentic history is absent from *L'Espoir*, as it is from *Les Voix du silence*; the absence constitutes the very problematic essence of the novel.

A close examination of *L'Espoir* in conjunction with Broué's and Thémime's view of the Spanish civil war and Merleau-Ponty's criticism of the art philosophy, raises doubts about the extent to which it can be viewed as a major departure in Malraux's work. Ethically, it furnishes no addition to the system of wartime values, the bond between warriors constructed in the earlier novels. Politically, with its emphasis on the imposition of order in an eternal and anachronistic context, it serves to demonstrate the consistency in Malraux's enthusiasm for Garine and his support for de Gaulle. The paradox of the novel lies in the way that support for a democratic cause and inclusion of esthetic elements act as a means of "fascination," in Claude-Edmonde Magny's term, which mask a remarkably constant authoritarian viewpoint. If any progression is visible at all, it is within a Nietzschean context, from the dour, unsmiling heroes of the early novels, modeled upon Nietzsche's evocation of Dürer's knight in *The Birth of Tragedy*, to an ideal similar to "that Provençal notion of 'Gaya Scienzia,' of that union of singer, knight and free spirit,"[33] but that progression itself removes the argument to a plane distinctly different from the traditional perspective of European humanism in the twentieth century.

Robert Sayre

"L'ESPOIR" AND STALINISM

L'Espoir represents a particularly important step in the evolution of Malraux's political vision, since it is his last novel before his total break with the Communist movement and eventual turn to Gaullism. It is at the same time the one in which his perspective is most closely associated with the institutionally dominant agent of Communism, the Stalinist Comintern. The latter is of course present in the first two of Malraux's novels of revolution, represented by the characters Borodine and Vologuine. Malraux presents their theses convincingly in the novels, and in his reply to Trotsky's critique of *Les Conquérants* he explicitly defends the International.[1] But while their author consciously espouses the politics of the Comintern, the novels themselves provide a picture that, at the very least, raises serious doubts about the Stalinist position. This is especially true in the case of *La Condition humaine*, the dénouement of which shows the savage repression of the Shanghai revolutionaries by Chiang Kai-shek as a result of Comintern directives. In an article published the year following *La Condition humaine*, Trotsky claims that in both this novel and *Les Conquérants*, "without realizing what the political relationships and consequences were, the artist here formulates a crushing condemnation of the politics of the Communist International in China, and with scenes and characters confirms . . . everything that the leftist opposition had explained with theses and formulas."[2] *La Condition humaine* has indeed often been considered *trotskysant*. Moreover, as Jean Lacouture points out in his biography, during the period immediately following its publication (1933–34) Malraux "considers himself, if not a Trotskyist, at any rate a sympathizer with that great exile."[3]

The sympathy with Trotskyism was short-lived, however. In April 1935, Malraux clearly signaled his break with oppositional Communism by neglecting to come to the aid of the persecuted Trotskyist Victor Serge. He seems to have come to a realization at that point that the Trotskyists could not win in their struggle against Stalinism and consequently must be abandoned in the interest of making an effective and unified attack against fascism. The change of orientation is already evident in *Le Temps du mépris* (1935), in which the relation between party direction, simple militants, and workers is represented as an unproblematic unity. In July 1936, then, when Malraux left for Spain, he had more than a year earlier adopted a perspective that brought him closer than ever before to the politics of Stalinism. *L'Espoir*, written in 1936–37, clearly shows its mark. Indeed, Lucien Goldmann's analysis of the novel leads him to assert that it is "a book written in a Stalinist perspective."[4] In this essay we wish to examine that thesis. We shall investigate the relationship of Stalinism to the novel—that is, attempt to determine precisely how Stalinism is embodied in its artistic structure. We will argue that as a whole *L'Espoir* incarnates the sensibility not of a Stalinist per se, but of a thoroughgoing fellow traveler of Stalinism.

The first way in which we might approach the question of Stalinism in *L'Espoir* is to consider the novel in terms of its silences—what is absent from it, what it leaves unsaid. At the most general level we might characterize what is absent from the novel as a whole dimension of the historical reality that the work portrays. The political dimension of the Spanish civil war is almost entirely absent from Malraux's novel. The war is treated predominantly from a military point of view, and as Goldmann points out, the conflicts between opposing tendencies within the government coalition are mainly limited to their military aspects.[5] In a literary work that is set in the civil war and that takes the latter as at least one of its principal subjects, such an omission is serious. Near the beginning of *Homage to Catalonia*, as he explains what he will include in his account of the war, George Orwell asserts: "It would be quite impossible to write about the Spanish war from a purely military angle. It was above all things a political war. No event in it, at any rate during the first year [i.e., the year in which the time span of the novel falls], is intelligible unless one has some grasp of the inter-party struggle that was going on behind the Government lines."[6]

By excluding the political dimension from *L'Espoir*, Malraux more specifically leaves out a development within the war that is crucial to its understanding. First, the revolutionary starting point of the war is occulted. In the first few weeks after the fascist uprising in the areas that had successfully repelled the fascist threat the workers and peasants set up revolutionary committees through which they exercised effective power. As the historian Pierre Broué terms it, "The armed counterrevolution sets off the revolution."[7] The popular resistance to the uprising stimulated the actual taking of power by the working class that had been impeded by weaknesses and divisions in the working-class parties in the early years of the Republic.

Second, and even more important, the process that follows this revolutionary beginning is also totally absent from *L'Espoir*. The Comintern's position on the Spanish war was largely dictated by Stalin's policy of cultivating alliances with Britain and France, and therefore of seeking to demonstrate the nonrevolutionary intentions of the Communists. In addition, the Spanish revolution promised to be difficult, if not impossible, to bring under Stalinist control, since a large part of the Spanish working class owed allegiance to anarchism, left-wing socialism, or dissident communism. Consequently, from the very beginning the Comintern, working through its agents and through the Spanish Communist party (PSUC) energetically carried out its plan to turn back the Spanish revolution, to return to the previous status quo. Using as leverage the prestige of the Soviet Union and the promise of military aid, it worked with the most conservative elements of the government coalition to restore the previously existing social hierarchy, transferring power from the revolutionary committees back to parliamentary bodies, and replacing the egalitarian, popular militias by a traditional army. Thus in the strictest sense the Stalinist Comintern played a *counterrevolutionary* role in the Spanish civil war.[8]

Because their actual role flagrantly contradicted their overt ideology, the Stalinists naturally wished to hide what they had done. The most effective way to achieve this was by also hiding from the world outside Spain the revolutionary beginnings of the war. As Orwell points out: "Since the revolution had got to be crushed, it greatly simplified things to pretend that no revolution had happened. In this way the real significance of every event could be covered up; every shift of power from the trade unions to the central Government could be represented as a necessary step in military reorganization."[9] This picture of the Spanish civil war—as a defense of the Republic against fascism, a defense that was becoming increasingly effective militarily—is the one that was presented abroad by anitfascists and antifascist newspapers, by non-Communists as well as Communists, since the former hoped to attract greater support from Western countries by denying the revolutionary nature of the conflict. It is also the picture conveyed in *L'Espoir*. Although at the beginning of the novel the anarchist Puig dreams of a revolutionary upheaval, he dies on the first day of fighting without seeing it realized. And while the *hope* of revolution is often reevoked later on, the *reality* of it is absent from *L'Espoir*. A central presence in the novel, on the other hand, is the military reorganization referred to by Orwell.

Thus the suppression of the political and concentration on the military dimension eliminates from the universe of the novel a general sociopolitical process crucial to the period. But even more specifically, certain particular entities and events are absent from Malraux's fictional world, entities and events that are of the utmost importance for the period. In considering events that are absent from the novel, the relevant time span is not the period covered by it (July 1936 through March 1937), but rather the period from the beginning of Malraux's engagement in the war up to the date of completion and submission to the publisher of his final manuscript (July 1936 through November 30, 1937).[10] For until that last date Malraux was free to modify what he had already written and to add new material that might be influenced by events currently taking place. The events that we have in mind—which, if they had appeared in the novelistic world, would have thrown an entirely different light on it and thereby significantly modified it—are first of all the Moscow trials of the old Bolsheviks, the first and second of which took place in August–September 1936 and January 1937 (thus falling even within the time span of the novel).

Even more directly significant were the extensions of Stalinist repression and terror in Spain. After having caused the POUM—an organization of anti-Stalinist Communists who strongly denounced the Moscow trials—to be excluded from the government in December 1936, the Stalinists called for its dissolution and the arrest of its leaders in May 1937 and realized their aim in June. One of those arrested, Andrès Nin, was tortured and assassinated by the Soviet secret police. Indeed, following the May events in Barcelona—in which the Communist-dominated governmental forces met with insurrectional resistance when they attempted to take the telephone exchange from the anarchist (Confederación Nacional del Trabajo; CNT) union that had controlled it—large-scale Stalinist repression of *all* non-Communist revolutionaries was instituted in Spain. During the May events several non-Communist leaders were abducted and killed; afterward, with the installation of a Communist police chief in Barcelona, many other arrests, abductions, tortures, and assassinations of anarchists, Trotskyists, and members of the POUM followed. The repression extended throughout Spain; the POUM was assimilated with fascism and its members in the army summarily sentenced and shot as traitors. In August mass arrests of anarchists in Aragon took place, and the press censorship already in effect was extended to cover any criticism of the Soviet Union. The situation was summarized dramatically by John MacGovern, a member of the British Independent Labour party who visited Barcelona as part of a delegation in November: "Russia has bought Spain. In exchange for Russian aid in arms, the Comintern has been given a tyrannical power that it uses to imprison, torture and kill socialists who do not accept the Communist line. There are two international brigades in Spain: one is fighting on the battlefields . . . the other is an international Cheka made up of gangsters working for the Comintern."[11]

The series of events to which we have briefly referred all occurred within the time span terminated by the submission of *L'Espoir* for publication, and the general situation described by MacGovern obtained at the time it was submitted. Yet Malraux chose to exclude from his novel any important allusion to them. Anarchists are present in *L'Espoir* (although in far smaller numbers than Communists; Malraux significantly underrepresents them in relation to their actual importance), but the repression of anarchists—with the exception of a single, passing reference to a lesser case[12]—does not figure in it. The novel presents one Soviet character, Golovkine, but he is only a journalist, and there is no agent of the Comintern or of the Soviet secret police.

Moreover, and very significantly, the POUM as a whole is nonexistent in the novel. How can we explain this difference in treatment of anarchism and the POUM? First of all, simply the large numbers of anarchists and the importance of the anarchist organizations in Spain would have made it extremely difficult not to portray them at all, whereas the POUM was numerically small enough to be neglected. Equally important, however, is the nature of the two groups. The POUM was a Communist organization close to (but not identical with) the Trotskyism that Malraux had just abjured. One of the things that most clearly characterized and defined it was its outspoken criticism of the Stalinist deformation of communism in the name of an authentic communism. Such a group could not exist in the fictional universe of Malraux, a non-Communist who had opted for Stalinism as an effective force, since its very existence would point to the unpleasant realities that Malraux did not allow to enter that universe and would represent a telling critique of Stalinism *from within* the Communist perspective. As we shall see, Malraux does allow a certain questioning of Stalinism in the text, but only from non-Communist viewpoints. And this criticism is highly circumscribed and mitigated, reflecting the same reticence that led Malraux to advise Gide to postpone publication of his *Retour de l'URSS* in the interest of the antifascist cause.[13]

As for the anarchists, their presence is important in the novel because, in contrast to the POUM, at least at one level they point up realities that Malraux wishes to underline. Treated almost exclusively in military terms, they act as a foil for the Communists. Their disorganization and lack of discipline discredit them in the context of the novel's value scheme and provide a contrast that adds luster to the virtues of the Communists.

Turning now from the absences or silences of *L'Espoir* to consider the *presences* within it, the first and most elementary structural element we might note is the chronological découpage made by Malraux. The time span of the novel runs from the start of the civil war through the Republican victory at Guadalajara in late March 1937. It is significant that Malraux chooses to end the novel at this particular juncture, eight full months before his submission of the manuscript. By so doing he eliminates from its chronological range at least the most important, if not all, of the occurrences and processes that would be difficult to reconcile with his perspective. The first Moscow trials had already taken place when the novel ends, but the repression in Spain had not. Indeed, a period can be said to end with the battle of Guadalajara. According to Broué, it marks "the summit of the period during which 'organization and discipline had not killed enthusiasm and faith, while enthusiasm and faith relied on discipline and organization, and on arms as well.' . . . From that date on, the struggle against the revolution in the Republican zone in fact more and more lost its democratic appearance."[14] Since the overall movement of *L'Espoir* reveals the replacement of "enthusiasm and faith" by "discipline and organization" and seeks to demonstrate the necessity of this development, it is important that the novel stop at that historical point. For until then there continues to be a dialectical tension between the two; the second has not yet totally destroyed the first and fully revealed its own true nature.

The basic structure of *L'Espoir* is unmistakable. The first of three parts shows the courageous but unorganized and underequipped fighting in the early months of the war. Although at first the power of the "lyrical illusion" seems sufficient to the task (the fascists, thinks one combatant, "'have the leaders, they have the weapons . . . but they aren't getting through'"),[15] later in the section the text repeatedly points to the errors and inefficiency of the Republican troops, and it ends with a major defeat. The second part, which covers mainly the month of November, is a transitional one. In it discipline begins to assert itself over the "Apocalypse," and the necessary equipment to carry on effective technological warfare begins to arrive. It opens with Manuel (along with Heinrich, another Communist leader) reorganizing the demoralized remains of the troops routed at Toledo; near its end the same Manuel calls for and sees carried out the execution of deserters, including volunteers. The section is punctuated with the arrival of war materiel and triumphantly ends with the Soviet planes that save Madrid. In the last part, the militias have given way to a disciplined army organized principally by the Communists. And the equipment sent is being used in a manner worthy of its source: "The Republican tanks, with the orderliness of an exercise on Red Square, attacked" (*E* 575). The combination of the two is clearly responsible for the final victory at Guadalajara.

The novel's underlying structure, then, is patterned after this military evolution. The movement is from negative to positive, from weakness to strength, from anarchic inefficiency to effective discipline. In this respect, let us recall the comment by Orwell on the official war propaganda: "In this way the real significance of every event could be covered up; every shift of power from the trade unions to the central Government could be represented as a necessary step in military reorganization." Thus the basic structure of the novel serves to hide another, symmetrically opposed structure: the systematic dismantling by the Communists of the initial revolutionary gains. Here the movement is from positive to negative, from strength to weakness (of the workers and peasants), from egalitarianism to domination. And the transition in this process is simultaneous with the obverse, military one. According to Orwell, "the general swing to the Right dates from about October–November 1936, when the U.S.S.R. began to supply arms to the Government and power began to pass from the Anarchists to the Communists. . . . The Russians were in a position to dictate terms. There is very little doubt that these terms were, in substance, 'Prevent revolution or you get no weapons.'"[16] The novel's structure, therefore, functions in the same way as the official, Stalinist-dominated propaganda. It represents a transposition into artistic form of the function of concealment that characterized the propaganda in the foreign press.

This correspondence of function makes it clear why the Communist press received *L'Espoir* far more warmly than the earlier novels. Georges Friedmann, for example, in a 1938 review of the book in *L'Humanité*, praises it for (among other things) dramatizing the necessity of military organization and discipline and the primacy of military victory in the struggle between "fascism and democracies."[17] The coincidence between Malraux's novelistic world and the party line is almost complete.

Yet Malraux was clearly not himself a Stalinist, and *L'Espoir* can certainly not be called a Stalinist novel per se. An examination of its major characters and the relationships between them reveals rather the perspective of that characteristic intellectual figure in the period between the world wars: the fellow traveler of Stalinism. We will proceed on the assumption—accepted by most critics of Malraux— that *all* of the major characters in some way articulate the varied and contradictory aspects of the author's self. The configuration of all these characters must therefore be taken into consideration. But it must equally be recognized that two characters manifestly dominate the novel: Manuel and Garcia. The first plays a dominant role because he is identified with the structure of the novel; he follows precisely the same trajectory as the latter. Garcia, on the other hand, predominates by the sheer weight of his presence; he first appears somewhat late in the novel (*E* 115) but thereafter reappears regularly in important scenes of discussion, in which he is always given the most fully developed and compelling arguments. Moreover, he and Manuel have the last word in the work: he is the central figure in the next-to-last chapter, and Manuel in the last.

Of these two leading characters, one—Manuel—is a Communist and the other is not. Goldmann mistakenly identifies Garcia as a Communist too,[18] although Garcia's last conversation makes it evident that he is not (*E* 585–86). But Goldmann's error is in itself instructive. For while Garcia is never positively identified as a Communist, his discourse is not essentially different from that of the Communist characters, and in fact closely resembles it. This resemblance results from the elimination of the political dimension. Neither Manuel nor the less developed Communist characters engage in political discussion or reflection that would particularize them as Communists. Instead their concerns and affirmations are shown to be essentially the same as Garcia's; military organization for military victory is their common obsession. Some of the minor Communists express narrow, unconditional loyalty to their party, but this and this alone distinguishes and separates them from Garcia. In the case of Manuel we do not even find this differentiation. It is indeed striking that, while one of the two principal characters is a Communist, if he were not labeled as such early on in the novel we would not be able to identify him as one. We might, in others words, make the same mistake as Goldmann, in reverse. This profound ambiguity of political identification translates into the world of the novel the perspective of the fellow traveler. Garcia is the quintessence of the fellow traveler himself, and in Manuel we recognize not the Communist per se, but the Communist as seen by the fellow traveler.

At one point, when Manuel is talking with the older Communist syndicalist, Ramos, the text affirms that the relations between the two are changing, and that although Manuel was before "without political experience . . . he was beginning to acquire it" (E 105). Yet Manuel's actual education as illustrated in the novel is in no way political; it is an education in authoritarian leadership devoid of political content, in a purely military context. Thus Manuel's mentor comes to be not the syndicalist Ramos but the professional military officer Ximénès. Manuel is placed with the latter by the party itself (E 194), since the lesson it wants him to learn can be taught as well by a non-Communist as by a party member. (In general, Communists in the novel are almost exclusively portrayed in their relations with non-Communists, rather than among themselves.) The Communist Heinrich eventually summarizes that lesson for Manuel, with little difference except in tone of voice: " 'From the day you accept a position of command in the army of the proletariat, you no longer have a right to your soul. . . . Your heart you can keep; that is something else. But you must lose your soul.' . . . The vocabulary was almost that of Ximénès, but the tone was the hard one of Heinrich" (E 484). Garcia, who functions as mentor in the novel as a whole, that is, as mentor of the novel's intended reader, teaches a similar lesson. We might say that Garcia indirectly instructs Manuel, for the latter in fact learns (through Ximénès) how to put in practice what the former articulates in theory.

Although he is not a Communist, Garcia's lesson is indistinguishable from the Stalinist position, both in detail and in general tenor. When he tells Magnin, " 'We are not the revolution' " (E 136), he is faithfully espousing the Stalinists' line, which claimed that no revolutionary situation existed in Spain, and that the question of revolution could only be addressed after the war had been won.[19] Garcia's argument does not fully elucidate their position and does not openly acknowledge its source; it rather alludes to what anyone within the situation would recognize as the specific line of the official Communists. Moreover, in several passages Garcia seems to defend—again in rather vague terms—the Soviet Union and Stalin against criticisms (E 357, 463, 466).

More generally, Garcia consistently advocates the radical theory of *Realpolitik* first elaborated by Machiavelli and eventually adopted by the Stalinists: "'Action can only be thought of in terms of action. Political thinking only compares one concrete thing with another, one possibility with another possibility . . . one organization or another organization'" (E 250). Garcia here postulates the absolute (rather than partial and problematic) separation of the personal, the moral, and the ideal from the collective, the political, and the immediately possible, and he implicitly devalues the former. This position has been affirmed and utilized by Stalinism and its aftermath: it continues to function in the ideological justification of "actually existing socialism." But as Marcuse (among others) has demonstrated, it lies at the basis of modern Western "one-dimensional" ideology as well. Against this pervasive modern ethos, Marcuse affirms the power of negative thinking, of utopia, of that which does not yet exist.

It follows from Marcuse's critique of "positive thinking" that the primary role of the intellectual is a critical one. Conversely, Garcia's conception of the intellectual is in keeping with his general postulate: "'The strength of a thinker lies neither in his approbation nor in his protest . . . it lies in explanation. Let the intellectual explain why and how things are thus and so, and let him protest afterward if he thinks it necessary (but as a matter of fact it will no longer be necessary)'" (E 464). For Garcia the intellectual's function is purely analytical. The true intellectual analyzes existing phenomena; in addition he may ask by what actually existing means these phenomena can be modified. But he must not bring moral considerations to bear upon them. In this way the question of the relationship between ends and means in terms of values is declared a false one. The only appropriate mode of reflection on ends and means becomes the mode of efficiency. We are presented with what amounts to a technical conception of the intellectual. Stalinism, of course, asked precisely this of its intellectuals: that they provide expert knowledge without raising questions of value.

This conception of the value-free intellectual, as well as the one-dimensional elimination of the not yet real or immediately possible, are also potent forces in bourgeois ideology, however. This perhaps goes a long way toward explaining the fact—astonishing at first thought—that non-Communist readers of Malraux are often insensitive to the sinister implications of Garcia's line of reasoning. In his commentary on *L'Espoir*, for example, Pol Gaillard waxes eloquent on the nobility of Garcia, going so far as to assert, "If the twentieth century could have, like the seventeenth, its ideal 'honnête homme,' the typical representative of the best that a free, progressive culture produces, it would be he."[20] We could be inclined, on the contrary, to see in Garcia a twentieth-century Mephistopheles rather than its *honnête homme*!

Garcia and Manuel, of course, are not the only important characters, and they do not represent the sole viewpoint in *L'Espoir*. There exists a whole series of critical characters, that is, characters who in one way or another question the main line of affirmation in Garcia/Manuel. Moreover, Stalinism and Stalinists (though the terms are never used) are treated in a negative as well as a positive light. In the character of Karlitch we are shown a type of Communist very much associated with the rise of Stalinism: the type that is attracted by armed power and imposed order. Karlitch was an officer in the White Russian army before changing allegiance, and (just as Manuel comes to be fascinated by police dogs, fighting cocks, and so forth) he takes pride in shining his Cossack boots. He demonstrates the affinity, several times alluded to in the novel, between Stalinist Communism and the fascism it is combating. Enrique and Pradas, on the other hand, are presented as another negative type: the narrow-minded bureaucrat who puts total, uncritical fidelity to his organization above all else. This type is compared with that of the *curé* or *abbé*, thus underscoring the affinity of Party faithful with a negative aspect of institutional Christianity.

Moreover, a number of the book's leading characters—most important, Hernandez, le Négus, old Alvear, Scali, and Magnin—pose substantial challenges to the position of fellow traveler of Stalinism. Yet in each case their challenge is largely undermined or devalued. Hernandez, although he agrees with the Communists' position on land collectivization, refuses to aid them in imprisoning on trumped-up charges an anarchist who is following an opposite policy. In so doing he affirms the necessity of relating means and ends in terms of values. And his claim to Garcia that "'men die only for what does not exist'" (*E* 250), affirms the power of the ideal and utopian that Marcuse opposes to the dominant modes of discourse. Equally telling is le Négus's direct critique of Stalinist politics. In the one passage in which the anarchist-Communist split is dealt with politically, albeit very briefly, le Négus expostulates, " 'No bureaucrats in place of delegates, no army to put an end to armies, no inequality to end inequality, no deals with the bourgeois'" (E 236). But both le Négus and Hernandez are portrayed as making a mystique of sacrifice, to the point of displaying suicidal impulses; they are shown to be more concerned with realizing themselves in terms of their personal ethic than with accomplishing something concrete for the Spanish masses.

Alvear, a retired professor of art history, also raises questions about Communist practice. He asks Scali:

What guarantees that the gains economic liberation would bring you will be greater than the losses brought by a new society that is threatened on all sides and obliged because of its fear to use constraint, violence, perhaps denunciation? Economic bondage is heavy to bear; but if to destroy it it is necessary to strengthen political, military, religious bondage, or bondage to the police, then what does it matter to me? (E 377)

This passage illustrates on the one hand Malraux's doubts concerning the Soviet Union, and on the other the severe limits he imposed on criticism of it. In the passage the Soviet Union remains unnamed and the dangers referred to are spoken to in the conditional and future tenses, as if they had not yet actually occurred. Scali—a fellow art historian—later rearticulates Alvear's argument, and at the end of the novel we learn that he has become "almost anti-Communist" (E 585). But his revolt also is undermined; he is associated with the anarchists, already thoroughly devalued, and with Hernandez, whose death is seen (by Garcia) as a direct result of his erroneous viewpoint (E 467). As for old Alvear, he shares the suicidal impulse of the other critical characters, and the fact that he is reading Don Quixote suggests that his protest, though noble, is as absurdly irrelevant as that of Cervantes' protagonist.

Of the critical characters, Magnin is the only one who is directly present—along with Garcia, Manuel, and Ximénès—at the end of L'Espoir. Early on in the novel, after having identified himself as a left-wing socialist, Magnin responds to Garcia's " 'We are not the revolution'" with " 'Well, let's be the revolution!'" (E 137). This opposition to the Stalinist line is similar in nature to that of Alvear; Magnin speaks of the revolution in Spain as a future possibility, thus implicitly denying its present reality. Moreover, shortly afterward Magnin recognizes that his party is weak in comparison with that of the Communists, and admits that in the name of effectiveness Communist practice can be justified: " 'All of that could be defended'" (E

186). He is forced to accept (albeit with sadness) the point of view of Garcia, that "'action is action, and not justice'" (*E* 187). Thus he passes from the camp of the critical to that of the fellow travelers, and later will make his air squadron part of Spanish aviation (that is, part of the Communist-dominated Popular Army), naming the Communist Attignies as political commissar.

Within the universe of *L'Espoir*, then, the critical characters suffer a fate that is the novelistic equivalent of a Stalinist catchword: they are, as it were, relegated to the "dustbin of history." And parallel to Manuel's transformation is Magnin's: from criticism to the stance of fellow traveler. We do not mean, of course, to underestimate the critical elements in *L'Espoir*. Their presence in the novel clearly distinguishes it from a vulgar piece of Stalinist apology. They demonstrate that Malraux was far from unaware of the problematic nature of his commitment. But they are nonetheless pushed into the background and, if not canceled, at least neutralized by the overall development of the novel. It is Garcia who has the final word, putting them into perspective at the end. When asked what he thinks of the Communists, he cites Guernico's phrase: "'They have all the virtues of action—and those virtues alone,'" and adds, "'but at the moment it is a question of action'" (*E* 585). Since in *L'Espoir* the primary value is effective action, the conclusion of the syllogism would be that within the novelistic world the Communists have all the virtues. Yet the journalist Shade, another critical character of lesser importance, exhorts his readers: "'Let us tell the fascists to get out of here . . . and tell the Communists the same thing tomorrow, if necessary'" (*E* 454), and this imperative would seem to define the provisional nature of the fellow traveler's solution. Objections and opposition to Stalinism must for the moment be put in parentheses, and this is precisely what the novel does with them.

But in addition to the neutralization of criticism in the novel, we must also note the nature and source of the criticism. In most cases it comes from intellectuals, and it is formulated in terms of the individual. The opposition is mounted in the name of a personal ethic, and focuses on dangers to freedom for the individual. Although this kind of criticism is crucial, what is missing is criticism from the point of view of a class—the very class in the name of which the Communists claimed to speak, but whose revolution they in fact crushed. Le Négus comes closest to making this critique, but he does not really do so since his opposition to Communist policy is presented as stemming from a desire to live authentically and freely in the present, even at the expense of losing, rather than from anger at betrayal of the revolution. The issue is thereby falsified, and the most telling critique, in the name of the revolutionary collectivity, remains unspoken.

Thus *L'Espoir* embodies—in terms of what it leaves out as well as what it includes and how it presents what it includes—the characteristic sensibility of an intellectual fellow traveler of Stalinism. As a whole it holds in a delicate balance the contradictions and hesitations, the voluntary blind spots and interiorization of propaganda, of the consciousness of the fellow traveler. It is perhaps one of the most complete and esthetically compelling literary transpositions of that highly volatile, transitional form of consciousness that characterized an important moment in the development of many intellectuals in the period between the two wars, and which in many cases did not survive World War II. Such was, of course, the case with Malraux himself.

In the course of his intellectual and artistic evolution, Malraux identified himself with Stalinism only for a relatively short period (1935–37), and only one of his works (or two, if we include the minor work *Le Temps du mépris*) reflects the specific dynamic of that identification. Yet in a deeper sense Malraux's vision as a whole—beyond the specific historical thematics—reveals a certain affinity with Stalinism. Beyond the vicissitudes of Malraux's process of development there remains an overriding continuity of vision, and it is at this level that we would situate the deeper affinity. In this sense a Stalinist coloration is present in the early novels as well as in *L'Espoir*.

The affinity with Stalinism lies in the elitist tendency that runs throughout Malraux's work: the cult of the hero and the purely passive conception of the people. The latter constitute a malleable mass to be manipulated by the leader-hero, whom they worship with quasi-religious devotion. In *L'Espoir* this hierarchical figuration of hero and masses is most perfectly incarnated in the famous scene of the descent from the mountain near the end of the novel. The wounded aviator-heroes are brought down from the heights like gods descending earthward. A few peasants serve them by carrying them down and providing food at great sacrifice, while others await them below and pay homage to the saviours who have risked their lives for the people. Although we would agree with Frohock that this scene contradicts the novel's propaganda thesis in that it provides a picture "of solidarity not within the Communist party but within the larger fraternity of Man,"[21] that solidarity is nonetheless a highly hierarchical and mythologized one. Consequently, at a deeper level it is entirely in keeping with Malraux's Stalinist commitment. It reproduces the relationship of leader and masses that was so well cultivated by the "little father of the people." A similar relationship, of course, characterizes fascist movements. So in this respect Malraux's work also reveals a supreme paradox: a hidden—and effectively repressed, let it be added—affinity with the fascist ideology that he always combated.

Susan Rubin Suleiman

MALRAUX'S WOMEN:

A RE-VISION

Re-vision—the act of looking back, of seeing with fresh eyes, of entering an old text from a new critical direction . . .

ADRIENNE RICH[1]

The thought that it might be time to take another look at Malraux's novels first occurred to me two years ago, while I was reading the passionate, angry few pages that Annie Leclerc devotes to him in *Parole de femme*. "Malraux the bombastic [*L'emphatique Malraux*]," she calls him—the repetitive proponent of conventional values, and first and foremost of the value of the hero: "The hero; it's me-me-me, for as long as possible. *My* mark, *my* takeover, *my* possession for eternity." Grandiose and ridiculous, ever the posturing male, Malraux's hero deserves all the scorn that a woman's word can heap on him.[2]

Leclerc exaggerates, of course; hers is not a critique but an attack, not a reading but a caricature. She bases her indictment on a few well-known quotations from *La Voie royale*, makes no distinction between Malraux and Perken, ignores the other novels, does away with ambiguities and contradictions. Malraux doesn't interest her; she merely uses him to make a point, then passes on.

And yet, her few acerbic words prompted me to think once again, in a way I had not thought before, about Malraux's novels and their contemporary significance. I had first read the novels in graduate school, at Harvard in the early sixties. After finishing each one, I would read the corresponding chapter in Frohock's *André Malraux and the Tragic Imagination*—an excellent book, I thought then, and still do. Years later, I reread *L'Espoir* with some care and wrote about it; but it was in a context that did not oblige me to rethink, only to expand and refine, my earlier reading. Malraux was, for me, a familiar and admired writer, exemplary in his concern for questions of the broadest human significance. Although the 1930s had receded into history and Malraux himself had undergone a metamorphosis (perhaps more than one) since those impassioned days, his novels remained for me, like those of Sartre, Camus, and a few others, representative of a kind of fiction—serious, urgent, eloquent—that I regarded with what might be called historical nostalgia: they were not repeatable today, but they were definitely worth saving.

Now along came Leclerc, telling me that he is not worth saving—not by or for women, in any case. And that made me pause. I, after all, had changed since the days in the Widener Library when I reflected with a certain exaltation over the bitter defeat of Garine or Perken, the tragic victory-despite-defeat of Kyo and Katow, or the hard-won education of Manuel. Could it be that they too had changed over the years or taken on a different meaning? I remembered the powerful conclusion of Frohock's chapter on *La Condition humaine*: "From their destinies [Clappique's, Ferral's and Gisors's] we know the power of the Absurd. But at the same time we have also seen Katow go out to die, and we know that there inheres in man's fate, in spite of all the possibilities of defeat, the possibility of the power and glory of being a man."[3] Might I find, after so many years, that when Malraux speaks of the problematic glory of man's fate, he is not speaking to me? Might I discover, in his novels, what Judith Fetterley sees in the whole expanse of American fiction by male writers: "In such fictions the female reader is co-opted into participation in an experience from which she is explicitly excluded; she is asked to identify with a selfhood that defines itself in opposition to her; she is required to identify against herself"?[4]

Clearly, a rereading—or rather, a re-vision as Adrienne Rich defines it: rereading from a new critical perspective—was in order. A feminist perspective? Yes, to the extent that the whole enterprise was provoked by my reading of contemporary feminist writers and critics and that its underlying question could not have been formulated outside a feminist problematic. At the same time I was, and am, extremely wary of the temptation that besets any critic with a strong ideological allegiance: to transform commentary into polemics and to start a critical investigation from foregone conclusions. I therefore decided to proceed as gingerly, and with as much verifiability, as possible; rather than attacking head-on the question of Malraux's heroes, about whom in any case a great deal has been written, I would look instead at Malraux's . . . heroines? No, his women. Who are they? Where are they? What do they do? Who speaks to them, to whom do they speak? And what difference does it make?

The Name and Its Absence

My first observation brought with it a shock of discovery: in Malraux's six novels, with their total cast of hundreds of characters, only five women are named. Of these, two have only a first name and are evoked in the most fleeting way: Perken, in *La Voie royale*, talks to Claude Vannec about the woman he once lived with, whose name was Sarah; Vincent Berger, in *Les Noyers de l'Altenburg*, had a servant named Jeanne. That leaves three women with full names and who appear as more than mere evocations: May Gisors, Valérie Serge, and Anna Kassner. I shall talk about them later.

And the others, those who appear without a name? The list is short enough to be mentioned almost in its entirety. In *Les Conquérants* the Genoese merchant Rebecci, mentor of the Chinese terrorist Hong, is married to "a quite beautiful native woman, gone to fat"[5]; she is later referred to, in a description by the first-person narrator, as "a fat Chinese woman" (*C* 36), and on the next page by another character as "his [Rebecci's] Chinese woman" (*C* 37). The German revolutionary Klein, who is killed by the terrorists, has been living in Canton with "a white woman"; when she comes to mourn over his mutilated body, she is referred to merely as "a woman," and later as "she" (*C* 191, 192); Garine and the narrator, who are present, do not speak to her. The dead wife of Nicolaïeff, the Russian czarist agent turned revolutionary, is evoked: "A sincere and respected terrorist, whose death was a strange story." (C 132) At one point, the narrator enters Garine's room and finds him buttoning his tunic while two naked women are lying on his bed: "two young Chinese women," "the women." (C 138)

In *La Voie royale* Claude Vannec's mother and grandmother are evoked by the impersonal narrator; they are designated respectively as "his mother" and "his [grandfather's, old Vannec's] wife." There is also the evocation of Claude's and Perken's first meeting in a brothel in Djibouti, where Claude saw Perken "beneath the outstretched arm of a big Negro woman draped in red and black." (VR 14) Toward the end of the novel, Perken has two Laotian prostitutes brought for him and Claude: they are "two women," "the little one" called "the other," who then becomes "she" (VR 156, 158)—she is the one Perken sleeps with. And all along, collectively, there are "the women"— the women who obsess Perken's memory and imagination, those in the Moï tribes, those by whom his friend Grabot has himself flagellated.

In *La Condition humaine* there is Hemmelrich's wife, "his Chinese woman" (CH 179) (as seen by Hemmelrich), who gets blown to bits by a grenade; there is an evocation of Katow's dead wife, "a little working girl who loved him," "that vacant [*vague*] idiot" (CH 209, 210). The Japanese painter Kama talks about his wife and daughter, for love of whom he says he paints. Ferral, to vent his frustration after being bested by Valérie, picks up a woman referred to only as "a Chinese courtesan" whom he humiliates by treating as a simple prostitute: "a girl with a sweet, lovely face," "that Chinese woman" (CH 231). Gisors at one point remembers his dead wife: a Japanese woman; and there are the various women Clappique meets: a "Philippine," a "Russian," etc.

In *Le Temps du mépris* there is the old woman who speaks at an anti-Nazi demonstration about her dead son, killed by the Nazis: "An old silhouette awkwardly bent over the microphone: mass-produced hat, black coat" (TM 155). In *L'Espoir*, there are a young militia-woman who brings food to the men fighting with Barca and Manuel; a nurse in a military hospital; a woman hostage who escapes from the Alcazar in Toledo and gives information to the Republican Lopez; a woman who during the bombardment of Madrid asks Guernico and Garcia for advice about whether to stay or leave. Toward the end Manuel speaks to Ximénèz about a woman he once loved passionately to no avail, and with whom he had slept the previous week with total indifference. In *Les Noyers de l'Altenburg* a woman throws bread to the French prisoners at Chartres; Vincent Berger admires the women on the street in Marseilles after he returns from a six-year stay in the Middle East; the soldiers in young Berger's regiment show photographs of their wives or girl friends—Leonard tells about the time he slept with a starlet at the Casino de Paris; Pradé talks to Berger about his son, who needs him to help him with schoolwork, and he also talks about his wife: "'The wife, what can she do? She's a girl from a large family. She's not intelligent.'" (NA 266) And there is the old peasant woman at the end, in whom Berger sees a symbol of humanity's eternal endurance.

Putting aside for the moment the three fully named women who appear in La Condition humaine and Le Temps du mépris and allowing for a few unnamed ones that I may have missed, the above gallery constitutes just about the entire cast of female characters in Malraux's fictional universe. But *characters* is of course not the right word: taking up the distinction made by Roland Barthes in S/Z, we can call them, at most, figures. In order to have a character, Barthes remarks, there must be a proper name; it is the name that unites a series of dispersed traits, or seems, into a stable configuration, a character with a personality and a biography—and only a character, hence someone with a name, can be the "object of a destiny."[6] A figure is a different thing altogether: "It is not a combination of semes concentrated in a legal Name, nor can biography, psychology or time encompass it: it is a nonlegal, impersonal, nontemporal configuration of symbolic relationships."[7] Presumably, a named character can also function as a figure, "an impersonal network of symbols"[8]; but a figure cannot become a character—not without a name.

If we call the women enumerated above figures, we must ask what they are figures of; what do they symbolize? Wives, prostitutes, mothers, providers of food or care, they are the eternal feminine as pictured by the male imagination. A Chinese woman, a Japanese woman, a white woman, a woman: like the hat of the old mother at the demonstration, they are one in a series, interchangeable and anonymous. Shadowy presences or fleeting evocations, they exist as extensions of, in relation to, seen or imagined by, men who possess a name as well as a past and a future. We are given Rebecci's entire biography, but all we know of his *Chinoise* is that she was once beautiful and is now fat; Nicolaïeff's life story is before us, but about his wife we know that she was a terrorist whose death was a "strange story." We know Gisors intimately; of his wife, we know only that she was not, like May, "à demi-virile," but made possible for Gisors a love that was tender, serene, and sweet. Above all, we know that she is dead; there are a great many dead or absent wives in these novels, very few who are *there*. Nor, I would contend, is their absence explicable only by the fact that Malraux wrote chiefly about war and revolution, two activities in which the presence of women is rare. That would certainly not account for the considerable number of dead wives and mothers, or for the apparently nonexistent ones like Vincent Berger's wife (young Berger's mother) in *Les Noyers de l'Altenburg*, who is never mentioned. Whereas the father-son (or its variant, grandfather-grandson) relation is privileged in almost every novel— Claude and his grandfather in *La Voie royale*, Kyo and Gisors in *La Condition humaine*, Jaime Alvear and his father in *L'Espoir*, the three generations of Bergers in *Les Noyers*, not to mention the large number of spiritual father–spiritual son relations ranging from Rebecci-Hong or Gisors-Tchen to Ximénès-Manuel—Malraux's heroes seem to have experienced no affective ties at all to their mothers. The absence of women in their emotional life is thus attributable to more than the mere circumstantial *données* of the fictions.[9]

Of the unnamed women who are present in the novels, it may be accurate to say that they are not so much figures as *figurantes*: they are extras on a stage where men are the objects of destiny.

Silence

The chief characteristic of an extra is silence. Malraux's men are inveterate talkers, but they rarely address a word to a woman. Talking to a woman is, of course, difficult when there are so few of them around. But there is something else at stake here too—a kind of fundamental incompatibility between what a man has to say and what a woman can understand or cares about. "To have a man's heart and not to notice that one is explaining it to a woman who doesn't give a damn is quite normal," says Garine (*C* 65). After sleeping with his "two young Chinese women" Garine buttons his officer's tunic and gives instructions to his boy to show them out and pay them. He then tells the narrator: "'After you've been here for a while, the Chinese women get on your nerves a lot, you'll see. The best thing is to sleep with them and forget about it, so you can keep your mind on serious things'" (*C* 138). Oriental prostitutes are not people one talks to, especially if one is a Garine or a Perken. But Garine doesn't talk to Klein's "white woman" either: he watches her embrace Klein's mutilated body, then tells the Chinese attendant: "'When she's gone, you cover them all'" (*C* 192). About Tchen, May says: "'I didn't really know him: he couldn't stand women'" (*CH* 334). We know, however, that Tchen frequented prostitutes; what he evidently could not stand was the *company* of women.

Quite a lot has been written about the eroticism of Malraux's adventurer or terrorist heroes: Garine, Perken, Ferral, Tchen. Eroticism is, as the eroticists themselves explain it, first of all a need to dominate the other, to use the other as a means of gaining possession of oneself. Thus Ferral: "He derived his pleasure from putting himself in the place of the other, that was clear; of the other, compelled: compelled by him. In reality he never went to bed with anyone but himself, but he could do this only if he was not alone" (CH 232). The woman in such a situation is obviously there to be negated, and she must be silent. It is true, as Lucien Goldmann and others have noted, that Malraux—or rather, the implied author of La Condition humaine—does not endorse eroticism as a positive value[10]; on the contrary, he shows that Ferral's drive to dominate women is merely the sexual side of a more general drive to impose his will on others, just as Perken's eroticism is the sexual counterpart of his desire to "leave a scar on the map." Furthermore, in both instances the adventurer's project ends in failure.

The adventurer's scorn of women, his refusal to talk to them or allow them to speak—in other words, to consider them as fully human beings—is thus not attributable to the author of La Condition humaine; indeed, one can cite Valérie's letter to Ferral, in which she proclaims her refusal to be "only a body," as proof to the contrary. What seems to me more significant, however, is that even Malraux's revolutionaries, the men of goodwill like Kyo, Katow, Hemmelrich, Kassner, Garcia, or Manuel, find it extremely difficult to communicate with women. Leaving Kyo and Kassner aside for the moment, since theirs is the most fully developed relation with women (I shall discuss them in the next section), let us look at a few others.

Garcia and Guernico, walking on the street during the bombardment of Madrid, are stopped by a woman who tugs at Guernico's sleeve and asks whether he thinks she should leave the city. The dynamics of the brief scene that ensues are interesting enough to warrant reproducing it in full:

A woman plucked Guernico's sleeve and addressed him in French. "Do you think I ought to leave?"

"She's a German comrade," Guernico explained to Garcia, but did not answer her.

"He says I ought to go," the woman went on. "He says he can't fight properly when I'm around."

"He is surely right," Garcia said.

"But I just can't go on living if I know he's fighting here . . . if I don't even know what's happening . . ."

Another accordion playing the "Internationale" droned an accompaniment to the words; a second blind man, begging bowl on lap, was carrying on the tune from the point where the first had dropped it.

They're all alike, these women, Garcia thought to himself. If that one goes, she'll take it hard at first, but she'll see it through; whereas, if she stays, he'll be killed. He could not see her face; she was much shorter than he and her face was screened by shadows of the passers-by.

"Why do you want to stay?" Guernico's voice was gentle.

"I don't mind dying. . . . The trouble is, I've got to eat well, and now that won't be possible. I'm pregnant . . ."

Garcia did not hear Guernico's reply. The woman drifted away on another stream of shadows. (E 303)

Concentrating on the exchange between the woman and the two men, we note the following: she asks Guernico a question, to which he does not reply, turning instead to Garcia to explain who she is. The woman rephrases her question, and this time Garcia replies curtly that her husband is surely right (in asking her to leave). She responds by talking about her feelings, allowing her voice to trail off at the end of the sentence. Garcia's attention turns to the sound of the accordion in the background; then he thinks to himself that women are all alike and that she might end up causing her husband's death. He does not tell her his thoughts, however: he seems clearly scornful of her typically feminine lack of good sense, and indeed he does not address a word to her again. Guernico's question to her elicits a reply which shows courage (she is not afraid to die), but which also reinforces the impression that she is vacillating (notice the points of suspension), and again that she lacks good sense: since she is pregnant, the answer to her own question should be evident. Garcia is no longer interested, however, and doesn't even hear Guernico's rejoinder. After the woman disappears into the shadows, the two men resume their conversation, which is long and philosophical.

This is a minor incident in a lengthy novel, but it is not insignificant. It is one of the very rare scenes in L'Espoir where a woman speaks, or, what is even rarer, where a woman speaks to express her feelings. True, Garcia's indifference may not be due only to her being a woman—she is, after all, a total stranger and he has many things on his mind—but there is no mistaking the scornful tone of the phrase "they're all alike these women [Toutes les mêmes]," which explicitly marks her sexual difference. Even more important, this difference represents, in his eyes, a potential threat of death for her husband: women can be dangerous; in any case, they hamper the serious activities of men.

In La Condition humaine besides Kyo there are two other revolutionaries who either are or have been married: Hemmelrich and Katow. Hemmelrich lives with a Chinese woman and has a child by her; the child is seriously ill. After a first attempt to bomb Chiang Kaishek's car, Tchen and his two friends seek shelter in Hemmelrich's store. He refuses to let them stay, fearing that if the police find them there with their bombs, they will kill the woman and child. After the three leave, Hemmelrich goes upstairs to the bedroom where the sick child is, hating himself meanwhile for having let down his comrades: "His Chinese woman was sitting, her eyes fixed on the bed; she did not turn around" (CH 179). Hemmelrich does not speak to her; he speaks to the child, then goes downstairs again. He thinks, with increasing fury and frustration, about the misery of his present and past life. The only thing that keeps him from going out and joining the terrorists is the thought that his wife and child depend on him. A little later, Katow arrives and Hemmelrich confides to him his sense of guilt and also his anger; the misery of his life is somehow summed up by his wife, in whom he sees a poor humiliated creature like himself:

"Devotion, yes. And everything she can. The rest—what she hasn't got—is all for the rich. When I see people who look as if they're in love, I feel like smashing them in the face." (CH 207)

Katow, who for reasons of his own understands only too well how Hemmelrich is feeling, tries to reassure him:

". . . If you believe in nothing, *especially* because you believe in nothing, you're forced to believe in the virtues of the heart when you come across them, no doubt about it. And that's what you're doing. If it hadn't been for the woman and the kid you would have gone, I know you would. Well, then?"
"And as we live only for those virtues of the heart, they gobble you up. Well, if you've always got to be eaten it might as well be them." (CH 208–209)

It is not clear whether "them" in Hemmelrich's reply refers to "virtues of the heart" or to women like his wife—devoted, alien, and mute—who are the immediate subject of the conversation. But it hardly matters, since the "virtues of the heart" belong to those women. Hemmelrich is saying that he is tied down by his wife (or rather, that he is "eaten up," and the choice of that image is not insignificant),[11] that he accepts his situation, but is not happy about it. Katow, in the meantime, thinks but does not dare to say out loud: "'Death will free you'" (CH 209). Hemmelrich is in fact "freed" shortly afterward, when the woman and child are killed by a grenade attack on the store. He then throws himself into the battle: "His shoulders thrust forward, he pushed ahead like a tugboat toward a dim country of which he knew only that one killed there, pulling with his shoulders and brain the weight of all his dead, who, at last, *no longer prevented him from advancing*" (CH 255; my emphasis).

Later he escapes to the Soviet Union, where he finds happiness working in an electric plant.

As for Katow, he understands Hemmelrich's problem because he has experienced a similar one. He too was married once:

> Having returned from Siberia without hope, beaten, his medical studies shattered, and having become a factory worker, convinced that he would die before seeing the revolution, he had sadly proved to himself that he still possessed a remnant of life by treating a little working girl who loved him with deliberate brutality. But hardly had she become resigned to the pains he inflicted on her than he had been suddenly overwhelmed by the tenderness of a creature who could share his suffering even as he made her suffer. From that moment he had lived only for her, continuing his revolutionary activity through habit, but carrying into it the obsession of the limitless tenderness hidden in the heart of that vague idiot: for hours he would caress her hair, and they would lie in bed together for days on end. She had died, and since then. . . . (CH 209–10)

Katow will find his apotheosis in the gesture of self-sacrifice that links him to the two men for whom he gives up his cyanide pill and consents to be burned alive. For him as for Hemmelrich, it is the revolution that provides dignity and genuine communion with others—and those others are men, generically opposed to the "vague idiot" with whom he once spent his days. This opposition is, curiously, echoed and reinforced by one of Kassner's internal monologues while he is in the Nazi prison: remembering his martyred comrades in China, Russia, and Germany, Kassner exclaims "'You, my companions, it is what exists between us that I call love'" (TM 107).

Katow and Hemmelrich both choose (if that is quite the right word) women who are below them socially and intellectually, and whose death signifies liberation and the possibility of self-fulfillment for the revolutionary hero. Their humiliated companions bear at least some resemblance to the wordless prostitutes over whom Garine, Perken, and Ferral assert their manhood. Although the revolutionary is not an eroticist, his relations with women are not altogether different from those of the adventurer. As an older "Clappique" told Malraux in a conversation in Singapore, reported in the Antimémoires, "'The first characteristic of the adventurer is that he is unmarried [d'abord, un aventurier est célibataire!]'"[12] Unhampered by a woman, free to act—that seems also to be the ideal state toward which the revolutionary hero tends.

When the narrator of Les Conquérants first meets Nicolaïeff, he makes a remark which I find extremely illuminating in this context: "'The fat man speaks French with a very slight accent. His tone of voice—despite his clipped answers, you'd think he was speaking to a woman, or was about to add, "My dear fellow," his calm face, the unctuousness of his manner, made one think of an ex-priest'" (C 96–97). What is not only implied here but is taken for granted is that when men speak to women, they do not speak as they do among themselves. The "unctuous" intonation of a man speaking to a woman is enough to feminize him, make him appear less masculine (an "ex-priest"). Not speaking to women, or speaking to them in a special way, these are but two aspects of a single phenomenon: the fundamental scorn that Malraux's heroes feel toward women and their deep-seated fear of them.[13]

Three Women

Not for nothing was Malraux a brilliant writer, however. If on some level he and all his heroes shared in "the fundamental misogyny of almost all men" (CH 54), he seems to have had the necessary lucidity to realize it, and—like his creature Kyo—to be ashamed of it. We can read his treatment of Valérie Serge, May Gisors, and Anna Kassner as a compensatory gesture, a way of righting the balance, as it were. At the same time, their stories—or rather, their episodes, for they ultimately play a small part in the two novels in which they appear—repeat in different modes the dominant theme of separation, of an inalterable and unbridgeable difference between the sexes; they also repeat, rather unexpectedly, the valorization of the masculine that we have already encountered elsewhere.

Valérie's is the mode of irony. In this woman, in whom Ferral senses "a pride akin to his own" (CH 117), the eroticist adventurer meets an adversary to his own measure. Valérie is beautiful, rich, articulate—a woman who earns her own way and speaks her mind. During a conversation in his bedroom, shortly before they make love, Ferral tells her that a woman must of necessity give herself, and a man must of necessity possess her; to which she replies: "'Hasn't it occurred to you, dear, that women never give themselves (or hardly ever) and that men possess nothing? . . . Listen, I'm going to say something very wicked—but don't you think it's the story all over again of the cork which considered itself so much more important than the bottle?'" (CH 120). By insisting on leaving the light on while they make love, so that he can watch her face as she reaches orgasm, Ferral seeks to assert the superiority of the "cork" over the "bottle." Valérie then retaliates with the famous scene of the canaries, in which Ferral plays the role of dupe while she plays that of director; whereupon Ferral does her one better and transforms her hotel room into an enchanted forest full of tropical birds: "Through hatred he would have offered Valérie his handsomest gift" (*CH* 223). But the aim of the gift is clear: "It was necessary above all that, if Valérie told the story of the cages—she would not fail to do so—he would only have to tell the end in order to escape ridicule" (*CH* 220–21).

It is in this context of a somewhat bitter drawing-room comedy, where what matters above all is the protagonists' image in the salons, that Ferral—and the reader of *La Condition humaine*—reads Valérie's letter:

"You know a good many things, dear, but you will probably die without its ever having occurred to you that a woman is *also* a human being. I have always met (perhaps I shall never meet any who are different, but so much the worse—you can't know how thoroughly I mean 'so much the worse'!) men who have credited me with a certain amount of charm, who have gone to touching lengths to set off my follies, but who have never failed to go straight to their men friends whenever it was a question of something really human (except of course to be consoled)." (*CH* 217)

Valérie, in her mocking way, seems to be pointing her finger here not only at Ferral but at all of Malraux's heroes; wasn't it a hero, after all, who said that to keep one's mind on "serious things," that the best thing is to "sleep with them and forget about it"? Isn't it true that not a single one of Malraux's heroes—not an adventurer, not a revolutionary, not Gisors the philosopher, not Alvear the art historian, not even Kyo or Kassner—ever talks to a woman about any of the "truly human things" that preoccupy them so persistently, and about which they talk to each other with such urgency and eloquence?

At the same time, it is worth noting that by humiliating Ferral, Valérie adopts a quasi-masculine stance: she will certainly not convert him to her point of view; she merely asserts her own power in a struggle where both self-respect and public image are at stake. Her gesture is a declaration of war with all the aggressiveness that such declarations imply. If we admire her, as we are surely meant to do, it is because she is a woman with masculine pride and self-assertiveness. For that very reason, however, it seems clear that she can never have any but an adversary relationship to men.

May and Anna are quite different; they are the only two women in Malraux's novels who have what might be called an egalitarian love relationship with a man. Goldmann devotes some lyrical pages to his celebration of the love between Kyo and May; theirs is, in his words, "one of the purest and most beautiful love stories to have been described in the important works of the twentieth century."[14] According to Goldmann, the love that Kyo and Kassner feel for their wives is the counterpart to their feeling of authentic revolutionary community with their fellow men. The love between man and woman, in other words, is the private aspect of the more generalized love that unites men in "virile fraternity." This is an attractive interpretation, one that allows Goldmann to explain why adventurers (for example) are not able to love women; what it fails to take account of is the very precarious nature of the love relationship as it is actually experienced by the two men in question (we never know exactly how the women feel, since Malraux maintains a strict internal focalization on the men when they are together), and the possibly problematic rather than integrative relation that exists, in Malraux's novels, between heterosexual love and virile fraternity.

The love between Kyo and May is placed at the outset under the sign of ambiguity—of at least two ambiguities, in fact. First, there is the ambiguity of May's appearance: "Her blue leather coat, of an almost military cut, accentuated what was virile in her gait and even in her face. . . . Her very high forehead as well had something masculine about it, but since she had stopped speaking she was becoming more feminine" (CH 48–49). When May speaks, she appears to Kyo like a man (here we find a familiar paradigm—to be fully feminine, the woman must be silent); at the same time, it is her sensual mouth, with its full lips ("le léger gonflement de ses lèvres"), that most clearly marks her as a woman.

The other ambiguity is more complex: it has to do with Kyo's sense of closeness to her and at the same time with his feeling of total separation from her. The alternation of these two feelings defines Kyo's relationship to May (and hers to him? We cannot be sure)—which may be one reason why Gisors, after Kyo's death, thinks of their love as an "amour intellectuel et ravagé" (CH 333).

Kyo's greatest feeling of alienation from May comes, understandably enough, after she tells him that she finally slept with one of her colleagues at the hospital where she is a doctor. Although their marriage is not based on sexual exclusiveness and although he knows that her act had no more than passing significance for her, he cannot help feeling angry and jealous. What is more important in our context, however, is his discovery, after her "confession," that May had begun to recede from him way before—that it was not her infidelity, but time and habit, that would eventually separate her from him. The passage in which this realization hits Kyo should be quoted almost in full in order for its impact to be felt (significantly, Goldmann does not include it in his extensive quotations from the novel when he discusses Kyo and May):

He continued nevertheless to look at her, to discover that she could make him suffer. For months, whether he looked at her or not, *he had ceased to see her;* certain expressions, at times . . . Their love, so often hurt, uniting them like a sick child, the common meaning of their life and their death, the carnal understanding between them, nothing of all that existed before the fatality which discolors the forms with which our eyes are saturated . . . He remembered a friend who had had to watch the disintegration of the mind of the woman he loved, paralyzed for months; it seemed to him that he was watching May die thus, watching the form of his happiness absurdly disappear like a cloud absorbed by the gray sky. *As though she had died twice—from the effect of time, and from what she was telling him.* (CH 51; my emphasis)

Kyo's alienation from May, in other words, is not the temporary alienation of a husband angry at his wife; it is a much more deeply anchored thing, against which even his love for her is no protection. And it is a thing that *kills* her—not once, but twice. May is also, in a sense, a dead wife. Finally, as if this weren't enough, Kyo realizes that something else separates her from him: not anger or hatred, not jealousy, not even the destructive power of time, but a feeling without a name that suddenly transforms her into something incomprehensible: "This body was being invested with the poignant mystery of a familiar person suddenly transformed—the mystery one feels before a mute, blind, or mad being. *And she was a woman. Not a kind of man. Something else . . .* She was getting away from him completely" (CH 54; my emphasis).

The fundamental alienation between men and women is here orchestrated in a tragic mode. Kyo's reaction, when he realizes his separation from May, is to want to clasp her to him: "To lie with her, to find refuge in her body against this frenzy in which he was losing her entirely; they did not have to know each other when they were using all their strength to clasp their arms around their bodies" (CH 55). Sexual union would be a way of escaping from the awareness of a more irremediable separateness. This union is prevented, however, for at that point the bell rings and Clappique enters; Kyo then goes out, and it is only later, while walking with Katow, that he is able to rediscover (or perhaps to reason himself into believing?) his sense of closeness to May: "Since his mother had died, May was the only being for whom he was not Kyo Gisors, but the most intimate complicity" (CH 57).

The same alternation between alienation and communion (where, paradoxically, May's presence provokes the former, her absence the latter) occurs in the only other scene that Kyo shares with May, shortly before he is arrested and killed. His refusal to allow her to go with him to the meeting is in one sense revenge for her earlier infidelity, and they both understand it as such; at the same time it is an attempt on his part to protect her. After she finally lets him leave, he realizes that their kind of closeness does not allow for either revenge or protectiveness, and he returns to get her: "Before opening the door he stopped, overwhelmed by the brotherhood of death, discovering how insignificant the flesh appeared next to this communion, in spite of its urgent appeal. He understood now that the willingness to lead the being one loves into death itself is perhaps the complete expression of love, that which cannot be surpassed" (CH 204).

Paradoxically, the love Kyo feels for May can find its ultimate expression only in death. Could their love story be a revolutionary version of *Tristan et Iseult*? That might explain why Goldmann found it so powerful and pure; but as readers of Denis de Rougemont know, the source of Tristan's love is narcissism.

It seems to me significant that Kyo's final, "fraternal" communion with May is explicitly contrasted by Kyo himself with the derisory quality of merely carnal love. One critic has remarked that Kyo's and May's marriage is a fraternal, rather than a conjugal, union.[15] I think it more exact to say that Kyo's heterosexual desire (which is mentioned in both of the scenes he has with May) is constantly deflected or sublimated toward a "higher goal," this higher goal being that of the same-sex (even if not homosexual in the usual sense) communion of revolutionary *brother*hood: *virile* fraternity.[16]

The same sublimation, I would argue, occurs in the Kassner–Anna marriage in *Le Temps du mépris*. The revolutionary activist Kassner, after being imprisoned by the Nazis and thought dead by his wife, returns home to her and their child. The couple's reunion is extremely awkward: "He knew that he should take her in his arms in silence, . . . but he felt uncomfortable with the old gestures of affection, and there are no others" (TM 173). Kassner realizes how much she has suffered in his absence, and how much she will continue to suffer (for his return is temporary, and he will have to leave again to be killed sooner or later), but that very realization separates him from her: "This suffering which made her cling to him with eyes full of desire for congeniality, for gaiety—yes, this suffering which he was causing her separated him from her atrociously" (TM 174). As they talk and as she has a chance to express her sadness even while affirming that she accepts the life she has chosen, he begins to feel closer to her. They caress each other gently as they talk; then Kassner has a sudden "epiphany" as he thinks about the meaning of his life and of his approaching death—he must go out with Anna, walk with her in the street. The novel ends as he is waiting for her near the door.

Here, as in *La Condition humaine*, the revolutionary hero, already marked by death, subordinates the heterosexual drive (if that is still the right word—Kassner, unlike Kyo, doesn't seem to feel any physical desire for his wife) to a more mystical communion with his fellow men. Although he apparently includes Anna in this communion, it is striking how often in this novel we encounter what James Greenlee has called the "redundantly masculine" expression of virile fraternity.[17] At the demonstration where he goes to look for Anna, Kassner hears an old woman tell the crowd about the imprisonment of her son; he sees a number of women in the crowd whom he mistakes for Anna. Yet, when at the end of the episode he must sum up for himself the meaning of this experience (Malraux has told us in the preface that this is a novel with only two characters, "the hero and his sense of life"), his way of expressing it is characteristically single sex: "No human speech went so deeply as cruelty. But virile fraternity could cope with it, could follow cruelty to the very depths of blood, to the forbidden places of the heart where torture and death are lurking" (*TM* 165). Earlier, in his prison, he had already stated (in a sentence I quoted earlier) that genuine love was what existed between him and his (male) comrades. After he is released, he looks at the pilot who is flying him to safety and feels a strong bond with him: "Their common action joined the two men like an old and firm friendship" (*TM* 131).

After this, and despite Kassner's love for his wife, there seems little doubt that the word *homme* and its derivatives (e.g., *humain*) are to be understood in this novel (perhaps in all of Malraux's novels?) in a gender-specific sense. What this means as far as women— even beloved women—are concerned is, of course, problematic. At one point during the demonstration Kassner looks at the crowd and finds in it an expression of "the passions and the truths which are given only to men gathered together" (*TM* 164). In his mind, the exaltation of his communion with the "men gathered together" becomes joined with his "invisible woman," who is hidden from him by the crowd. But it is significant that the process is later repeated in reverse, when Kassner's reunion with Anna expands until they become joined with the crowds of the street: individual—specifically, sexual—union with the beloved women is rejected, or at least deferred, in favor of "men gathered together." It is almost as if, in order to participate in Kassner's love, Anna had to become a man.

May, in her appearance and actions, was already "à demi-virile." Valérie, in whom Ferral recognizes a pride similar to his own, chooses the male arena of contest and one-upmanship in which to assert herself. Without wishing to indulge in paradox, one might well advance the proposition that the only women *characters* in Malraux's fictional universe—the only women deserving of a name and of either hateful or loving recognition by men—are men in disguise.

Conclusion

The foregoing raises a number of questions, and first of all this one: What difference does it make? What is the usefulness of rereadings such as the one I have been practicing, given that they only confirm what might seem by now an all too familiar fact: the literature of adventure and heroism, whether in the past or in our own time, has been overwhelmingly male—written by men, about men, for men, embodying male fantasies, and founded on the most enduring male fantasy of all: the fantasy of a world without women.[18] Is there really a point in demonstrating, as if no one had noticed (even if they didn't talk about it) that Malraux's novels are exclusively masculine fictions? Yes, there is. It is one thing to notice something and leave it unexpressed, or cover it up like a guilty secret; it is quite another to examine it and attempt to state its significance. The fact that (to my knowledge, at least) none of the hundreds of articles, books, special issues of journals, and commemorative pieces devoted to Malraux since his death—not to mention the thousands that appeared while he was still alive—has seriously questioned or sought to explore the implications of the status of women in his works is indicative of a certain critical blindness.

Perhaps it is merely a sign of critical timidity: one does not wish to expose oneself to ridicule, to accusations of belaboring the obvious or of tilting at straw men. One therefore keeps still, or one talks about Malraux and tragedy, Malraux and history, Malraux and revolution, Malraux and art, Malraux and the human condition, and the metamorphosis of the gods. It took an openly polemical, patently one-sided attack by a woman not afraid of ridicule to shake me out of my own complacency.

The usefulness, indeed the necessity of such shake-ups for and by women readers and critics has been emphasized by recent works of feminist criticism. Judith Fetterley, whose work I referred to earlier, calls on women to become "resisting readers," in order to counteract a tradition in which "as readers and teachers and scholars, women are taught to think as men, to identify with a male point of view, and to accept as normal and legitimate a male system of values, one of whose central principles is misogyny."[19] And this theme was already sounded ten years ago by Elaine Showalter, in an essay, "Women and the Literary Curriculum": "Women are estranged from their own experience and unable to perceive its shape and authenticity . . . they are expected to identify as readers with a masculine experience and perspective, which is presented as the human one."[20] Whence the need not only for the study of literary works by women writers, which present a different perspective—the influence of books like Showalter's *A Literature of Their Own*, or Gilbert and Gubar's *The Madwoman in the Attic*, which aim to map a hitherto unexplored, feminine territory in the literary landscape, suggests that such study is now well underway—but also for a reappraisal of the "masculine experience . . . which is presented as the human one."

Does this mean that from now on, every time I teach Malraux, I shall insist only on the *macho* or antifeminine aspect of his work? Not at all. Shortly after I finished writing the bulk of this essay, I lectured to an advanced undergraduate literature class at Harvard on *La Condition humaine*. With only two lectures scheduled for this complex novel, I could hardly devote more than a few minutes to the question of women. The nods of recognition I saw among the women students in the class—and the almost grateful looks with which they greeted my remarks on the absence of the name and on the woman's silence in Malraux's novels—showed me that this was not merely an academic question. For these students it was important that it *not* be passed over in silence or with an offhand observation.

At the same time, I would not wish to see such questions, or such rereadings, become territorialized as an exclusively feminist—or feminine—concern. Rather than denouncing Malraux (or any antifeminine writer) as the enemy, which Fetterley tends to do, we can analyze him as a symptom; and today that kind of analysis is as urgent, as important, for men as it is for women. What is it, in our culture and history—some would even claim in our biology—that has obliged men to prove their masculinity always and only through the repeated affirmation that they are "not female"? Why is misogyny a transcultural and transhistorical phenomenon, apparently as universal as the incest taboo? Is the need to negate woman—which is always, in the last instance, the need to negate one's mother—a permanent feature of male psychology? Questions such as these, which are prompted by but go far beyond the rereading of writers like Malraux, are being raised today increasingly not only by women, or feminists, or students of literature, but by any number of anthropologists, sociologists, psychologists, and cultural historians, male and female, who seek to understand our past and the direction of our future. If it is true, as Walter J. Ong (who is not a feminist) recently wrote in the conclusion of an important and thought-provoking book, that "The entire history of consciousness can be plotted in relation to the always ongoing male-female dialectic,"[21] then it behooves all of us to attend to that dialectic. What is at stake is not only our words, but our world.

Brian Thompson

FROM FASCINATION TO POETRY:

BLINDNESS IN

MALRAUX'S NOVELS

Days of Wrath

BY ANDRÉ MALRAUX

TRANSLATED BY HAAKON M. CHEVALIER

MCMXXXVI

RANDOM HOUSE · NEW YORK CITY

Beneath Malraux's constant preoccupation with the visual arts, beneath his constant effort in the novels to convey to the reader the visual experience of his characters, lies an equally constant preoccupation with the very opposite of vision: blindness. It is present, literally or figuratively, in each of Malraux's novels—not to mention his critical works on art[1]—a somber counterpart to vision and all that vision represents for Malraux.

L'Espoir, perhaps the most visual of Malraux's novels, ends with an evocation of a blind beggar whom Manuel recalls encountering: "'The headlights had suddenly lit up the hands that the blind man was stretching forward, immensely enlarged by their projection because of the slope of the Gran Via, made bumpy by the cobblestones, broken by the sidewalks, crushed by the rare war vehicles that were still circulating, long like the hands of destiny'" (*E* 858).[2]

This is surely one of the most striking pictures which Malraux's visual imagination conjures up in the novels. And *imagination* is the right word here: despite the apparent precision and accuracy of the description, the image could not actually occur, nor could it be perceived in such detail from a moving automobile; it comes directly from Malraux's inner vision, and is thus all the more significant, leading progressively to a seemingly natural association between the blind man's hands and the "long hands of destiny."

This association between blindness and destiny is a constant with Malraux, but we must keep in mind what he means by destiny. Perhaps the most concise definition that Malraux himself gives for his concept of destiny is found in *Les Voix du silence*: it is "all that which imposes on man the awareness of his condition" (*VS* 628). In a less well known text, which appeared in the art review *Verve* shortly after the publication of *L'Espoir*, Malraux elaborates on what he means. Destiny is "man's awareness of those forces outside himself that shape his ends; the 'sorry scheme of things' with its vast indifference to men, and with its mortal perils; time and the universe, death and the tyrant earth."[3] The emphasis shifts in the novels from one aspect of man's condition, of the "sorry scheme of things," to another, but blindness functions throughout as an image of destiny in its various guises.

In *L'Espoir*, for example, the final image has been preceded and prepared by the entire experience of Jaime, which marks several important scenes in the novel. A study of Jaime's blindness will throw light on the thematic importance of blindness in the novel as a whole.

Jaime Alvear is a young engineer, a militant socialist for whom fighting for the Popular Front is essentially an experience of fraternity, both in life and in death. In the first scene in which he plays an important part we see him helping to break down the gate of the Alcazar with a battering ram. He is later assigned to the international air squadron, accompanied by his black basset hound, Raplati—soon the squadron's mascot. Jaime's flamenco songs accompany bombing missions, including that over the Alcazar during which he meets his fate.

The first indication we have of the imminent encounter with destiny is the plane's entrance into the "indifference" of the larger universe—one important element of man's condition: it is "lost in the indifferent gravitation of worlds," (*E* 555) whereas down below the rebels and their adversaries are caught up in "the absurd rhythm of

earthly things." (E 555) The bombing raid succeeds, the Alcazar sur-
renders, but Jaime's jubilation is short-lived, for the agent of his particular fate is closing in: enemy fighter planes.

Through Malraux's dramatic use of the montage technique, we immediately cut to the Jefatura, leaving Jaime's fate in suspension, then
back to the airfield where Marcelino's plane is anxiously awaited.
Scali and Raplati pace up and down; Jaime is also aboard. The dramatic tension of this scene is heightened by the race between the increasingly rapid fall of night and the returning plane. The final, complete darkness figures Jaime's injury: "It was Jaime, climbing down a
good while after the others. His hands out in front, trembling, with a
comrade to guide him: an explosive shell at eye level. Blind" (E 569).
It is Jaime's hands which first reveal his blindness, just as Grabot's
blindness in La Voie royale is confirmed when he stretches a hand
out in front of him.

Jaime is profoundly transformed by his blindness. The fraternal action of the earlier episode of the battering ram is replaced by relative
solitude. He no longer mixes with the other pélicans, to say nothing
of the crowds in the streets. He cannot even stand the presence of his
own dog, assimilating him, no doubt, to a seeing-eye dog. His flamenco singing has been silenced; he spends his time more passively,
listening to the radio.⁴ We see him alone, next to the window, which
is, significantly, "closed upon the night" (E 673).

Leclerc's drunken ranting and raving finally draws Jaime out of his
solitude, providing an occasion for the narrator to define the relationship of the other fliers to their blind comrade. Leclerc is berating
Scali when "'No kidding?'" resounds from the other end of the
room—the first time Jaime has spoken out since he was blinded: "It
seemed that he had just recovered the voice of his former songs,
muted as if something in it, too, had become blind. They all knew
that each time they took off they were threatened by his injury. He
was their comrade, but also the most threatening image of their destiny" (E 582). Jaime gropes slowly toward Leclerc; the other fliers
move aside as if terrified by the thought of touching him. For them
his blindness has become associated—indeed, almost identified—
with destiny, as it surely is for Malraux. Their reaction is deeper than
the simple, rational thought that they could also be injured in combat. House, with several machine-gun bullets in each leg, elicits no
such response. It is the specific injury to the eyes and the resulting
blindness—with its corollaries of solitude, dependence, and vulnerability—which make Jaime an image of destiny, a reminder of the pre-
cariousness of the human condition.

Another aspect of destiny which Jaime embodies becomes clear during the important conversation between Scali and Jaime's father, both art historians, on the force and value of art in the face of death. Jaime's blindness is evoked by Alvear's resemblance to his son, a resemblance accentuated by the lighting, which makes him appear to be wearing dark glasses. Scali, also wearing glasses, happens to sit on Jaime's favorite spot, facing the library of books on painting full of thousands of pictures that Jaime can no longer see. The blind man is thus cut off from the appreciation of art—or, at least, visual art—as "anti-destiny."[5] Is this perhaps one of the reasons blindness has become an image of destiny for Malraux, for whom the visual arts are so essential?

Jaime's blindness is so painful for Alvear that he would trade the entire Republican cause for his son's sight. He dare not place much hope in eventual recovery, yet two images in the scene figure his hope and its eventual realization: Alvear hears the "Internationale" being played outside, " 'this song of hope played by a blind man.' " (*E* 706) He turns off the light and opens the window. The complete darkness of the room makes Jaime's blindness tangible for Scali and Alvear. When the latter switches the lights on again the darkness is dispelled, prefiguring Jaime's recovery.

After the moving scene in which Jaime begins to recover his sight he heads back to the airfield, once more surrounded by his friends, "completely crazy, whistling like orioles." (*E* 790) From an image of destiny in his blindness and isolation, he has once more become an active participant in the "virile fraternity" that is Malraux's answer to destiny in *L'Espoir*. He is a concrete example of man's hope.

Malraux seems to throw an ironic light on such good fortune, however. On the way back to the airfield, Jaime and his friends pass huge figures of Donald Duck, Mickey Mouse, and Don Quixote—the abandoned floats from a children's parade which evoke a modern fairy-tale world "where all those one kills come back to life." (*E* 791) Is Malraux perhaps gently suggesting that Jaime's cure is just such a fairy-tale "resurrection,"—a wish fulfillment in the world of the imagination, not in the real world where the Marcelinos and the Hernandezes have not come back to life?

However that may be, Jaime's blindness has transformed him into an image of destiny. Destiny in its various guises—the indifference of the universe, man's solitude, death—is the real enemy in *L'Espoir*, and Jaime's blindness has helped to make it concrete and tangibly present to the reader.[6]

Injury to the eyes, whether real or imagined, is a constantly recurring motif throughout Malraux's novels. Gardet's face injury in the plane crash makes Pujol and others fear for his eyes; even more than the dead Arab volunteer behind him, he represents for the Spanish peasants of Linares "the face of War" and in a moving scene they salute him with raised fists.[7] So, too, soldiers of the International Brigade had earlier risked their lives by standing up under enemy fire to salute comrades returning with face wounds.

Injury to the eyes is the most terrifying and feared aspect of imminent death. Perken imagines his eyes rotting away after death. Souen is terrified most by the thought of his eyes being burned in the boiler of the locomotive:

"To be burned alive," he said. "To be burned alive. The eyes too; the eyes, you understand . . ."
"The eyes, too," Souen kept repeating, in a lower voice, "the eyes too . . ." (CH 408)

So, also in Le Temps du mépris Kassner is obsessed by a nightmare in which a vulture rips away chunks of his flesh, "without ceasing to look at his eyes, which it coveted" (TM 33). The mere threat to the eyes seems to cause more fear than the actual piecemeal devouring of the rest of the body.

It is the eyes which show the first effects of the poison gas used on the Russian front in Les Noyers de l'Altenburg. Throughout the evening before the attack, the German professor who has invented the gas appears as an inhuman technician, explaining in technical terms the development of combat gases. He is eloquent in elaborating the effects of his new gas upon the eyes, and his evident enthusiasm is so presented as to make the description doubly atrocious. His "antlike walk" associates him, like the insects in La Voie royale and in Möllberg's Africa, with fatality. The lighting in the entire scene is also carefully handled so as to underline the ominous attack upon humanity—especially the human eye—about to take place. Early in the scene Vincent Berger looks out the window and sees the crosses of an Orthodox church gleaming in the sun. As darkness falls, a lamp is lit; its effect seems to prefigure that of the gas upon the eyes: "The light of the lamp had all at once made the window opaque and black" (NA 122). When Berger again looks out, the crosses of the church are black against the sky. The next day we witness with Vincent Berger the actual results of the gas, which are so atrocious that they call forth the "apocalypse of fraternity" which closes the central section of the novel.

The professor's inhuman enthusiasm is not far from the intentional violence to the eyes which seems to hold a special fascination for Malraux. It is the most common torture or punishment to be found throughout the novels. Malraux seems almost to have collected accounts of such incidents in the course of his readings and travels.

In *Les Conquérants* Garine and the narrator find Klein after he has been tortured and killed. Garine approaches the corpse to close the eyes, in the final act of fraternity that Malraux himself was later to anticipate. He withdraws his hand in horror from Klein's blank white stare: "'I think they cut off his eyelids . . .'" (*C* 136). The effect of the mutilation itself is increased for the reader by Garine's reaction, which he later recalls with distaste: "'I had for him a man's friendship. . . . To discover the absence of eyelids and to think that one was about to touch eyes . . .'" (*C* 137). Garine seems to be more affected by the torture inflicted on the eyes than by Klein's death. He comes back to it still later with a shudder at the mere thought: "Never to see anything! . . ." (*C* 138).

The gouging out of eyes becomes almost a commonplace in Malraux's fiction. Kassner addresses an imaginary discourse to his "Russian friends with torn-out eyes [*aux yeux arrachés*]" (*TM* 47). Scali shows an Italian prisoner photographs of downed Republican pilots, their eyes gouged out by fascist torturers.

In *La Voie royale* Grabot, who has already intentionally blinded himself in one eye in order to have a superior officer punished, almost has the other gouged out, and is finally totally blinded by the Moïs, who throw his eye to the dogs. For Perken, Grabot is a double corpse: his blindness is juxtaposed and equated in seriousness with his probable castration. The fact that it is Perken who makes the comparison is significant, for from what we know of his interest in eroticism, castration would be the most terrible and humiliating fate imaginable to him.[8]

In *La Condition humaine* Malraux uses a comparison to blinding in order to express the acute humiliation that Valérie inflicts upon Ferral. It is a negation of his entire being: "She had struck him in his most sensitive spot, as if she had put out his eyes in his sleep: she was negating him" (*CH* 339). Here, too, there is perhaps an implicit link between the figurative blinding and, if not castration, at least sexual frustration: Ferral has just come to Valérie's hotel to satisfy his "unlimited need" to be preferred, to dominate and subjugate his partner sexually. He feels his humiliation as equivalent to an attack upon his manhood.

In all these cases, the eyes are seen as central to the person, signs of one's very being and humanity. Violence done to the eyes is violence done to one's dignity, one's integrity, one's very person.

Malraux's characters seem to share his penchant for telling stories about such humiliating tortures. Garine, in a mood of frustration and depression, recalls the story of Basil II, an eleventh-century Macedonian emperor: "'What I've done, what I've done! Ah, la la! It reminds me of the emperor who used to put out the eyes of his prisoners, you know, and send them back to their country in bunches, led by one-eyed guides; they, too, through fatigue, would gradually go blind. A fine picture-book image for what we're up to here'" (C 138). Another of Malraux's characters had already told a fuller version of the story in his early *Voyage aux îles fortunées*. The episode fascinated Malraux, for he comes back to it in *Les Voix du silence* (VS 172) and again in *Le Monde chrétien* (MC 34), where he also notes that two-thirds of the Byzantine emperors met the same fate.

Ferral recalls a story told to him by Clappique in which an Afghan chief punishes a neighboring chief for having raped and returned his wife with a note: she was not as good as he had heard. Having captured the offender, the first chief has him bound in front of his naked wife, then gouges out his eyes. Having seen and disparaged her charms, he shall never see them again. Just as Valérie's earlier (sexual) humiliation of Ferral is compared to putting out his eyes, so here gouging out the eyes is a punishment for a sexually oriented humiliation, and it is directly linked in Ferral's imagination to his own revenge. Several pages later he takes obvious pleasure in recalling with Gisors the punishment meted out under the early Chinese empires to unfaithful wives. He is so engrossed in imagining Valérie with her hands chopped off, her eyes put out, tied to a raft and set afloat that he momentarily forgets that the wives' lovers were also blinded and abandoned in the same way (CH 347).

Physical mutilation, whether of oneself or of another, often has sexual connotations—especially, perhaps, when it is a question of the eyes. Even Oedipus' blindness was due in part to his incestuous relationship with his mother. With no pretension to special psychoanalytic insights, we can nonetheless note the importance and permanence of this motif in Malraux's works.

In addition to bearing witness to a constant fascination in Malraux, how do the various manifestations of blindness combine in the novels and contribute to the expression of their major themes? We have seen that in *L'Espoir* blindness is identified with destiny, in Malraux's sense of the word: whatever makes man conscious of his condition. Throughout the novels blindness comes to represent, to make present, one aspect or another of man's condition as Malraux sees it—his vulnerability, his dependence on forces outside himself, his solitude, and the impossibility of fully communicating with others.

The shadows of the blind beggar's hands at the end of *L'Espoir* are associated with the hands of destiny, and Manuel looks forward to the "destins aveugles" which no doubt still await him. We could perhaps imagine a personified Destiny, blindfolded like the traditional figure of Justice. But the fundamental association between blindness and destiny for Malraux is seen not from the point of view of destiny but rather from that of the man subject to destiny. The blind man, like Jaime, figures man's subjection to destiny rather than destiny's action in the world.

The blind man is the image of man's vulnerability and defenselessness, for he cannot see danger coming, much less defend himself against it. Kassner, for example, is reduced in his prison cell to "a life of a blind man in danger" (*TM* 26), and is completely at the mercy of his guards. When they open his cell door, he is, ironically, blinded by the light and cannot begin to defend himself against their blows. So, too, Hemmelrich's wife in *La Condition humaine*, equally defenseless all her life, is characterized as "a blind, martyred dog" (*CH* 312). For Malraux, a "blindman's defense" is hardly a defense at all, a desperate last effort, doomed to failure. Thus adventure is for Claude Vannec a blindman's defense against death, which is inexorable in any case (*VR* 41).

Man's dependence on forces outside himself is similarly figured by the special dependency of the blind man. While approaching the Moï village in search of Grabot, Claude must drag his feet to avoid stepping on sharpened bamboo spikes. Every time he raises his foot, his muscles contract: "Linked to danger by them, Claude was descending to the life of a blind man," which is for Malraux a "slave's dependency" (*VR* 102). This passage foreshadows, of course, the gruesome discovery of Grabot's blindness and slavery. The import of the association is then further deepened, for Grabot becomes for Claude and Perken the image of man's dependency on forces beyond his control—so much so that Claude cannot stand looking at him and feels the urge to shoot him to get rid of "this proof of his human condition" (*VR* 124).[9]

The image of the blind man's dependency on his guide serves in *L'Espoir* to express the dependency of a bomber pilot on his lead plane[10]—a dependency which is in turn explicitly related to fatality: "Leclerc, attached to the plane of the group leader in the general unleashing, like a blindman to his guide, possessed by the feeling of no longer being separate from it, threw himself into the barrage with the fatality of a tank" (*E* 668). The blind man is thus the image not only of man's vulnerability but also of his dependency on forces or constraints beyond his control, which is yet another aspect of the human condition as Malraux sees it.

A further important element in Malraux's vision of the human condition is man's fundamental solitude, resulting largely from the difficulty—if not impossibility—of communicating meaningfully with others.[11] Here again the image of blindness manifests a universal aspect of man's fate. The blind man is quite obviously deprived of one of the means of communicating with his fellow men—perhaps even the principal means, for Malraux—for he cannot *see* others. Language for Malraux often seems to be a deficient and untrustworthy means of communication, despite the fact that he is a writer and that large portions of his novels are given over to dialogue and discussion. Many of the most important scenes involving real understanding and communication in the novels depend on what is *seen* rather than on what is said. The blind man is obviously cut off from this visual communication with others, and his specific infirmity is magnified by implication to figure the solitude and incommunicability characteristic of the human condition as a whole.

Moreno, in *L'Espoir*, equates blindness and the solitude he experienced while awaiting death in a fascist prison: "'They say being blind is a universe; being alone is another, believe me. [. . .] The two worlds do not communicate with one another'" (*E* 625). A literal example of just such a lack of communication is Claude's attempt to talk to Grabot. The blind Grabot is a "prisoner of his walled-in head," and Claude—who is himself limited to his own world of visible forms— cannot put himself in Grabot's place and establish communication with him: "'How can you convince a blind man?'" (*VR* 121). Claude shuts his own eyes and tries in vain to penetrate into the universe of the blind, which remains incommunicable. Claude himself had earlier been bound to just such an incommunicable world, that of his project of finding and removing sculptures from temples along the Royal Way. As long as he had conceived and nurtured the plan alone, he had been bound to "an incommunicable universe, like that of the blind man or the madman" (*VR* 42).

In *La Condition humaine* Kyo makes a similar connection between blindness and insanity as images of incommunicability, and he relates them to his earlier experience of fundamental human solitude. Following May's avowal that she has slept with another man, she appears to Kyo with all the mystery of the mute, the blind, and the insane. What he had assumed to be full communication and mutual understanding has proven illusory. He realizes that he does not fully know her, that there remains an unbridgeable gap between her and the knowledge he has of her, and he recalls his experience with the recording of his own voice which he could not recognize—the experience which, according to Malraux himself, gave the novel its title (VS 628).

Blindness thus plays a central role in showing forth the dark side of the human condition throughout the novels: solitude, incommunicability, humiliation, vulnerability, dependency. Its pervasive presence surely reflects a deep-seated fascination or obsession with blindness in Malraux himself.[12] Far more important for us here, however, is the transformation that this biographical raw material undergoes in the process of artistic creation, which transcends and universalizes the purely personal. The pervasive image of blindness in the novels helps them to convey a vision of the human condition which far transcends their author's personal make-up and situation. The raw material of biography has become poetry.

Mary Ann Frese Witt

MALRAUX'S SHAMANISM:

INITIATORY DEATH AND

REBIRTH

The figure of the shaman, man of visionary and sacred powers in cultures throughout Asia, Africa, Russia, and North America, seems to have exerted a fascination and something of a shock of recognition on Malraux. Leo Frobenius, a model for Möllberg in *Les Noyers de l'Altenburg* and whose discussion of shamanism Malraux must have read,[1] defines the shaman by his rebellion against reality and by his use of ego power,[2] qualities that apply to Malraux himself as well as to many of his heroes. A more recent expert on shamanism, Mircea Eliade, identifies the shaman's qualities in language that seems to echo Malraux: "The shaman stands out by the fact that he has succeeded in integrating into consciousness a considerable number of experiences that, for the profane world, are reserved for dreams, madness, or *ante mortem* states."[3] The effort to integrate visionary experience into consciousness is one of the threads binding together the protean Malraux—adventurer, revolutionary, man of action, writer, art theoretician. It is also at the base of a problem that preoccupied the author of *La Tentation de l'Occident*: how to integrate the visionary, mystical knowledge of the East with the West's obsession with rational knowledge and power. Malraux might have asked himself, Can a modern European shaman exist?

A reply is given in Malraux's last work of fiction by an otherwise unidentified "Russian friend" of Vincent Berger's son. Dostoevski, Mirabeau, Hölderlin, and Poe (as opposed to Pushkin, Robespierre, and Goethe) were shamans, and something of a shaman, he reports, was Vincent Berger.[4] There are three other references to shamanism in *Les Noyers*: Vincent Berger's imprudence is said to be the reverse side of his shamanism (*NA* 57), his ability to dispel the sadness of his fellow soldiers is a result of his shamanism (*NA* 159), and the "shamanism" of the inventor of the lethal gas is "upsetting" (*NA* 172). These sparse remarks and cryptic comments are simply enough to alert the reader to search elsewhere for clues to the nature of shamanism.

Frohock has demonstrated how the pattern of withdrawal, enlightenment, and return basic to the initiation of shamans (as discussed by Richard Chase in *The Quest for Myth*, 1949) also defines the life experience not only of the three Bergers and the ethnologist Möllberg in *Les Noyers*, but also of most of Malraux's fictional heroes from *Lunes en papier* on.[5] In the course of the sacred rituals he undergoes throughout his life, the shaman in fact realizes the essence of the great nature myth that haunted European culture from *The Golden Bough* through *The Wasteland*: that of death and rebirth. Leaving the world of the senses, the shaman enters into an ecstatic, deathlike trance during which he receives illumination on the secrets of life and death. Returning to life renewed and reborn, the shaman is equipped to serve as spiritual guide to his fellows. A comparative reading of Malraux's texts in the light of Eliade's and Frobenius's discussions of shamanism suggests that several of Malraux's heroes not only follow the general shamanic pattern in the course of their destinies but also *specifically* undergo experiences comparable to shamanic initiation. These are of two types: (1) the ritual climbing of the "world tree" or "cosmic tree" and (2) initiation by ritual death during enclosure or "burial" in a hut or underground cave and reemergence as ritual rebirth. The first of these appears only in *Les Noyers*, although related tree symbolism appears throughout Malraux; the second, of prime interest here, is most evident in *Les Noyers* but has important antecedents in the experience of earlier fictional proto-shamans.

A basic meeting ground of myths and religions—a point stressed by Eliade throughout his work—is the concept of a lost paradise and a fall: a primordial *illud tempus* when human beings lived in harmony and communication with the gods, the animals, and their own kind, followed by a rupture leaving humanity mortal and fallible, cut off from the secrets of heaven and nature, fallen into linear time and history.[6] *In illo tempore* man had the freedom to climb a mountain, a ladder, or a tree to heaven when he wished. A prime function of the shaman is to return, through ecstatic experience, to the paradise of primordial man. One of the ways in which he may accomplish this is by the ascent of a sacred tree, symbolizing the cosmic tree at the center of the world, a kind of umbilical cord from heaven to earth standing for "the universe in continual regeneration, the inexhaustible spring of cosmic life."[7] The shaman's sacred drum is also made from the wood of this tree. Surely, Vincent Berger's mystical vision of the great trees "that bloomed out into eternal life" (*NA* 152), his intuition of the relationship between the wood of the trees and the wood of the gothic statues in Altenburg, and his groping faith in "fundamental man" parallel the knowledge gained by the shaman from his sacred ascent of the world tree. His visionary experience standing in contradiction to Möllberg's argument, delivered at the Altenburg colloquium, that the world's cultures rise and fall with no continuity among them, Berger in a sense defeats the African ethnologist on his own grounds. The non-Western intuition of the eternal and fundamental, taking place at a center of Western culture, annuls the analytical European's conclusions from his African experience.

Shamanism is in many cultures a hereditary state, and the Berger men are all apparent heirs. Yet if the right to become a shaman is inherited, the neophyte shaman must also undergo a rite of initiation, a rite that may be repeated several times during his life. To be initiated is to transcend historical time, to relive the sacred beginnings, to participate in the vital myths of the culture. Initiation comports an ontological change: the initiate dies to the profane world to enter the sacred to be reborn into this world. In many cultures the initiate is enclosed in a cave (representing both a grave and the womb of Mother Earth) for several days and is sometimes tortured or symbolically killed before emerging back onto earth. The experience of rebirth is not only physiological but cosmological. According to Eliade, "It is not the repetition of maternal gestation and physical birth, but a temporary regression to the virtual, precosmic world—symbolized by night and darkness—followed by a rebirth analogous to a 'creation of the world.'"[8] The analogy with the central event of the Christian religion is obvious. A professed agnostic, haunted all his life by the presence of the sacred, Malraux uses Christian symbols with those of archaic and other religions to explore a fundamental experience which he already suggests in the early *farfelu* novels and which he envisions himself undergoing in *Lazare*. Initial forms of the death-illumination-rebirth sequence, before its elaboration in *Les Noyers de l'Altenburg*, appear most clearly in certain scenes, particularly the last one, in *La Voie royale*, in the prison scene of *La Condition humaine*, and throughout *Le Temps du mépris*. The metaphors of enclosure in the first and the prison settings of the other two serve something of the function of the shaman's cave. The modern prison cell, as Michel Foucault has noted, has a peculiar archetypal value: "In that closed cell, temporary sepulchre, myths of resurrection easily take form."[9]

The death of Perken in *La Voie royale* and the central scene of *La Condition humaine*—the schoolyard prison where Kyo and Katow, with their comrades, prepare to die—portray not an actual figure of death and rebirth but a portrayal of the absurdity of death preceded by a form of illumination and accompanied by a suggestion of some sort of continuity. Perken, although he is with Claude in the open forest, envisions himself to be closed in through a series of similes. An inaccessible railroad seems to bind him and his former hopes like a "prisoner's chain."[10] Smoke coming from the Moï settlement cuts off the horizon like a "gigantic grill" (*VR* 163), and the tribesmen, the power of the forest, and the threat of death fuse in "a hopeless, superhuman imprisonment" (*VR* 163). He compares himself to a prisoner closed in the world of men as if in an underground cave; he feels that he is descending into an "elementary" world; he imagines his own corpse, his rotting flesh (*VR* 164). Yet along with this cluster of images of enclosure, anguish, and death, Malraux introduces a new element:

As Perken opened his eyes the sunlight flooded them, devasting light, yet vibrant with joy. . . . But now the world of men, even the solid earth drifting past beneath him with its trees and animals, had lost their meaning: he only knew that white immensity, the kingdom of the light, and a tragic inward exultation that little by little overpowered his senses, throbbing with the muffled tremor of his heart (*VR* 164–65)[11]

Touched by a form of mystical illumination, Perken is even said to be eager to "flee from his body." If he must finally succumb to death, there is nonetheless the suggestion that something of his transcendent experience will live on in Claude, with whom he leaves "the desperate fraternity that was wrenching him out of himself" (*VR* 168).

This element of continuity, along with a marked analogy with ritual death, become more important with the prelude to the deaths of Kyo and Katow in *La Condition humaine*. Imprisoned, watching the guard come for the execution of each fellow prisoner in the scene that gives the novel its Pascalian title, Kyo seems to prepare for his death by imitating it—lying down, crossing his arms over his chest, immobile, assuming "precisely the position of the dead." Outer reality disappears for a time as the reader enters into Kyo's thoughts, objective time ceases—and then suddenly returns—as shown in the following passage.

O prison, place where time ceases—time, which continues elsewhere . . . NO! It was in this yard, separated from everyone by the machine-guns, that the Revolution, no matter what its fate or the place of its resurrection, was receiving its death-stroke; wherever men labor in pain, in absurdity, in humiliation, they were thinking of doomed men like these, as believers pray . . .[12]

Kyo's ritual death brings him the enlightenment that enables him to complete his suicide with serenity. The martyrs of the revolution will ensure, through their sacrifice, the resurrection of the revolution. (The scene is filled with religious terms.) Thus Kyo dies with faith in a kind of rebirth. Katow undergoes the same experience in a different way. During the intense sequence in which he passes his cyanide, giving "more than his life" to his two comrades, the loss of the two capsules in the dark is like a relapse into solitude, redeemed by the fraternal handclasp, the recovery of the cyanide and the exclamation, "O resurrection!" (*CH* 366). Katow's march to his execution, his shadow larger than life, is also a figure of resurrection. Like that of Kyo, his prelude to death is a ritual and poetic triumph. Transmitting more of themselves than the dying Perken does to Claude, Kyo and Katow leave their comrades with a sense of spiritual solidarity and assurance of continuity.[13]

With *Le Temps du mépris* Malraux for the first time portrays a hero whose ritual death is not a prelude to actual death but a means to rebirth and survival. The cell in the Nazi prison where Kassner is held captive is described as "a rather large dark hole,"[14] and his ordeal there reads in some ways like an extended treatment of the prison scene in *La Condition humaine*. Unlike the Shanghai prisoners, however, Kassner is held in solitary confinement, a fact that precipitates his descent into a subjective, timeless world peopled by a series of surrealist visions. Like Kyo, Kassner lies down on the cell floor and crosses his hands over his chest in the position of a corpse. Gradually his chaotic visions transform themselves into a triumphant illumination: "Beyond the cell, beyond time, there was a world which triumphed even over suffering, a twilight world, swept clear of primitive emotions, in which all that had made up his life glided with the invincible movement of a cosmos in eternity" (*TM* 56).

Following this vision, Kassner abandons his corpse position to stand up and replaces his inner music of funeral hymns with the "Internationale." But the triumph here, only in the second chapter of the novel, is temporary. Returning to struggle with the deathlike cell and its visions once more, Kassner will be "resurrected" not by his efforts alone but through the help of others: first the "fraternal tapping" from the cell next to his saving him from madness and then the sacrifice of the unknown comrade who identifies himself as Kassner, permitting the real Kassner to be freed.

The death-rebirth pattern stated in chapter two becomes enlarged to encompass the entire novel. Thus the first five chapters portray Kassner's "death" along with his "gestation" (it is stressed that he was in the dark hole for *nine* days); chapter six, in the airplane headed toward Prague, is a time of suspension between death and life, and chapter seven portrays Kassner's "rebirth" or "resurrection." The latter takes place in both a collective and a private sphere. As most critics have stressed, *Le Temps du mépris* is a propaganda novel, and Kassner's ritual death and rebirth is on one level a reinitiation into socialist solidarity out of solipsistic isolation. This is clear both from the method of Kassner's liberation and from the sense of new solidarity he experiences at the meeting he attends. But Kassner's story, however awkwardly it may handle certain literary problems, is more than a piece of propaganda. The struggle of the private individual, both in prison and out, receives more attention than that of the Communist organizer. His first impressions while walking the streets of Prague—of a woman ironing, of people and shops—are those of a man seeing familiar life with totally new eyes: "It was he who had come from hell and all this was simply life" (*TM* 139). When he at last finds his wife, Anna—significantly, not at the meeting but in their apartment at home—much of the joy in their reunion centers around their child, and Anna speaks of the experience of birth. " 'Men do not have children'" (*TM* 170), Kassner reflects, but have the same need to experience joy through "reality." Reborn himself, Kassner wishes to ensure the continuity of rebirth through action. His political commitment thus seems rooted in a deep private experience. Like the shaman, he emerges from ritual death better equipped as a spiritual guide.

Vincent Berger's vision of the world upon debarking in Marseille after his years in Asia and failed adventure in Turkestan parallels almost exactly that of Kassner in Prague—it is as if he were observing the simple, everyday acts of European humanity for the first time. Returning to Europe (perhaps to time and history after the "eternity" of Asia), Berger is to be intimately involved with death five days later with the suicide of his father Dietrich. Vincent's recollection (seen in flashback in conversation with his uncle Walter at Altenburg) is especially of the closed room where his father died, the room where no one, himself included, dared to chase away death by opening it. Vincent at last achieves a certain triumph by the simple gesture of pulling the curtains. What he sees from the window prefigures, through simile, his vision of the walnut trees: "And from the simple presence of the people passing there, hurrying in the morning sunlight, as alike and as different as leaves, there seemed to well up a secret that did not only come from death still crouching behind his back, a secret that was much less that of death than of life—a secret that would not have been less heart-gripping if man had been immortal" (NA 93).

Walter Berger responds to this with an anecdote from his own experience recapitulating the enclosure-darkness-death/opening-light-life sequence. Accompanying the mad Nietzsche, whom he claimed as a friend, on a train from Turin to Basel, Walter feared a crisis when the train entered a long, dark tunnel. Instead, what emerged was a "sublime" song—Nietzsche's poem "Venice" set to his own music. Attempting to explain himself more fully, Walter compares the dark train compartment to Pascal's prison: "'In the prison of which Pascal speaks, men have managed to draw forth from themselves an answer that pervades, if I dare say so, with immortality those who are worthy of it. And in that railroad car . . . the millenniums of the starry sky seemed to me as eclipsed by man as our poor destinies are eclipsed by the starry sky'" (NA 97).

What we have in the two recounted experiences are two types of rebirth, or resistance of the human species to mortality, the one "simply life," on the order of "fundamental man," the other art, the sublime moments of culture. Walter, the esthete, along with most of the Altenburg intellectuals, can only admit the latter; Vincent, the intellectual turned activist, searches for the former; it will be up to Vincent's son the narrator to attempt to synthesize the two.

Discussion during the Altenburg colloquy, "Permanence and Metamorphosis of Man," offers two images of the same order. The art historian Stieglitz tells the assembly of an imprisoned friend for whom only three books could "withstand" the atmosphere of prison: *Robinson Crusoe, Don Quixote,* and *The Idiot,* three versions of the story of a man's struggle to emerge from solitude and rediscover community. Here it seems possible that resistance to mortality and the rediscovery of fundamental man may take place through art. Möllberg, in his long speech, uses the example of certain African ritual killings of the king (in a cave) with the "resurrection" of the new king, as one proof of the radical discontinuity between our own civilization and one whose sense of fatality is based on the movements of the stars. Ironically, it is through his own experiences of ritual death and resurrection (linked to the previously discussed tree vision) that the "shaman" Berger will be able to affirm his intuition of continuity.

Vincent Berger's central experience as a German lieutenant on the Russian front in World War I creates yet another form of death and rebirth experienced through enclosure-illumination-eternity/opening-resistance-continuity. Hidden, or buried underground [terré] in a "vast cave striped with light" (NA 183), the soldiers of the 132nd brigade speak to Vincent's ears with a voice linking them to men of other times and places: "the slow and deep voice of the people in the face of mystery, that voice . . . of the sorcerers of old" (NA 194); "voices of indifference and centuries-old dreams, voices of types of work" (NA 199); "the voice of the only species that has learned—and so badly—that it can die" (NA 202). It is as if Vincent must now be initiated with a collective death and rebirth as a complement to his previous solitary experiences. As at Reichbach and Altenburg, the death and rebirth cycle is associated with trees. After emerging from the trench, making his way toward the place where the Russians have been gassed, Vincent's perception of death is first of all of dead trees: "Apple trees pruned by man, killed like men, dead more than other trees because they were fertile" (NA 218).

Into the landscape of death rush soldiers covered with leaves, resisting the inhumanity of the gas attack by a desperate attempt to save the Russian soldiers. It is the attempt to save the enemy from the forces of inhumanity more than the success of the operation that saves the German soldiers from a kind of death in life. Into this struggle of life against death, Malraux introduces Judeo-Christian symbols of renewal: Vincent finds on a soldier's chest the dove and the crucifix of the Huguenot cross "like a friendly face" (NA 226). The gassed landscape appears to have been struck by a "Biblical punishment" as definitive as the stroke of creation, but at the same time, in the glowing of the sun, to begin to reanimate itself with a "secret life" (NA 234). The moment of death and defeat ends paradoxically in triumph.

Writing from his prison camp, bringing together the themes of his father's life and the Altenburg colloquium in a search for "what resists the fascination of nothingness" (NA 250), the youngest Berger recounts his own wartime rite of initiation. The long episode in which the narrator and his three companions in their armored tank fall into a pit on the road to Flanders and manage to extract themselves with the tank is in many ways the most ambitious of the book. Even more than with the World War I soldiers in their trench, Malraux's language transforms the event into a ritual death and rebirth: " 'The earth reverberates with the noise of the free tanks that pass all around our death'" (NA 274), observes Berger. The face of his companion Pradé takes on "the livid solemnity of the faces of the dead" (NA 279). Malraux plays on the double meaning of fosse (ditch, grave) in an image suggesting that the four are sacrificed, dead and buried: "We are flattened out against the wall of our common ditch (grave): Berger, Léonard, Bonneau, Pradé—one single cross" (NA 281). Finally, as the four companions lay down to sleep following their escape the narrator suggests that they have been and still are dead: "Perhaps we will come back to life again tomorrow" (NA 285).

The "grave" in which the four find themselves trapped recalls the "large dark hole" in which Kassner underwent a symbolic death. Kassner's cell had nothing but a ventilation hole for an opening; the pit, also perceived metaphorically by the soldiers as a cell, has an inaccessible skylight: " 'We are as if in those cells that are lighted only by an inaccessible skylight; prisoners do not escape through the ceiling'" (NA 282). Kassner, in his fantasies, envisioned the starry sky both as a symbol of victory over imprisonment and as a superhuman reflection of eternal imprisonment. The four soldiers here, trapped in a hole in the earth with no view but of infinity, find themselves quite literally in the Pascalian prison as it was defined by Walter Berger, "thrown at random between the profusion of matter and that of the stars" (NA 99).

Yet these prisoners emerge victorious. The death and rebirth motif here takes on a new dimension. Rebirth is in this case not a poetic triumph or mystical union with the revolution but, first of all, an actual event, an act of will accomplished by men working together. As Berger emerges from the ground, he leaves death to meet regenerating life: " 'But the night is no longer the sepulcher of the grave; the living night appears to me like a prodigious gift, like an immense germination'" (NA 284). Berger emerges from the tomb/womb of Mother Earth with an utterly fresh perception of reality.

More clearly than the other sequences discussed, Berger's ordeal follows the pattern of shamanic initiation. Buried and as if dead in the tomb/womb of Mother Earth, enlightened by the infinite vision of a cosmic night, Berger's reemergence onto the earth becomes assimilated with a sense of cosmic rebirth (also called an "aube biblique"), described by him the morning following the event: " 'But, this morning, I am only birth. I still bear within myself the irruption of the earthly night on coming out of the ditch (grave), that germination in the darkness deepened with constellations in the holes of fleeting clouds; and, as I saw that full and rumbling night surge out of the ditch (grave), now there rises from the night the miraculous revelation of the day'" (*NA* 289–90).

Berger's rite of initiation has given him knowledge not of a rational order but cosmic, mystical, "fundamental." He now knows the "meaning of the ancient myths of people brought back from the dead"; he bears within him a "sacred and simple secret" (*NA* 291). The Asiatic or African shaman must pass through death in order to be able to interpret the mysteries of life. The European "shaman" must have an intimate knowledge of human mortality before he can intuit the permanent qualities of human life. By the end of *Les Noyers de l'Altenburg* the narrator has gained in his own right an insight into the mystery of the fundamental unity and continuity that lay at the heart of his father's experience. The book written from prison is his testimony to the dual powers of life and art to combat the temptation of nothingness.

Ralph Tarica

ON DREAMS AND THE HUMAN MYSTERY IN MALRAUX'S "MIROIR DES LIMBES"

Time and again in *Le Miroir des limbes* Malraux communicates an obsessive need in him to probe the "mystery" of man—a mystery so profound that only an allusive, interrogative style can suggest its nature and sustain the author's discourse. This mystery has little to do with the private secrets of individual men. We know how distrustful Malraux is of the psychoanalytic approach to investigating that mystery: "What man hides, and which is often merely pitiful, has been too easily confused with what he does not know about himself" (*ML* 8).[1] There are doubtless many good reasons to explain why Malraux shuns the "merely" psychological. For one thing, he appears to bear a grudge against a field that has set about with much zeal unearthing the long-forgotten demons in humanity without simultaneously awakening the long-forgotten gods. For another, psychology has tended to study human beings in a cosmic vacuum, as though the world did not exist and have its own meaning. It is clear that for Malraux any study of the human dilemma or mystery must be carried out in the greater context of human presence in the world, to which we are inextricably joined.

Since the appearance of W. M. Frohock's work on Malraux we have become accustomed to thinking of Malraux as something of a poet as well as an important writer and an influential contemporary thinker and critic. There is really no work of Malraux's that does not manifest a strong poetic urge. That urge is still very much in evidence in the essays of the 1960s and 1970s that now constitute *Le Miroir des limbes*. Indeed, would any other than a highly metaphorical language and structure be capable of bearing the weight of representing Malraux's intuitive perception of the mystery?[2] But these later essays further oblige us, more than ever, to think of Malraux as a mystic as well. I do not mean this simply in the loose, rhetorical sense that he is interested in dramatizing curious coincidences and enigmas (he does that too, of course) but in the literal sense that he may actually *believe* that there are mysterious forces at work in the world, revealing themselves to men.

The subject of Malraux's interest in the mystical is a vast one, encompassing as it does such notions as the unreal, the imaginary,[3] the absolute, transcendence, the intemporal, the sacred, and the divine. In his voluminous art criticism some of these notions are subjects in their own right and are treated in relatively orderly fashion, whereas in *Le Miroir des limbes* they only occasionally surface to become the central focus of Malraux's discourse. For the most part, they remain a subliminal preoccupation, part of a background atmosphere propitious for sustaining a certain spiritual tone—but a tone which is the dominant one of the book. Contributing to this tone we find abundant references, of both a serious and playful nature, to a variety of mystics and mystical phenomena: sorcerers, witches, prophets, seers, palm readers, card readers, geomancers, pythonesses, gurus, religious mystics, trances, mental telepathy, and so on.[4]

With no intention of oversimplifying an extremely complex subject, we might nonetheless find it useful for practical purposes to try reducing this preoccupation of Malraux's to its constituent parts. We might depict it in terms of an interplay between a perceiver and the perceived, linked at the contact point of perception. This would give use, on the one hand, a creative mind seeking transcendence—the artist, visionary, conqueror, dreamer—and on the other, the contents of his dreams: "l'autre monde," the transcendental world of the imag-

inary and the sacred. Their point of contact, the terrain of the interplay between the two worlds, is the dream itself.

It is that dream I would like to consider in the pages that follow.
Malraux's references to dreams (*rêve, rêver, rêveur, songe*) appear
throughout *Le Miroir des limbes*, with particular frequency in certain pages of the "Antimémoires," "Hôtes de passage," and "Lazare"
sections. My concern here, within the limited scope of these pages,
will be to explore the general thrust of the dream image and then to
relate it to one of the most recurrent themes of the book: Malraux's
intuitive understanding of his own life and of his sense of a personal
destiny.[5]

Throughout *Le Miroir des limbes* the dream metaphor appears in
several types of traditional commonplaces, corresponding to the gram-
matical functions of verb, noun, and adjective. The verb *rêver*, in one
frequent usage, conveys the notion of longing or wishing, of looking
forward to something as the result of absence or nostalgia. In a section from *Les Noyers de l'Altenburg*, Malraux writes of Vincent
Berger's isolation in Asia as follows: "How often, in Afghanistan, had
he dreamed of what he would first want to see again [in Europe]. . . .
After a few months of central Asia, accompanied by the endless trot
of his Afghan horses, he dreamed of walls covered with posters, or of
inexhaustible museums" (*ML* 36). After Malraux's *La Condition
humaine* was adapted for the stage, "I discovered the theater, and
dreamed of writing, after someone or other, an *Alexander in India*"
(*ML* 557). African leaders: "are they dreaming of African unity?" (*ML*
701); hippies "dream of India, of Buddhism" (*ML* 770).

The corresponding noun—dream as the object of desire—also appears with considerable frequency. Malraux talks to de Gaulle about
"the secret dream of a good part of France" (*ML* 98); he recalls Méry
and "his dream of a civilization for which death would be a stoical
suicide" (*ML* 474). The implication in most of these instances is that
the object of desire is an ideal outside the scope of realization: "Ex-
emplariness belongs to the dream, to fiction" (*ML* 907).

Our third form of the image is the adjectival *dreamlike*, or the in-
finitely more expressive, despite its commonplace usage by the surrealists, *oneiric*. There are several instances of this usage in Malraux's descriptions of decor, usually in contexts of deserted places of
this sort: "No one in the little square, as intimate as a dream" (*ML*
804). The silent procession of his motorcade through an explosive colonial capital, Cayenne, has something "oneiric" about it (*ML* 133),
as does the sheer size and emptiness of the Chinese city of Canton.
But most of the examples occur in the context of sacred places,

where the dreamlike quality is supported by references to the unreal and to the pure. The sacred tree of the Queen of Casamance, in Africa, standing in a wide clearing in the midst of a village having "unreal cleanliness," rises out of "oneiric purity" (*ML* 521). Most such examples have to do with India and with the sense of the sacred that so deeply stirs Malraux during his visits there. Jaipur is "a most oneiric place," a mass of construction seemingly abandoned by genies, "the most unreal city of Moslem India," where the façades on a street remind him of stage sets for the *Thousand and One Nights* (*ML* 85–86).[6] Malraux's trip to the caves of Ellora further elicits not only dream imagery but the kind of specific references that link dreams to the imaginary and the sacred. In this oneiric place someone has sculpted the prayer: "'Oh Lord of all gods, teach me *in dreams* how to carry out the works that are in my mind'" (*ML* 221; Malraux's emphasis).

There is another traditional usage of the dream metaphor to express what is not real—but here Malraux's notion of dreams departs significantly from the commonplace one. In his lengthy exposition on Hindu beliefs in the "Antimémoires," he appears to be particularly attracted to the notion of *maya* and to the distinction between what is truly real and what is merely appearance or illusion. Recounting the experiences of the Hindu ascetic, Narada (the story had appeared earlier in *La Métamorphose des dieux*), Malraux writes: "It is not because it was a dream that Narada's second existence does not count: it is because it was as real as the first" (*ML* 213). The explanation is that in Hindu belief everything that is subject to time is *maya*, illusion, unreal. This is, of course, a belief that appeals to Malraux as well. Throughout Malraux's work we find a number of variations on this theme: "Belonging to the realm of mystery is everything that escapes time" (*ML* 821).

But the development of Malraux's argument here, and the recurrent usage of certain of the dream metaphors, suggests that what interests him is not so much the notion that reality is a dream as that dream is a reality. To put this in a somewhat different way, irreality expressed by dream contains a truth that transcends that of ordinary, ephemeral reality, so that dream must be considered a privileged state of perception. Malraux clearly rejects, then, the Western notion, expressed in the commonplace metaphor, that dream signifies that which cannot be taken seriously. Describing the "unreal" atmosphere inside the great temple of Madura, with its figures of paper animals contributing to its air of fantasy, Malraux writes: "Europe believes that what does not imitate what it considers real represents a dream. These figures no more imitated a dream than those of the royal gate of Chartres imitate the kings of France" (*M* 218). For India, a land where people still believe that the world has a meaning invisible to the senses, this privileged state of dream allows for communication with the sacred: "Nowhere had I felt to such an extent that all sacred art presupposes that the people to whom it is addressed hold as a certainty the existence of a secret of the world, a secret which art transmits without revealing, and in which it allows them to participate. I was in the nocturnal garden of the great dreams of India" (*ML* 221).

The belief that dreams are a privileged state of perception and the refusal to equate dreams with what is not serious for materialistically minded people also extends to Malraux's sense of his own life. I would now like to turn to that subject.

One of the major themes of *Le Miroir des limbes* is that the events in Malraux's life are not merely disconnected, accidental fragments but parts of a continuous and unified whole, an adventure that he does not fully comprehend but one that imbues the consciousness of his own life with a sense of awe and mystery. This idea is not shared by most men. His melancholy friend Méry, for whom he has the greatest respect and affection, has a pessimistic streak in him that leads him at one point to say: "My friends, or what passes for such, say that they always feel like themselves. They say that the lives of other people seem to us like a dream. That may be. But I, too, seem like a dream to me" (*ML* 363). Malraux counters this attitude by pointing out that the impression of discontinuity in life—characteristic of a Buddhist stance which may have influenced Méry—is contradicted by an even more powerful Indian concept, that of reincarnation, which accepts as a given the "eternity of the human being" (*ML* 364) until the *final* release from life. Malraux's attitude might be stated as follows: One should not say that the self is constantly changing, but rather that the self is constantly being reborn. The first attitude stresses discontinuity, and is fatalistic; the second—Malraux's characteristic attitude—stresses the unity of the self while allowing for dynamism and creativity.

What does life hold in store for us? A young man does not know the man he will become. What will some future self produce? Young Rembrandt cannot know what pictures he will paint as an old man. And yet we know that our destiny is out there, waiting to be revealed to us by the passage of time.

Unlike his friend Méry, Malraux is passionately curious to know what life holds in store for him. Without that curiosity, there can be no sense of destiny to bestow meaning upon one's present life and no sense of adventure to give it excitement. The episode in which Malraux must face a Nazi firing squad at Gramat, only to be spared for some unknown reason, becomes in his book one of the important landmarks in his sense of a destiny transforming life into an adventure and removing it from the realm of empty dreams (for which Malraux usually reserves the term *songes*): "My life was one of those human adventures that Shakespeare explains by calling them dreams [*songes*], but which are not dreams. A destiny that was fulfilling itself in front of a dozen rifles, among so many other destinies, as fleeting as the earth" (*ML* 179). And so, in the face of the mystery that confronts him on such a personal terrain, he becomes intensely curious: "What was about to happen to me furiously interested an insignificant part of myself, like the will to get out of the water when one is drowning" (*ML* 179). He had shown this same overwhelming curiosity when, some time before, after being wounded and captured by the Nazis and carried through the village on a stretcher, some disembodied part of him watched himself about to undergo his final fate: "I would not see our victory. What sense did this life have, would it ever have? But I was sucked up by a tragic curiosity for what was waiting for me" (*ML* 168). It is, of course, the experience of imminent death that provides the most intense moments of this curiosity, and he recalls, in the context of this same experience at Gramat, his own father's experience a few days before committing suicide: "My father had told me that death inspired in him an intense curiosity" (*ML* 181).[7]

One of the primary functions of the dream metaphor in *Le Miroir des limbes* is to convey Malraux's sense of wonder and astonishment—factors in his "intense curiosity"—as he witnesses the unfolding of a mysterious destiny. But even beyond its figurative expressiveness, dreaming has an active significance as a tool for acceding to knowledge. Since an integral part of a truth remains mysterious, lying beneath a surface appearance and remaining inaccessible to analysis of an objective sort, the manner of reaching it must also involve an instinctive approach, in which Malraux seems determined to prod the unconscious into a full collaboration with consciousness. Malraux makes it clear that in offering his "Antimémoires" to the public, he is in essence attempting to communicate not merely the events in his life, for which memory might have been adequate, but the meaning of that life. To this effect he writes: "When we are faced with the unknown, certain of our dreams have no less significance than our memories" (*ML* 11). This can in part be explained by the fact that dreams reach a deeper level of the mind than memory. A former inmate in a Nazi camp, explaining her return to normal life after the Liberation, certainly confirms this notion when she tells

Malraux: "I came out of memories more quickly than out of dreams" (*ML* 500).

It is not, however, so much the feeling of depth in dream that Malraux finds intriguing as the feeling that dreams collaborate with destiny, that they are privileged signs informing one of what life has in store—in short, premonitions. One of the great dreamers to whom Malraux refers several times in the course of *Le Miroir des limbes*, T. E. Lawrence, is quoted as stating of daydreamers that "'the dream virus also gives rise to action'" (*ML* 12). Out of context, this phrase would probably be interpreted by most readers as meaning that great deeds are preceded by a necessary period of reflection during which the idea that will eventually take form will be conceived, incubated, and hatched. That is certainly the likely sense of the image when Malraux, later referring to the ambitions of Alexander the Great, quotes Lawrence as saying in effect that daydreamers with power are dangerous: "'Watch out for dreamers when they are awake and dispose of the means of fulfilling their dreams'" (*ML* 568). But at the beginning of the "Antimémoires," the reference has to do with a curious quirk, that so fills him with wonder, that so much of his life has been foretold by his own previous fiction—by, that is, the product of his literary dreaming.

Even for an agnostic—and Malraux insists on more than one occasion that he is an agnostic—to have undergone the startling experience of seeing his own fiction come true must make it seem inescapably evident that there is an essential mystery working itself out in life. Malraux calls our attention to several of these experiences at the beginning of the "Antimémoires." The name of his last fictional hero was Berger; that was to become his own military name during the Resistance years. The family of the fictitious Bergers was Alsatian; the real Malraux was soon to become commander of the Alsace-Lorraine Brigade; his second wife was to die in a clinic on an avenue named Alsace-Lorraine, and his third wife lived in another city on a street with the same name. There are many other coincidences to which Malraux does not specifically allude at the beginning of the "Antimémoires" but which readers of Malraux familiar with his novels will be quick to recognize. Two of his fictitious characters of the 1930s, Kyo and Kassner, undergo interrogation scenes; he would himself undergo one after his capture by the Nazis.[8] The description of what it feels like to undergo execution by firing squad—couched in metaphorical language that underscores the bizarreness of the experience[9]—is presented in *L'Espoir* in the Hernandez episode; he would himself undergo a similar experience in Gramat, again expressed in terms of the absurd and the bizarre—with, of course, the difference that he is saved at the last moment by an inexplicable change of heart on someone's part (a mystery that remains). Inmates in a Nazi prison in the fictional *Temps du mépris* communicate from one cell to another through coded thumps on the walls; Malraux's fellow inmates in a real Nazi prison will likewise devise a communication system through their walls. In *La Condition humaine*, Clappique's failure to keep an appointment will lead to Kyo's capture; the fact that Malraux is twenty minutes late in meeting with a Resistance agent, Violette, will lead to her capture (*ML* 916–17). In "Lazare" the cries of the sick in his hospital will remind him of the moaning of the condemned prisoners he invented for *La Condition humaine*: "The moans of the Salpêtrière echo those of the prison yard in Shanghai" (*ML* 926). There are other examples as well.

Malraux apparently believes in the premonitory capability of his own literal dreaming as well. We find at least two instances of dream reported in *Le Miroir des limbes* that support this notion. He recalls the first in the context of the firing-squad episode at Gramat:

They present arms to those about to be shot. A recent dream came back to me: I was in a ship's cabin whose porthole had just been carried off; the water came gushing in; faced with my life which was now irremediably over, which would never be anything more that it had already been, I burst out in a fit of laughter (my brother Roland died shortly afterward, in the sinking of the *Cap-Arcona*). I had often brushed against violent death. (*ML* 170)

The common ground for the dream and reality here is the experience of witnessing oneself at the mercy of death. But the dream ends with a laugh, a premonitory sign that he would not die here, and that his "real" experience is somehow a sham one. The explanation that he had often faced a violent death—reminiscent of Katow's stoic attitude toward death just before his execution in *La Condition humaine*—would corroborate the feeling that he should not take the threat of the firing squad at face value, and that feeling proves to be correct. The other premonitory sign, after its elements have been transposed a bit, is equally correct: his brother would soon die in a shipwreck.

In the other instance, which Malraux frankly describes as an encounter with the supernatural, the premonitory accuracy of the dream is even more astonishing. This dream takes place in the winter of 1944; it is reported in support of the reliability of two women mediums who have independently recognized a stain on an ancient piece of fabric as being Alexander's blood:

A dark woman looks at me very gently, inclining her head. It is my sister-in-law, although she only half resembles her, and is wearing her hair—

pulled back from either side of the part in the middle—in a way I have never seen on her. A solemn voice, a bit ironic, which is neither the voice of an ordinary dream nor the voice of a state of wakefulness, articulates very distinctly: "And now, here is your third wife." (*ML* 571)

The morning after the dream he receives a telegram saying that his wife Josette is in mortal danger. Shortly he arrives at her house, only to find that she has already died as the result of a terrible train accident. Later he will learn of the death of his brother, and later still he will marry his dead brother's wife.

Many of Malraux's readers will no doubt retain a grain of skepticism in the face of these mystical claims. To play devil's advocate for a moment, we might recall his well-known penchant for mythomania, which would probably not exclude stretching an element in dream a bit to dramatize his own self-awareness and make his story livelier, too. Even beyond that, it would hardly be difficult to find any number of good rational reasons to challenge the notion that his life is informed by a central mystery.[10] For one thing, a few coincidences among a myriad of events are probably not sufficient to establish the existence of hidden forces. For another, the forward progression from premonitory dreams (either of the literal or fictional type) to fruition in reality can only be considered part of the story, and only a small part at that; for the opposite movement—the transposition from real-life experience to fictional discourse—must surely account for considerably more episodes in the fiction than the converse. While no one has ever claimed that all of Malraux's fiction is based on real-life episodes, there is no scarcity of critical evidence to show that he did quite often work from real models.

As it turns out, this latter objection may be beside the point, for some of the real-life experiences reported in *Le Miroir des limbes* have an undeniable, often powerful mystical content in their own right. There are even two major examples of real, mystical life experiences that Malraux would eventually transpose into fiction. One of them, that particular epiphany which he himself consecrates as the motif of the "'return to earth' which has played a large role in my life, and which I have often tried to transmit" (*ML* 74), prepares the reader early on in the book for the tone of awesome mystery that will serve as the most persistent point of reference throughout, until the last reported confrontation with death in the "Lazare" section. His first real experience of it took place during the return flight to Bône, in Algeria, after that most exotic air expedition of his in the company of Corniglion. A flight over the Queen of Sheba's ruined city in the Arabian desert is followed by a visit to Ethiopia and then by an almost fatal struggle between their airplane and a savage storm through which the two adventurers must fly. As transposed into fiction, first in *Le Temps du mépris* (Kassner flies back to Prague after his release from a Nazi prison) and later in *Les Noyers de l'Altenburg* (Vincent Berger returns to Marseille after traveling through the deserts of central Asia), the act of returning comes across as an experience of momentary alienation, the shock of which allows for a sense of rediscovery. Europe will be suddenly viewed as a civilization of shop windows, of hands that work but whose palms also suggest lines of destiny at work, of women without veils who seem defiantly free, and so on. Here is a portion of the passage found in *Les Noyers de l'Altenburg*, as retold in *Le Miroir des limbes*:

And from the simple presence of the people passing there, hurrying in the morning sunlight, as alike and as different as leaves, there seemed to well up a secret which did not only come from death still crouching behind his back [Vincent's father has just committed suicide], a secret that was much less that of death than of life—a secret that would not have been less heart-gripping if man had been immortal. (*ML* 27–28)

The presence of a mystery is thus revealed—not its true essence, of course, for that remains secret, but its presence, associated with both life and death in the morning light. The effect upon Vincent, as it was for Kassner, is that of an exhilarating liberation from time. This effect will also come across in *Le Miroir des limbes*, with perhaps the difference that the exhilaration is associated more explicitly with the sense that a true miracle has occurred: a voyage to death has been followed by the inexplicable grace of a return to life.

The other major example is the freeing of Malraux's tank from a tank trap, and from the certain death that would come to its crew from the Nazi artillery fire being aimed at it. The event is reported as taking place in reality early on in the war, in 1940; it was transposed into fiction as part of the final section of *Les Noyers de l'Altenburg* where, as we remember, the escape from death is followed by a prolonged meditation on the miracle of the rebirth of life. That entire retelling is repeated in *Le Miroir des limbes*, ostensibly to provide a point of comparison between Western and Eastern attitudes toward death. The members of the tank crew represent a modern Western mentality—devoid of spirituality and terrified by an imminent death because death has no meaning in our culture—while for Hindus Shiva's cosmic dance has a very precise meaning: that of the necessary cycle of life and death, thoroughly understood and accepted in India and more real than any material phenomenon. But like the return to earth motif, this second motif also serves Malraux's purposes in providing a context where the author can report on a return to life after a brush with death, filled with a sense of wonder that his destiny is following a path strewn with miraculous events and that his life is truly an adventure.

These two examples suggest that Malraux does not really need either premonitory dreams or premonitory fiction to experience, and communicate, the revelation of a personal destiny. Life itself is sufficient to give off intimations of a profound mystery working itself out, at least for someone like Malraux who is disposed to believe, first, that the world does have a meaning; second, that the world provides occasions where the confrontation with death allows for that meaning to be glimpsed, if not revealed; and, finally, that like the artists, visionaries, and adventurers that populate the pages of his book, he is one of those persons endowed with the power to receive signals and to express them to others. Malraux never really attempts to prove that his intuitive perceptions have any objective validity. Indeed, his often repeated claims that he is an agnostic would make it appear that even he would like to reject the mystical but that the sheer weight of the evidence makes it impossible to do so: "I have encountered the supernatural. I tend to brush it aside; it tends to come back" (ML 570). What resistance can he oppose to the power of that inner voice in him, far deeper than memory and in touch with (and, perhaps, at the source of) a total meaning which he cannot quite lay bare but which he is absolutely certain is there? Toward the beginning of *Lazare* he writes, in full awareness of what his book will be: "I leave, and then come back to, the fragments of this book where my memories, my obsessions, my premonitions jostle each other" (ML 838). Toward the end he admits to the impossibility of the ultimate task: "The revelation is that nothing can be revealed" (ML 930). And yet the book ends with a reference to the Zenlike attitude of irony and reconciliation that precedes the final illumination, which is sure to come.

To say that Malraux is disposed to believe that the world has a meaning may mean nothing more than that he wants it to have one. He is fond of quoting someone who cannot be accused of sacrificing scientific objectivity to mysticism, Albert Einstein, as saying (several versions of this statement appear throughout the book): "'What is most astonishing is that it is almost certain that the world has a meaning'" (ML 633). As to why Malraux may want it to have a meaning, the clearest reason given seems to be that only by engaging in a dialogue with the transcendental, with "that which is not involved with man" or "that which does not exist," can man establish a relationship with an absolute, which is alone capable of ordering human civilization. Malraux offers as negative evidence the notion that mod-

ern civilization has entrusted the creation and safeguarding of satisfactory human values to science and politics, both of which have
proven woefully incapable of doing either. Again, the point of encounter must take place at the frontiers of death, but most western-
ers are too terrified of death to engage in a fruitful dialogue with it,
either through lucid reflection or through the kinds of dream jour-
neys that Malraux takes to death and back.

There may be no better explanation to account for Malraux's interest in mystical communion than the statement we find at the beginning of the "Antimémoires": "Our mind invents its stories of Puss-
in-boots and coachmen that change into pumpkins at dawn, because
neither the religious person nor the atheist is completely satisfied
with appearance" (*ML* 14). From this point of view, *Le Miroir des
limbes* can be seen as having as one of its goals to distinguish between apparent truth and profound truth: "'The secret of things,
which is not in their appearance, . . .' says Aristotle" (*ML* 823). Appearance is the mask we in the West call the "real," concealing a secret truth—"unreal" because it has no material existence—that in-
fuses reality with life and gives it its meaning, and whose agent of
revelation is dream in its various aspects: religion, myths, fairy tales,
works of art and other mystical acts and documents that have as
their goal the release of man from his human condition by linking
him to the forces of the cosmos.

In addition to everything else he may be in *Le Miroir des limbes*—
biographer and autobiographer, historian and memorialist, praiser of
great men, moralist for our times—Malraux is also, more than ever,
the shaman figure that he saw in his character Vincent Berger[11]
and that W. M. Frohock subsequently identified with Malraux himself.[12] Whether it be through the creation of fiction, the reporting of
literal dreams, or the disposition to place his psyche in a ready state
of reception for whatever signs in life the world is transmitting to
him, Malraux's dreaming can be seen as an act of probing, with a
characteristically intense curiosity, at the frontiers of death, in search
of the secret meaning that will explain human existence in the world.
The search for that meaning—a meaning which will be the gift that
he will bring back to humanity—is perhaps the goal that gives his
own life meaning and that transforms it, for himself and for us, into a
long and noble adventure.

MAJOR WORKS OF

ANDRÉ MALRAUX

THROUGHOUT THE TEXT, THE FOLLOWING WORKS ARE REFERRED TO BY THE
INITIALS OF THEIR TITLES IN BRACKETS

La Tentation de l'Occident (Paris: Grasset, 1926). *The Temptation of the West*, tr. Robert Hollander (New York: Vintage, 1961).

Les Conquérants (Paris: Grasset, 1928). *The Conquerors*, tr. Winifred S. Whale (New York: Harcourt, Brace, 1929).

La Voie royale (Paris: Grasset, 1930). *The Royal Way*, tr. Stuart Gilbert (New York: Smith and Haas, 1935).

La Condition humaine (Paris: Gallimard, 1933). *Man's Fate*, tr. Haakon M. Chevalier (New York: Smith and Haas, 1934).

Le Temps du mépris (Paris: Gallimard, 1935). *Days of Wrath*, tr. Haakon M. Chevalier (New York: Random House, 1936).

L'Espoir (Paris: Gallimard, 1937). *Man's Hope*, tr. Stuart Gilbert and Alastair McDonald (New York: Random House, 1938).

Les Noyers de l'Altenburg (Lausanne: Editions du Haut-Pays, 1943). *The Walnut Trees of Altenburg*, tr. A. W. Fielding (London: John Lehmann, 1952).

La Psychologie de l'Art, 3 vols. (*Le Musée imaginaire, La Création artistique, La Monnaie de l'Absolu*) (Geneva: Skira, 1947–1950). *The Psychology of Art* (*The Museum without Walls, The Artistic Act, The Twilight of the Absolute*), tr. Stuart Gilbert (New York: Pantheon Books, 1949–1951).

Saturne: Essai sur Goya (Paris: Gallimard, 1950). *Saturn: Essay on Goya*, tr. C. W. Chilton (New York and London: Phaidon, 1957).

Les Voix du silence (Paris: Gallimard, 1951). *The Voices of Silence*, tr. Stuart Gilbert (New York: Doubleday, 1953).

Le Músee imaginaire de la sculpture mondiale, 3 vols.: I. *La Statuaire* (Paris: Gallimard, 1953). II. *Des Bas-reliefs aux grottes sacrées* (1954). III. *Le Monde chrétien* (1954).

La Métamorphose des dieux (Paris: Gallimard, 1957). *The Metamorphosis of the Gods*, tr. Stuart Gilbert (New York: Doubleday, 1960).

Antimémoires (Paris: Gallimard, 1967). *Anti-Memoirs*, tr. Terence Kilmartin (New York: Holt, Rinehart and Winston, 1968).

Les Chênes qu' on abat (Paris: Gallimard, 1971). *Felled Oaks: Conversation with de Gaulle*, tr. Irene Clephane (New York: Holt, Rinehart and Winston, 1972).

Oraisons funèbres (Paris: Gallimard, 1971).

La Tête d'obsidienne (Paris: Gallimard, 1974). *Picasso's Mask*, tr. June Guicharnaud and Jacques Guicharnaud (New York: Holt, Rinehart and Winston, 1977).

Lazare (Paris: Gallimard, 1974). *Lazarus*, tr. Terence Kilmartin (New York: Holt, Rinehart and Winston, 1977).

La Métamorphose des dieux, 3 vols.: I. *Le Surnaturel* (Paris: Gallimard, 1977. Published in 1957 as *La Métamorphose des dieux*). II. *L'Iréel* (1975). III. *L'Intemporel* (1976).

Le Miroir des limbes (Paris: Gallimard, Collection "Pléiade," 1976). (Includes *Antimémoires* and *La Corde et les souris*.)

L'Homme précaire et la littérature (Paris: Gallimard, 1977).

BOOKS IN ENGLISH ABOUT

ANDRÉ MALRAUX: A SELECTION

BLEND, CHARLES D., *André Malraux: Tragic Humanist* (Columbus, Ohio: Ohio State University Press, 1963).

BLUMENTHAL, GERDA, *André Malraux: The Conquest of Dread* (Baltimore: Johns Hopkins Press, 1960).

BOAK, DENIS, *André Malraux* (London: Oxford University Press, 1968).

FROHOCK, W. M., *Malraux and the Tragic Imagination* (Stanford: Stanford University Press, 1952; rpt. 1967).

GANNON, EDWARD, S. J., *The Honor of Being a Man: The World of André Malraux* (Chicago: Loyola University Press, 1957).

GOLDBERGER, AVRIEL, *Visions of a New Hero: The Heroic Life According to André Malraux . . .* (Paris: Lettres Modernes, 1965).

GREENLEE, JAMES W., *Malraux's Heroes and History* (De Kalb: Northern Illinois University Press, 1975).

HEWITT, JAMES R., *André Malraux* (New York: Ungar, 1978).

HORVATH, VIOLET M., *André Malraux: The Human Adventure* (New York: New York University Press, 1975).

JENKINS, CECIL, *André Malraux* (New York: Twayne, 1972).

KLINE, T. JEFFERSON, *André Malraux and the Metamorphosis of Death* (New York: Columbia University Press, 1975).

LACOUTURE, JEAN, *André Malraux*, tr. Alan Sheridan (New York: Pantheon, 1975).

LANGLOIS, WALTER G., *André Malraux: The Indochina Adventure* (New York: Praeger, 1966).

LEWIS, R. W. B., ed., *Malraux: A Collection of Critical Essays* (Englewood Cliffs, N.J.: Prentice-Hall, 1964).

PAYNE, ROBERT, *A Portrait of André Malraux* (Englewood Cliffs, N.J.: Prentice-Hall, 1970).

RICHTER, WILLIAM, *The Rhetorical Hero: An Essay on the Aesthetics of André Malraux* (London: Routledge & Kegan Paul, 1964).

TARICA, RALPH, *Imagery in the Novels of André Malraux* (Rutherford, N.J.: Fairleigh Dickinson University Press, 1980).

WILKINSON, DAVID, *Malraux: An Essay in Political Criticism* (Cambridge, Mass.: Harvard University Press, 1967).

NOTES

Introduction: Malraux's Quest

1. The best overall biography of Malraux is Jean Lacouture's *André Malraux: Une vie dans le siècle* (Paris: Le Seuil, 1973; rev. ed., Paris: Le Seuil, Collection Points, 1976). Lacouture puzzles over some of the remaining enigmas in his article "Sur quelques inconnues 'biographiques,'" in the excellent Malraux issue of *Les Cahiers de L'Herne*, No. 43, edited by Michel Cazenave (1982), subsequently referred to as *L'Herne*. All translations below are mine.

2. These early works are analyzed in relationship to the period and to Malraux's later evolution by André Vandegans, *La Jeunesse littéraire d'André Malraux* (Paris: Jean-Jacques Pauvert, 1964).

3. André Malraux, *La Condition humaine*, in *Romans* (Paris: Gallimard, Pléiade, 1947), p. 226. Hereafter abbreviated *CH*.

4. Léon Trotsky, "La Révolution étranglée," *La Nouvelle revue française* (April 1931), pp. 488–500; reprinted in *L'Herne*, pp. 38–44. Malraux's "Réponse à Trotsky" appeared in the same issue of the *NRF*, pp. 501–7, and is reprinted in *L'Herne*, pp. 45–48.

5. For an account of Malraux's making of *Sierra de Teruel*, see Denis Marion, *André Malraux*, Collection Cinéma d'aujourd'hui (Paris: Seghers, 1970), and John Michalczyk, *André Malraux's "Espoir": The Propaganda/Art Film and the Spanish Civil War*, Romance Monographs no. 27 (University, Mississippi: Romance Monographs Inc., 1977).

6. On this entire period, see Suzanne Chantal's account of Malraux's relationship with Josette Clotis, *Le Coeur battant: Josette Clotis– André Malraux* (Paris: Grasset, 1976).

7. See Père Pierre Bockel's article, "Métaphysique de l'agnosticisme," in

Malraux: Etre et dire, ed. Martine de Courcel (Paris: Plon, 1976), as well as his book, *L'Enfant du rire* (Paris: Grasset, 1973).

8. Interview with Kommen Becirovic for Yugoslavian Radio-Television and the Belgrade weekly *Nin* (May 5, 1969); reprinted as "Consolation ou apaisement, je ne crois pas . . . ," *L'Herne*, pp. 15–21.

9. Michel Cazenave, "La Métamorphose," *L'Herne*, p. 210. In a footnote to this passage Malraux confirms Cazenave's intuition: "Lien entire l'Espagne et la guerre en France. Certainement." In a 1947 speech following the presentation of his film, *Espoir*, Malraux explained:

When I was making this film, there was still the great dream of the "Internationale." The gesture of disdain with which Russia eliminated the "Internationale" from among its official songs swept away at once all the dreams of the nineteenth century. For better or worse, we are from now on bound to France. It is upon her that we must build Europe, and not against her; not upon her alone, not upon such or such a country, but upon the countries understood and recognized, and we now know that by wanting to be less French, we will not be more man, we will simply be more Russian. ("De l'Espagne à la France," *L'Herne*, pp. 201–2)

10. Malraux's speech on December 15, 1965, at the Palais des Sports in Paris. Published in *Espoir* no. 2 (1972); cited by Michel Cazenave, "La Métamorphose," *L'Herne*, p. 209.

11. Malraux, footnote to Cazenave, "La Métamorphose."

12. Malraux saw his cultural politics as a means of liberation. In an interview with Fanny Deschamps (*Elle*, March 9, 1967) he stated:

If I can say to myself, when I die, that there are 500,000 more young people who, thanks to my action, have seen a window open through which they will escape the harshness of technology, the aggressiveness of publicity, the need to make more and more money for their leisure activities, most of which are vulgar or violent, if I can tell myself that, I will die happy, I assure you. (Cited by Françoise Dorenlot, "Une unité de pensée?" *L'Herne*, p. 457)

13. The period was not only politically difficult but personally trying; Malraux's two sons were killed in an automobile accident in 1961.

14. Shinichi Ogasawara, "Les deux engagements de Malraux," *L'Herne*, p. 225.

15. Jean Lacouture, "Sur quelques inconnues," *L'Herne*, p. 179.

16. Françoise Dorenlot, "Une unité de pensée?" *L'Herne*, p. 454.

17. Roger Stéphane, *Fin d'une jeunesse* (Paris: Table Ronde, 1954), p. 62.

18. André Malraux, *Les Voix du silence* (Paris: Gallimard, 1951), p. 628; hereafter abbreviated *VS*.

19. André Malraux, interview with Jacques Legris (1975), published under the title "A propos des *Hôtes de passage*," *L'Herne*, pp. 156–63. The passage quoted is on p. 162.

20. Ibid.

21. André Malraux, interview with Kommen Becirovic, *L'Herne*, p. 16.

22. According to Jean Lacouture, *Le Miroir des limbes*, which regroups the definitive versions of these texts, was "the book dearest to Malraux, the most significant." ("Le biographe et sa cible," *Le Magazine littéraire*, September 1973, p. 34; cited by David Bevan, "L'Expression de la transcendance," *L'Herne*, p. 428.)

23. *Antimémoires* (Paris: Gallimard, 1967), p. 17.

24. *La Tête d'obsidienne* (Paris: Gallimard, 1974), p. 245.
25. T. Jefferson Kline, "Le Pont des arts," *L'Herne*, p. 325.
26. Pierre Bockel, *L'Enfant du rire*, p. 23.
27. According to Père Bockel, Malraux told him one day: "I am agnostic: I have to be something or other, for do not forget that I am very intelligent . . . but you know better than I that no one escapes God." (*L'Enfant du rire*, p. 126, cited by Charles Moeller, "Malraux et le vide de Dieu," *L'Herne*, p. 445.)

Malraux Criticism: Two Exemplary Modes

1. W. M. Frohock, *André Malraux and the Tragic Imagination* (Stanford: Stanford University Press, 1952); hereafter abbreviated as *F.*
2. Lucien Goldmann, "Introduction to a Structural Study of Malraux's Novels," *Towards a Sociology of the Novel*, tr. Alan Sheridan (Cambridge: Cambridge University Press, 1975); hereafter abbreviated as *G.* Originally published as *Pour une sociologie du roman* (Paris: Gallimard, Collection Idées, 1964).
3. André Malraux, *Les Conquérants* (Paris: Grasset, 1928), p. 173.
4. See Susan Rubin Suleiman's essay, "Malraux's Women: A Re-vision," elsewhere in this volume.—EDS.
5. Mary Ann Frese Witt explores this notion in her essay, "Malraux's Shamanism: Initiatory Death and Rebirth," elsewhere in this volume.—EDS.

Asia Out of Focus: Decoding Malraux's Orient

1. In Drieu La Rochelle's phrase, Malraux's novels testify to "un transfert direct de la réalité dans le récit." *Les Critiques de notre temps et Malraux* (Paris: Garnier, 1970), p. 49. See also Gaëtan Picon, *Malraux par lui-même* (Paris: Seuil, 1953), pp. 13, 14, 23–29.
2. Walter Langlois, *L'Aventure indochinoise d'André Malraux* (Paris: Mercure de France, 1967).
3. Jean Lacouture, *André Malraux: Une vie dans le siècle* (Paris: Seuil, 1973).
4. W. M. Frohock, *André Malraux and the Tragic Imagination* (Stanford: Stanford University Press, 1952), pp. x, 88. C. J. Greshoff, *An Introduction to the Novels of André Malraux* (Rotterdam: A. A. Balkema, 1975), stresses the "elliptic mind which cannot tell a story" (p. 65) and notes Malraux's effort to "transfer a cinematic *optique* into the novel" (p. 67).
5. Jean Carduner, *La Création romanesque chez Malraux* (Paris: Nizet, 1968); Franz J. Albersmeier, *André Malraux und der Film: Zur Rezeption des Films in Frankreich* (Bern: Herbert Lang; Frankfurt am Main: Peter Lang, 1973).
6. André Malraux, *Les Voix du silence* (Paris: Gallimard, 1951), p. 66. Hereafter Malraux's works will be abbreviated as follows: *C* (*Les Conquérants*); *CH* (*La Condition humaine*); *VR* (*La Voie royale*). All are published in *Romans* (Paris: Gallimard, Collection Pléiade, 1976). All translations are mine.

Malraux's Saint-Just

1. André Malraux, *Les Chênes qu'on abat . . .* (Paris: Gallimard, 1978), p. 127; hereafter abbreviated as *CA.* The English translations are mine.

2. Malraux evokes Michelet's image of Saint-Just, "the archangel of death," in his preface to Albert Ollivier, *Saint-Just et la force des choses* (Paris: Gallimard, 1954), p. 12; hereafter the preface will be abbreviated as *SJ.*

3. André Malraux, letter of July 4, 1947, in Emile Lecerf, *André Malraux* (Paris: Richard-Masse, 1946, 1971), p. 16.

4. Gaëtan Picon, *André Malraux* (Paris: Gallimard, 1945), p. 22.

5. See Wilbur M. Frohock, *André Malraux* (New York: Columbia University Press, 1974), pp. 11–12.

6. Albert Ollivier was editor of the review *Le Rassemblement,* founded by Malraux.

7. Malraux refers to this aphorism in his preface to *Oraisons funèbres* (Paris: Gallimard, 1971), p. 11.

8. Pierre Galante, *Malraux* (Paris: Paris Match et Presses de la Cité, 1971), p. 196.

9. See Jean-Pierre Gross, *Saint-Just: Sa politique et ses missions* (Paris: Bibliothèque Nationale, 1976), p. 64.

10. *Malraux: Paroles et écrits politiques 1947–1972* (Paris: Plon, 1973), p. 27.

11. See, for example, André Malraux, vol. 3 of *L'Espoir, Oeuvres* (Paris: Gallimard, 1937), pp. 158, 270, 384–86.

12. Interview by *Der Spiegel* (October 1968), in *Malraux: Paroles et écrits politiques,* p. 91.

13. James W. Greenlee, *Malraux's Heroes and History* (De Kalb: Northern Illinois University Press, 1975), p. 33.

14. Eugene Newton Curtis, *Saint-Just: Colleague of Robespierre* (New York: Columbia University Press, 1935), p. 226.

15. André Malraux, *Les Conquérants,* vol. 1 of *Oeuvres* (Paris: Gallimard, 1928), p. 152; hereafter abbreviated *C.*

16. See Gross, *Saint-Just,* pp. 63–64, 338.

17. See Lecerf, *André Malraux,* p. 51; Denis Boak, *André Malraux* (Oxford: Clarendon Press, 1968), p. 204; and Alex Madsen, *Malraux: a Biography* (New York: William Morrow, 1976), pp. 299–300.

18. *Les Critiques de notre temps et André Malraux* (Paris: Garnier Frères, 1970), p. 28.

19. Ibid., p. 29.

20. Fréderic J. Grover, *Six entretiens avec André Malraux sur des écrivains de notre temps* (Paris: Gallimard, 1978), pp. 110–15.

21. Greenlee, *Malraux's Heroes,* p. 44.

22. *Les Critiques,* p. 28.

23. André Malraux, *Antimémoires* (Paris: Gallimard, Collection Pléiade, 1976), p. 339.

Malraux and Tragedy: The Structure of *La Condition humaine*

1. In this connection see particularly Francis Fergusson, "Oedipus Rex: The Tragic Rhythm of Action," *The Idea of a Theatre* (Princeton, 1949).
2. It would have been considerably more so had the chapter Malraux excluded at this point been left in the book. In addition to a possible overemphasis upon Clappique, however, any addition here would have disturbed the balance between sections. For this chapter see "Un Chapitre inédit de *La Condition humaine*," *Marianne*, 13 décembre 1933.

This essay was first published in the *Romanic Review*, 44 (Oct. 1953), no. 3, pp. 208–214.

Malraux, Faulkner, and the Problem of Tragedy

1. Maurice E. Coindreau, "William Faulkner," *La Nouvelle revue française*, 36 (June 1931): 927. All translations are mine.
2. See, for example, Jean-Paul Sartre, "American Novelists in French Eyes," *Atlantic Monthly* 179 (August 1946): 114; Marius-François Guyard, "Faulkner le Tragique," *Etudes* 286 (1951): 182; Stanley D. Woodworth, *William Faulkner en France (1931–1952)* (Paris: M. J. Minard, 1959), p. 41.
3. W. M. Frohock, *André Malraux and the Tragic Imagination* (Stanford: Stanford University Press, 1952), pp. 90–92.
4. Gaëtan Picon, *André Malraux* (Paris: Gallimard, 1945), p. 117.
5. Cf. Bert M-P. Leefmans, "Malraux and Tragedy: The Structure of *La Condition humaine*," *Romanic Review* 44 (1953): 208–14, reprinted in this volume.
6. For a broad overview, see W. M. Frohock, "Malraux: The Tragic Sensibility," *Dalhousie French Studies* 2 (1980): 89–100.
7. André Malraux, *Le Temps du mépris* (Paris: Gallimard, 1935), p. 8.
8. Gaëtan Picon, *Malraux par lui-même* (Paris: Editions du Seuil, 1953), p. 66.
9. Cf. Charles D. Blend, *André Malraux: Tragic Humanist* (Columbus: Ohio State University Press, 1963), p. 66.
10. André Malraux, "L'homme et la culture artistique," *Les Conférences de l'U.N.E.S.C.O.* (Paris, 1947), p. 87.
11. André Malraux, preface to Manès Sperber, . . . *qu'une larme dans l'océan* (Paris: Calmann-Lévy, 1952), p. xx.
12. See W. M. Frohock, *The Novel of Violence in America* (Dallas: Southern Methodist University, 1950), pp. 164–65.
13. Cf. Sorin Alexandrescu, "William Faulkner and the Greek Tragedy," *Romanian Review* 24, no. 3 (1970): 102–10.
14. William Faulkner, *Sartoris* (New York: New American Library, 1964), p. 284.
15. For an account of tragic situations and the tragic vision in Faulkner criticism, see John Lewis Longley, Jr., *The Tragic Mask: A Study of Faulkner's Heroes* (Chapel Hill: University of North Carolina Press, 1963), pp. 171–73.

16. Frederick L. Gwynn and Joseph L. Blotner, eds., *Faulkner in the University* (Charlottesville, Va.: University of Virginia Press), p. 35.
17. Ibid., p. 38.
18. Ibid., p. 51.
19. Ibid., p. 118.
20. Ibid., pp. 96–97.
21. Ibid., p. 185.
22. Cf. Jean-Marie Domenach, *Le Retour du tragique* (Paris, 1967), p. 222.
23. William Faulkner, *Sanctuary* (New York: The Modern Library, 1932), p. 265.
24. William Faulkner, *Sanctuary: The Original Text*, ed. Noel Polk (New York: Random House, 1981), p. 152.
25. Cf. Elizabeth M. Kerr, "The Creative Evolution of *Sanctuary*," *Faulkner Studies* 1 (1980): 24.
26. Calvin S. Brown, "*Sanctuary*: From Confrontation to Peaceful Void," *Mosaic* 7 (1973): 94.

Malraux and Sartre: Dialogue on the Far Side of Despair

1. This statement was made by Sartre at a press conference held at the Venice Film Festival on the occasion of the showing of the film *Le Mur*. A transcription of the press conference was printed in *Jeune Cinéma* no. 25 (October 1967), p. 24. Translation mine.
2. Ibid.
3. Jean-Paul Sartre, *Le Mur* (1939; rpt. Paris: Gallimard, Collection Folio, 1974), p. 34. Translation, with occasional modifications, from *The Wall*, trans. Lloyd Alexander (New York: New Directions, 1969); hereafter abbreviated *M*.
4. *Jeune Cinéma* no. 25 (October 1967), p. 24.
5. Ibid.
6. Simone de Beauvoir, *La Force de l'Age* (Paris: Gallimard, 1960), p. 334. Translation from *The Prime of Life*, trans. Peter Green (Cleveland: World, 1962); hereafter abbreviated *FA*.
7. André Malraux, *L'Espoir* (1937; rpt. Paris: Gallimard, Collection Folio, 1978). Translation, with modifications, from *Days of Hope*, trans. Stuart Gilbert and Alastair Macdonald (1938; rpt. London: Hamish Hamilton, 1968); hereafter abbreviated *E*.
8. See W. M. Frohock, *André Malraux and the Tragic Imagination* (Stanford: Stanford University Press, 1952; rpt. 1967), p. 115.
9. Malraux's biographers seem to rely on the de Beauvoir account of this meeting, Malraux apparently having left no account of his own. See Jean Lacouture, *André Malraux: Une vie dans le siècle* (Paris: Seuil, 1973), p. 270.
10. Ibid.
11. Ibid., p. 271. English translation from *André Malraux*, trans. Alan Sheridan (New York: Pantheon, 1975).
12. *Huis clos/Les Mouches* (Paris: Gallimard, Folio, 1974), p. 236. English translation from *No Exit and Three Other Plays* tr. Stuart Gilbert and Lionel Abel (New York: Vintage, 1955), p. 123.

Malraux and Camus 1925–1960: Master and Disciple?

1. I have relied on the major bibliographical works, but mainly Raymond Gay-Crosier's exhaustive *Camus* (Darmstadt: Wissentschaftliche Buchgesellschaft, 1976), in my search for studies of the subject.
2. As indicated, my debt to Lottman is enormous. To footnote each of his contributions would turn the text into a thicket. Suffice it to say his contributions of factual information constitute the backbone of the biographical matter. I have referred to him in parentheses, however, each time that there is a quotation from his book, using the abbreviation *L*.
3. See John J. Michalczyk, "Camus/Malraux: A Staged Version of *Le Temps du Mépris*," *French Review* 50 (1977): 102–6. For other articles (and chapters of books) on Malraux and Camus, see Raymond Gay-Crosier, *Camus*, which reviews all publications through 1975.
4. Frédéric J. Grover, *Six Entretiens avec André Malraux sur des écrivains de notre temps (1959–1975)* (Paris: Gallimard, 1978).
5. Camus said this to me in a conversation in 1958.
6. Jean Lacouture, *André Malraux: Une vie dans le siècle* (Paris: Seuil, 1973).
7. *Carnets Mai 1935-Février 1942* (Paris: Gallimard, 1962).
8. *Carnets Janvier 1942-Mars 1951* (Paris: Gallimard, 1964).
9. Camus let me read the typescript of these notebooks in 1958, with permission to quote from them. At that time, the notebooks for 1954–1958 had not been typed.
10. Albert Camus, *Essais*, ed. Roger Quilliot and Louis Faucon (Paris: Gallimard, Collection Pléiade, 1965), p. 258.
11. Albert Camus, *Théâtre, Récits, Nouvelles*, ed. Roger Quilliot (Gallimard, Collection Pléiade, 1962), p. 1713. All translations of Camus are mine.
12. Grover, *Six Entretiens*, pp. 145–46.

Before *L'Espoir*: Malraux's Pilots for Republican Spain

Research for the present study was supported in part by a grant from the National Endowment for the Humanities, for which the author is deeply grateful.

1. "Anti-Fascist Italians Among Pilots," *London News-Chronicle*, August 19, 1936.
2. W. M. Frohock, *André Malraux and the Tragic Imagination* (Stanford: Stanford University Press, 1952), p. 8.
3. The two most recent of these studies are Robert S. Thornberry, *André Malraux et l'Espagne* (Geneva: Droz, 1977), and Günther Schmigalle, *André Malraux und der spanische Bürgerkrieg* (Bonn: Bouvier Verlag, 1980).
4. The quotation and information here are taken from Blum's 1947 testimony before a postwar legislative commission of inquiry. See *Les Evénements survenus en France de 1933 à 1945*. Témoignages et documents réunis par la commission d'enquête parlementaire, vol. 1 (Paris: Presses Univ. de France, 1951), pp. 215–16. Blum gives further information about his efforts to help Spain on pp. 121–32, 217–29, and 251–62. Several members of his government have written mem-

oirs that give additional details. Their recollections of what tran-
spired at cabinet and ministers' meetings are especially valuable,
since no official minutes were ever kept. There are some chronological discrepancies in these accounts (written years after the events in
question), which we have corrected from references in contemporary
newspapers. For our narrative we have drawn primarily from Pierre
Cot, *Triumph of Treason* (New York: Ziff-Davis, 1944), pp. 338–47;
Jules Moch, *Rencontres avec Léon Blum* (Paris: Plon, 1970), pp.
189–217; André Blumel's memoir, "La non-intervention en Espagne," published as an appendix to Georges Lefranc's *Histoire du
Front populaire* (Paris: Payot, 1965), pp. 460–66; and John Dreifort,
Yvon Delbos at the Quai d'Orsay (Lawrence: University Press of
Kansas, 1973), pp. 31–54. Unless otherwise indicated, we have made
all translations quoted.
5. "Blum-la-guerre a dû reculer," *Action Française*, July 25, 1936.
6. Two conservative morning dailies broke the news of the arrival of
these two Spanish airmen seeking "l'assistance de la France pour ré-
tablir la situation" in Spain. See "Des officiers aviateurs espagnols au
Bourget," *Echo de Paris*, July 22, 1936, and "Deux aviateurs espagnols
arrivent à Paris en mission officielle," *Le Matin*, July 22, 1936. More
news of their mission appeared in most Paris papers during the next
several days.
7. Numerous Franco-era Spanish historians have given details about the
state of the Republican air force at the time of the insurrection, but
their information is often inaccurate. The most reliable brief appraisal (it is based on contemporary American military intelligence
sources) is to be found in chapter II: "Spanish Aviation Immediately
Prior to War," in the U.S. Army War College publication, *Spain* (no.
38894, dated 1938), pp. 3–6, which we are using here.
8. Cf. *Spain*, p. 4, and "Madrid Said to Distrust Men in the Air Force;
Fear of Desertions Limits Attacks by Plane," *New York Times*, August 18, 1936. According to the *NYT* correspondent, a pilot in the Republican air force had told him that "there are three planes for every
flier who would be completely trustworthy." A Spanish commander,
Hidalgo de Cisneros, later wrote that at the outbreak of the insurrection about 80 percent of the equipment of the air force stayed in government hands, while only about 35 percent of the officers remained
loyal to the Republic. See Ignacio Hidalgo de Cisneros, *Virage sur
l'aile* (Paris: Editeurs Français Réunis, 1965), p. 330.
9. The plane bringing Warleta and Aboal from Madrid had brought this
shipment of gold. For details, see "L'arrivée par avion au Bourget de
près de 19 millions d'or espagnol," *Le Matin*, July 26, 1936.
10. On Léo Lagrange, see Eugène Raude and Gilbert Prouteau, *Le Message
de Léo Lagrange* (Paris: Compagnie du Livre, 1950), in particular the
biographical essay, pp. 23–29, and Malraux's reminiscences of his
friend, pp. 179–83. On Lagrange's early involvement in helping Madrid, see "M. Léo Lagrange au secours des communistes espagnols,"
Action Française, July 25, 1936. According to those who knew Lagrange best, his basic political commitment was not at all Communist, but rather a kind of "socialisme humaniste" that was very close
to Malraux's position.

11. The most detailed and documented discussion in English of this flight of Italian antifascists abroad is to be found in Charles P. Delzell, *Mussolini's Enemies* (Princeton: Princeton University Press, 1961), pp. 42–84.

12. For details of Malraux's colonial experience, see Walter G. Langlois, *André Malraux: The Indochina Adventure* (New York: Praeger, 1966). An evaluation of Malraux's growing antifascism is to be found in the same author's "Le jeune Malraux et la 'fertilité' de l'idéal communiste," *Sud* [Marseille], no. 21 (1977): 51–62; and "Malraux à la recherche d'un roman: *Le Temps du mépris*," *Cahiers de l'Association internationale des études françaises*, no. 33 (May 1981): 203–17.

13. For details about the formation, programs and activities of GL, see in particular *No al fascismo*. Saggi a cura di Ernesto Rossi (Turin: Einaudi, 1963); *Giustizia e Libertà nella lotta antifascista e nelle storia d'Italia* (Florence: La Nuova Italia, 1978); and Elena Aga Rossi, *Il Movimento republicano Giustizia e Libertà e il partito d'Azione* (Milan: Cappelli, 1969).

14. Delzell, *Mussolini's Enemies*, p. 160. The most accessible work in English on Rosselli is Gaetano Salvemini, *Carlo and Nello Rosselli: A Memoir* (London: Dunstan, 1937). In Italian, see Aldo Garosci, *Vita di Carlo Rosselli* (Florence: Vallecchi, 1973). Rosselli's major writings have been collected under the title *Scritti politici e autobiografici* (Naples: Polis, 1944).

15. It was generally known that GL counted among its members a goodly number of army and navy officers of the previous regime, as well as intellectuals and professionals. See "Five Intellectuals Sentenced in Rome," *New York Times*, May 31, 1936. As for D'Annunzio, he was a skilled and daring pilot who began making propaganda flights as early as the summer of 1915, when he dropped pamphlets on Trieste. However, his August 9, 1918, incursion over Vienna was certainly his most striking and widely publicized such gesture. On the Milan flight and its aftermath, see in particular Edigio Reale, "Il volo su Milano," in *No al fascismo*, pp. 201–16. Concerning Viezzoli—who subsequently became a valued member of Malraux's squadron and who appears in *L'Espoir* as Marcelino, see the pamphlet issued shortly after his untimely death (copy in the Spanish civil war collection at Harvard) entitled "Un eroe dell'ala rivoluzionaria italiana: Giordano Viezzoli" (Paris, 1936).

16. "Il popolo spagnolo in armi per la difesa della rivoluzione," *Giustizia e Libertà*, 3, no. 30 (July 24, 1936).

17. This information was contained in a confidential report summarizing GL activities. It was sent to Rome on August 14, 1936, and is preserved in a file of the Italian Ministry of the Interior (n. 3571/b5408). Cited by Franco Fucci, *Ali contro Mussolini: I raid aerei antifascisti degli anni trenta* (Milan: Mursia, 1978), p. 110.

18. See Pablo de Azcárate, *Mi embajade en Londres durante la guerra civil española* (Barcelona: Arriel, 1976), p. 21.

19. Gaëtan Sanvoisin, "Assistance française à la guerre civile?" *Le Figaro*, July 24, 1936.

20. Cf. Pierre Causse, "La livraison de matériel de guerre à l'Espagne," *L'Intransigeant*, July 26, 1936; "Vingt avions prêts à partir," *Le*

Matin, July 26, 1936; and "Le livraison des armes au gouvernement espagnol," *Le Temps*, July 26, 1936.

21. Cf. Maurice Pujo, "Ce marché sanglant est-il conclu?" *Action Française*, July 23, 1936, and "Le Front populaire français osera-t-il armer le Front populaire espagnol?" *Echo de Paris*, July 23, 1936.

22. "Blum-la-guerre a dû reculer," *Action Française*, July 25, 1936.

23. The above information is contained in the remarkable report letter that de los Ríos sent to Giral shortly after the meeting with Blum and his ministers. This document, originally revealed by a Rome newspaper, was published in *Action Française* on December 11, 1936. The Spanish text is to be found in *Historia de la cruzada española*, ed. Joaquin Arraras, vol. 4 (Madrid: Ediciones Españolas, 1941), pp. 519–20. The most accessible English translation is in William Foss and Cecil Gerahty, *The Spanish Arena* (London: Hale-Gifford, 1938), pp. 372–75. Various French newspaper reports a few days later concerning the arrival in Paris of a few "aviateurs espagnols" suggest that Madrid made at least a token effort to furnish pilots as de los Ríos had requested. See notably "L'arrivée d'aviateurs espagnols en France," *Le Temps*, July 26, 1936.

24. "La question des livraisons d'armes à l'Espagne," *Paris-Soir*, July 26, 1936. For purposes of our discussion we have labeled conservatives those ministers in Blum's government who were opposed to sending help to Madrid.

25. My emphasis. The Spanish text (Arraras, *Cruzada*, vol. 4, p. 519) reads: "La resolución del Consejo ha sido no hacer ninguna entrega de Gobierno a Gobierno; pero las autorizaciones que se precisen para que la industria privada nos entregue y circule el material que adquirimos."

26. On this visit to Madrid by Malraux, see Walter G. Langlois, "Aux sources de *L'Espoir*: Malraux et le début de la guerre civile en Espagne," in *André Malraux 2: Visages du romancier* (Paris: Minard, 1973), p. 93–133.

27. The text of this interview appeared as "André Malraux über die Ereignisse in Spanien," in *Rundschau über Politik, Wirtschaft und Arbeiterbewegung* [Basel] 5, no. 34 (July 30, 1936): 1395. This valuable text was first cited in Schmigalle, *Malraux und der spanische Bürgerkrieg*, pp. 90–92.

28. See the anonymous spy's report dated July 28 and the August 14 summary cited in Fucci, *Ali contro Mussolini*, pp. 109–10.

29. Of course, news of this recruitment of foreign antifascists—particularly Italians—soon leaked out and provoked indignant reactions from conservatives. See, notably, Maurice Pujo: "La guerre civile espagnole va-t-elle devenir guerre générale?" *Action Française*, July 30, 1936.

30. For details of Rosselli's trip to Spain and his subsequent enlistment in the column of Italian volunteers based in Barcelona, see Aldo Garosci, "Le diverse fasi dell'intervento di *Giustizia e Libertà* nella guerra civile de Spagna," in *Giustizia e Libertà nella lotta antifascista*, pp. 367–97.

31. On this meeting, see Langlois, "Aux sources de *L'Espoir*," pp. 120–24. The quotations below are taken from "Avec un enthousi-

asme ardent 30.000 Parisiens affirment, à Wagram, leur solidarité avec le peuple espagnol," *L'Humanité*, July 31, 1936.

32. M. Picot de Pledran, "Les événements d'Espagne ont été évoqués à la commission des Affaires étrangères de la Chambre," *Action Française*, July 31, 1936.

33. Blum, in *Les Evénements*, pp. 378–79.

34. "Le gouvernement autorise sous certaines conditions le départ des volontaires pour l'Espagne," *Echo de Paris*, August 2, 1936.

35. The text of this contract has been published in various places, but the revelation was made in "Recrutement des mercenaires français," *Action Française*, August 20, 1936, from which we quote here.

36. On the Saba flight, see, among others, Robert Payne, *A Portrait of André Malraux* (Englewood Cliffs, N.J.: Prentice-Hall, 1970), pp. 201–18, and Pierre Galante, *André Malraux: Quel roman que sa vie* (Paris: Plon, 1971), pp. 96–137. For a little-known but revealing aviation text by Malraux, see "L'homme et le moteur," in *Gnome-Rhône Journal* 7, no. 38 (April 1934): 2–3, reprinted in *Mélanges Malraux Miscellany* 2, no. 2 (Autumn 1970): 17–19.

37. The quotations here are from the text of the contract signed by de Albornoz and published in *Action Française*, August 20, 1936.

38. See Cot, *Triumph of Treason*, pp. 342–44.

39. R. P. de T., "Nouvelles de l'aviation," *L'Intransigeant*, August 6, 1936. This initial announcement listed a certain Belguinda as one of the pilots, but later information suggests that this was a garbled version of the name of Abel Guidez.

40. R. P. de T., "Nouvelles de l'aviation," *L'Intransigeant*, August 7 and 9, 1936. A second Dewoitine was damaged during one of these subsequent convoys.

41. "Des avions pour l'Espagne," *Le Figaro*, November 10, 1936.

42. On the ferrying of the Potez, see Maurice Pujo, "Les avions de Pierre Cot [. . .] en route pour l'Espagne," *Action Française*, August 7, 1936; "Qui trompe-t-on?" August 8; and "Les marchands de canons ont avoué," August 9.

43. For the primary texts relating to this matter, see *Documents diplomatiques français, 1932–1939*, 2d series (1936–1939), vol. 3 (July 19–November 19, 1936) (Paris: Imprimerie nationale, 1966), pp. 110–11, 142–46.

44. Dreifort, *Delbos*, pp. 46–47.

45. The information and quotations above are from Maurice Pujo, "Histoire de vol et de voleurs," *Action Française*, August 12, 1936. Pujo originally claimed that Malraux's flight took place on Saturday, August 8 but later corrected the date to Friday, August 7 ("Nouveaux aveux," *Action Française*, August 13, 1936). Accounts are not clear about the number of Dewoitines that left for Spain at this time, but twelve seems to be the most probable number.

46. Incident related in Galante, *Malraux*, p. 148. Esparre's recollection that the event took place "par un bel après-midi d'été" at a time when "le ministère Léon Blum venait de décider la non-intervention" seems to confirm this August 8 date. So far as is known, the only other group of planes that Malraux himself led to Spain did not go to the peninsula until much later, in mid-October, and they went via Bordeaux, not Toulouse.

47. This episode is related in Mijail Koltzov's *Diario de la guerra de España* (Paris: Ediciones Ruedo Ibérico, 1963), pp. 9–11.
48. Koltzov, a prudent man, related these events in the third person, referring to himself as Miguel. There are indications in Koltzov's account and elsewhere that the ferrying of the last few planes was actually not completed until Sunday, August 9, after the embargo was officially imposed. Unfortunately the few available records are so contradictory that this question will probably never be resolved.
49. This unpublished telegram is in the United States Department of State Decimal File, 1930–1939, document no. 852.00/2589.

Authoritarianism and Esthetics: The Paradox of *L'Espoir*

1. See Charles D. Blend, *André Malraux: Tragic Humanist* (Columbus: Ohio State University Press, 1963); Joseph Hoffmann, *L'Humanisme de Malraux* (Paris: Klincksieck, 1963).
2. David Wilkinson, *Malraux: An Essay in Political Criticism* (Cambridge: Harvard University Press, 1967).
3. Lucien Goldmann, *Pour une sociologie du roman* (Paris: Gallimard, Collection Idées, 1964), p. 196. Translation mine.
4. Parenthetical references to *L'Espoir* (*E*) are to the Pléiade edition in André Malraux, *Romans* (Paris: Gallimard, 1947). All translations are mine.
5. The nonpolitical quality of Ximénès is reinforced by the fact that Malraux makes him a colonel in the Civil Guard. As George Orwell points out: "At the outbreak of war the Civil Guards had everywhere sided with the stronger party" (*Homage to Catalonia* [Harmondsworth: Penguin, 1962], p. 152, n. 2). Ximénès' rallying to the government in Republican Catalonia, therefore, marks more a continuation of military professionalism than a political choice.
6. See W. M. Frohock, *André Malraux and the Tragic Imagination* (Stanford: Stanford University Press, 1952).
7. For a detailed analysis of Hegel's Master-Slave dialectic and its application to the French heroic tradition, see Serge Doubrovsky, *Corneille et la dialectique du héros* (Paris: Gallimard, Collection Idées, 1963).
8. An aspect of World War I described admirably by Joseph Kessel, in *L'Equipage* (Paris: Gallimard, 1924).
9. The distinction between the professional soldier and the *guerrier* is analyzed in Roger Vercel's novel of World War I, *Capitaine Conan* (Paris: A. Michel, 1949).
10. In this context, the concept of "fraternité," often seen as the ethical base of the extended democracy in the novel, requires careful investigation. On one level, it appears to be more concrete than the value of the *dignité* of *La Condition humaine* and more democratic than the *fraternité virile* of *Le Temps du mépris*. In addition, it binds together not merely the leaders of the combatants, as in earlier novels, but also the Republican peasantry. At the same time, however, it is more frequently seen as the bond of a Republican elite, which admits the inclusion of the peasants and militiamen for a temporary period only and, in the case of the peasants, for almost esthetic reasons. *Fra-*

ternité appears as a predominantly elitist, temporary wartime morality which can hardly serve as a base for a return to traditional liberalism, but whose aim is to stifle a metaphysical disquiet. Rather, it is
part of that worrying tendency outlined by Saint-Exupéry in *Terre
des hommes*: "In a deserted world, we needed comrades: the taste
of bread shared between comrades led us to accept wartime values"
([Paris: Gallimard, Collection Livre de poche], p. 232). Finally, *fraternité* is shown to be vulnerable and fragile in its struggle against isolation, that isolation which is the norm in Malraux's work and still un-
resolved (see Malraux, letters to P. B., in Hoffman, *L'Humanisme de
Malraux*, p. 229, n. 31).

11. Hugh Thomas, *The Spanish Civil War* (New York: Harper, 1961);
Gabriel Jackson, *The Spanish Republic and the Civil War, 1931–
1939* (Princeton: Princeton University Press, 1965). Chomsky is careful to point out that later editions of Thomas's book, together with
subsequent treatment of the anarchists and agricultural policy, tend
to modify his original thesis.
12. Noam Chomsky, *American Power and the New Mandarins* (Har-
mondsworth: Penguin, 1969), p. 65.
13. Chomsky makes particular use of the excellent study by Pierre Broué
and Emile Thémime, *La Révolution et la guerre d'Espagne* (Paris:
Editions de Minuit, 1961).
14. Ibid., p. 188.
15. Ibid., p. 210.
16. Ibid., p. 253.
17. Ibid., p. 254.
18. Orwell, *Homage to Catalonia*, pp. 58–59.
19. Ibid., p. 60.
20. George Orwell, article in *Controversy* (August 1937) quoted by
Chomsky, *American Power*, p. 85.
21. Bertoni, quoted in Broué and Thémime, *La Révolution*, p. 216.
22. Robert Brasillach, *Histoire de la Guerre d'Espagne* (Paris: Plon,
1969), p. 216.
23. Jackson, *The Spanish Republic*, pp. 313–14.
24. Chomsky, *American Power*, p. 82.
25. George Santayana, "Justification of Art," in Eliseo Vivas and Murray
Krieger, eds., *The Problems of Aesthetics* (New York: Holt, Rinehart
and Winston, 1963), p. 515.
26. "Fidélité," preface to G. Bazin, *Van Gogh et les peintres d'Auvers
chez le docteur Gachet* (Paris: L'Amour de l'Art, 1952), p. 6. The
image is repeated in *Du musée* (Paris: Editions Estienne, 1955),
unpaginated.
27. André Malraux, *Les Voix du silence* (Paris: Gallimard, 1951), p. 602.
28. See Robert Brasillach, "André Malraux ou le mal de l'héroïsme," in
Portraits (Paris: Plon, 1935); Ilya Ehrenburg, "*La Condition humaine*," in *Duhamel, Gide, Malraux, Morand, Romains, Unamuno,
vus par un écrivain d'URSS* (Paris: Gallimard, 1934).
29. Maurice Merleau-Ponty, "Propos: La Politique paranoïaque," in *Signes*
(Paris: Gallimard, 1960), p. 327.
30. Maurice Merleau-Ponty, "Le Langage indirect et les voix du silence,"
Signes, p. 75.

31. Ibid., p. 77.
32. Ibid., p. 93.
33. Friedrich Nietzsche, *Ecce homo*, in *Collected Works*, ed. Oscar Levy (Edinburgh and London: J. N. Foulis, 1909–13), p. 96.

L'Espoir and Stalinism

An earlier version of this essay was published in *Mosaic* (1975).
 1. André Malraux, *Nouvelle Revue Française*, April 1, 1931; see *Malraux: A Collection of Critical Essays*, ed. R. W. B. Lewis (Englewood Cliffs, N.J.: Prentice-Hall, 1964), pp. 22–24.
 2. Leon Trotsky, *La Vérité*, April 6, 1934, as cited in Jean Lacouture, *André Malraux: Une vie dans le siècle* (Paris: Seuil, 1973), p. 205. The translation is mine, as are all subsequent ones.
 3. Lacouture, *Malraux*, p. 205.
 4. Lucien Goldmann, *Pour une sociologie du roman* (Paris: Gallimard, Collection Idées, 1964), p. 222.
 5. Goldmann, *Sociologie du roman*, pp. 220–21.
 6. George Orwell, *Homage to Catalonia* (New York: Harcourt, Brace and Co., 1952), p. 46.
 7. Pierre Broué, *La Révolution espagnole (1931–1939)* (Paris: Flammarion, 1973), title of chap. 6.
 8. See Broué, *La Révolution espagnole*, chap. 8. This role is also acknowledged in a recent analysis by Fernando Claudin, who was a leading member of the Spanish Communist party during the war: "Spain: The Untimely Revolution," *New Left Review* no. 74 (July–August, 1972).
 9. Orwell, *Homage to Catalonia*, p. 51.
10. See Robert S. Thornberry, *André Malraux et l'Espagne* (Geneva: Droz, 1977), p. 10.
11. As cited in L. Nicolas, *A Travers les révolutions espagnoles* (N.O.E., 1972), p. 188; on Stalinist repression, see also pp. 141–68, 178ff, and Broué, *La Révolution espagnole*, pp. 92–96.
12. The case in question is one recounted by Hernandez, in which an anarchist is falsely accused of robbery and prosecuted because he is carrying out land collectivization against Communist policy.
13. See Pol Gaillard, "L'Evolution de Malraux et l'évolution de la critique à l'égard de Malraux," *Les Critiques de notre temps et Malraux* (Garnier, 1970), p. 13.
14. Broué, *La Révolution espagnole*, p. 83; the quotation is from P. Broué and E. Thémime, *La Révolution et la guerre d'Espagne* (Paris: Editions de Minuit, 1961).
15. André Malraux, *L'Espoir* (Paris: Gallimard, Collection Folio, 1937), p. 84. Hereafter abbreviated *E*. The translations are my own.
16. Orwell, *Homage to Catalonia*, p. 53.
17. *Les Critiques de notre temps et Malraux*, p. 84; also see pp. 11–12.
18. Goldmann, *Sociologie du roman*, p. 217.
19. On the Stalinists' theory of two stages, see Claudin, "Spain: The Untimely Revolution," pp. 10, 16.
20. Pol Gaillard, *L'Espoir de Malraux: Analyse critique* (Paris: Hatier, Collection Profil d'une oeuvre, 1970), p. 56.

21. W. M. Frohock, *André Malraux and the Tragic Imagination* (Stanford: Stanford University Press, 1952), p. 117.

Malraux's Women: A Re-Vision

1. "When We Dead Awaken: Writing as Re-Vision," *College English* (October 1972), reprinted in *Adrienne Rich's Poetry*, selected and edited by Barbara Charlesworth Gelpi and Albert Gelpi (New York: W. W. Norton, 1975), p. 90.
2. Annie Leclerc, *Parole de femme* (Paris: Livre de poche, 1974), p. 27. Unless otherwise noted, all translations from the French are my own.
3. W. M. Frohock, *André Malraux and the Tragic Imagination* (Stanford: Stanford University Press, 1952), p. 89.
4. Judith Fetterley, *The Resisting Reader: A Feminist Approach to American Fiction* (Bloomington: Indiana University Press, 1978), p. xii.
5. André Malraux, *Les Conquérants* (1927), Livre de poche edition, p. 31. Hereafter page references to Malraux's novels will be given in the text using the following abbreviations: *C: Les Conquérants*, Livre de poche edition; *VR: La Voie royale* (1930), Livre de poche edition; *CH: La Condition humaine* (1933), Gallimard Folio edition; *E: L'Espoir* (1937), Livre de poche edition; *TM: Le Temps du mépris* (Gallimard, 1935); *NA: Les Noyers de l'Altenburg* (1948). English translations are my modified versions of the following: *The Conquerors*, trans. Stephen Becker (New York: Holt, Rinehart, and Winston, 1976); *Man's Fate*, trans. Haakon M. Chevalier (New York: Random House, 1961); *Days of Wrath*, trans. Haakon M. Chevalier (New York: Random House, 1936); *Man's Hope*, trans. Stuart Gilbert and Alastair Macdonald (New York: Grove Press, 1979). Some English translations (e.g., *Man's Fate*) omit certain passages I have quoted, and they often "erase" the effect of the original—as in the case where Hemmelrich speaks of his wife "gobbling him up," which Chevalier translated simply as her "getting the better of" him. In order to avoid overburdening the text with numbers, I have given page references only to the French editions.
6. Roland Barthes, *S/Z*, trans. Richard Miller (New York: Hill and Wang, 1974), p. 68. Barthes goes on to note that the exception to the rule about the necessity of the name is a first-person narrator who does not name himself but says "I": "to say *I* is inevitably to attribute signifieds to oneself; further, it gives one a biographical duration, it enables one to undergo, in one's imagination, an intelligible 'evolution,' to signify oneself as the object of a destiny." By that token, the narrator of *Les Conquérants* qualifies as a character, even though we don't know his name.
7. Ibid., p. 68. Here, as in the previous quotation, I have modified Miller's translation somewhat.
8. Ibid., p. 94.
9. Malraux's biographer, Jean Lacouture, has expressed surprise at the fact that there are so few mothers in Malraux's novels. He hints at a psychoanalytic explanation ("We touch here on one of the most obscure aspects of the life and ethics of André Malraux"), but unfor-

tunately there is not much concrete information on which to base one. We know that Malraux's parents separated when he was four years old and that he grew up with three women: his mother, his aunt, and his grandmother. His relation to his mother was certainly not close, and his childhood does not correspond to that of the "mother's favorite son," which Freud suggested was typical for men of great achievement. Malraux himself stated that, unlike most writers, he hated his childhood; Lacouture comments, "To repudiate one's childhood is almost tantamount to insulting one's mother." See Jean Lacouture, *André Malraux: Une vie dans le siècle* (Paris: Seuil, Collection Points, 1976), pp. 12, 132–33.

10. See Lucien Goldmann, "Introduction à une étude structurale des romans de Malraux," *Pour une sociologie du roman* (Paris: Gallimard, Collection Idées, 1964), pp. 175–78. According to James Greenlee, Malraux gives an "indictment of eroticism" not only in the character of Ferral, but as early as *La Voie royale* (Greenlee, *Malraux's Heroes and History* [De Kalb: Northern Illinois University Press, 1975], p. 53). Goldmann, more correctly to my mind, claims that in the first two novels "eroticism and domination constituted precarious but positive values," and that it was only starting with *La Condition humaine* that eroticism became a negative value.

11. The psychoanalyst Wolfgang Lederer has documented, in an important book, the nearly universal fantasy of women as devouring females, ready to eat men alive. See his *Fear of Women* (New York: Grune and Stratton, 1968), esp. the chapter entitled "The Snapping of Teeth."

12. André Malraux, *Antimémoires* (Paris: Gallimard, 1967), p. 378.

13. Lederer, through his extensive study of myth and folklore in both primitive and advanced societies, shows that misogyny is practically synonymous with the *fear* of women. Malraux himself has been accused of misogyny by his first wife, Clara Malraux (*Nos vingt ans* [Paris: Grasset, 1966], pp. 99–103). If she may be considered a less than friendly witness, one can turn to Josette Clotis, who was Malraux's devoted companion until her death and the mother of his two sons. In her private papers from the 1930s, quoted in a recent book that speaks admiringly of her passionate attachment to Malraux, Clotis noted about his attitude toward her: "He wants her to be discreet, serene, tactful: wants her to face him with admiring eyes, silent mouth, the brain of a happy, innocent bird. He says, 'You've understood nothing,' sometimes almost tenderly, sometimes with his hard voice, which can be so mean" (Suzanne Chantal, *Le Coeur battant: Josette Clotis–André Malraux* [Paris: Grasset, 1976], pp. 154–55).

14. Goldmann, *Sociologie du roman*, p. 177.

15. Greenlee, *Malraux's Heroes*, p. 66.

16. In fact, Malraux does not use the expression *fraternité virile* in *La Condition humaine*. He does, however, use the adjective *viril* twice in a single paragraph, which describes precisely Kyo's feeling of communion with his fellow (male) prisoners moments before his death: "This place of agony was no doubt the most weighted with virile love. . . . Already stared at by death, how could he not hear that mur-

mur of human sacrifice which cried out to him that the virile heart of man is at least as strong a refuge against death as the mind?" (*CH* 304).

17. Greenlee, *Malraux's Heroes*, p. 66. Jacques Lacan, in an early article, pointed out that the "moral connotations" of the term *virilité* are a good indication of the "prevalence of the male principle" in our culture ("Famille," in *Encyclopédie française*, 1948; quoted in Catherine Clément, *Vies et légendes de Jacques Lacan* [Paris: Grasset, 1981], p. 99).

18. The fantasy of a world without women, where men would exist in peaceful harmony among themselves, is at least as old as the myth of Pandora, which sees woman as the source of all discord and unhappiness. See Lederer, *The Fear of Women*, chap. 10; Catherine Clément, referring to the anthropological studies of Lévi-Strauss and Pierre Clastres, has remarked, "They both tell us how powerful, in every culture, is the dream of a world without women, where one could live together—that is, among men; an asexual world of warriors." Clément goes on to note that "in a culture where the male principle is predominant, androgyny is not an equal share of man and woman. It is male [*elle est homme*]." See Clément, *Vies et légendes de Jacques Lacan*, pp. 99–100.

19. Fetterley, *The Resisting Reader*, p. xx.

20. Elaine Showalter, "Women and the Literary Curriculum," *College English* 32 (1971), quoted in Fetterley, p. xxi.

21. Walter J. Ong, *Fighting for Life: Contest, Sexuality, and Consciousness* (Ithaca: Cornell University Press, 1981), p. 208.

From Fascination to Poetry: Blindness in Malraux's Novels

1. Cf. my "The Image of Blindness in Malraux's Meditations on Art," in *Mélanges Malraux Miscellany* 3, no. 2 (Autumn 1971): 16–25.

2. References to Malraux's works will be made using the following abbreviations. *A: Antimémoires* (Paris: Gallimard, 1967); *C: Les Conquérants, CH: La Condition humaine,* and *E: L'Espoir,* all in *Romans,* Pléiade edition (Paris: Gallimard, 1947); *MC: Le Monde chrétien* (Paris: Gallimard, 1954); *NA: Les Noyers de l'Altenburg* [*La Lutte avec l'Ange*], *TM: Le Temps du mépris,* and *VR: La Voie royale* (Geneva: Skira, 1945); *VS: Les Voix du silence* (Paris: Gallimard, 1951). Translations are my own.

3. André Malraux, "Portrayal in the West and the Far East," *Verve* 1, no. 3 (October–December 1938): 69 [trans. Stuart Gilbert].

4. Even this detail may be significant since we have been told that, due to limited publication of newspapers, "the destiny of Spain was no longer expressed except by radio" (*E* 463).

5. In response to my query on this point, Malraux noted that the art of the blind is music. "Etre artiste, *c'est* ressentir l'art comme anti-destin [To be an artist *is* to experience art as an anti-destiny]" (Note to the author, February 1, 1972).

6. The virile fraternity which Malraux proposes as an answer to destiny in *L'Espoir* is largely realized—both made real and perceived—by the very opposite of blindness: vision. See my "Visual Imagination in

L'Espoir," in *André Malraux: Metamorphosis and Imagination*, New York Literary Forum 3 (1979): 201–8.

7. In the version of this scene in *Lazare* (Paris: Gallimard, 1974), Malraux underlines this aspect of Gardet's wound (p. 208).

8. Clara Malraux, who had a serious eye injury as a child and kept a life-long fear of blindness, also compares blinding and castration: "Is castrating a man worse than blinding him?" (*Apprendre à vivre*, [Paris: Grasset, 1963], p. 73). She experienced her childhood injury as a humiliation, an attack on her very person. Her acute fear of blindness in a dark stairway in her home (pp. 12–13) may even have provided Malraux with an incident in *Les Conquérants*, Garine's impression of becoming blind as he makes his way up a dark stairway (C 158–59).

9. In the *Antimémoires* Malraux makes a similarly close association between blindness, slavery, and the human condition. In Indian thought, he tells us, the attachment to things is "the slavery of man, blind to the essence which transcends him and handed over by his blindness to the illusory universe. [. . .] The invincible agent of the maya is not divine action, it is the human condition" (A 202).

10. It is interesting to note that in German air force slang, which may have been familiar to Malraux in Spain, the second plane of a two-plane formation is called the *Holzauge* (wooden eye), although its pilot is responsible for keeping an eye out for enemy aircraft. The expression has passed into common parlance: "Holzauge, sei wachsam!" (Watch out! Be careful!).

11. Blindness is also the recurrent image for the incommunicability between cultures separated in time or space. See my essay, "The Image of Blindness in Malraux's Meditations on Art," *Mélanges Malraux Miscellany*, 3, no. 2 (Autumn, 1971), pp. 16–25.

12. In two extended interviews with me, Malraux was singularly reticent about the entire subject. In our second talk—largely reproduced in volume 4 of the Série Malraux, *Malraux et l'art* (Paris: Lettres Modernes, 1978) under the title "L'Art et le roman: L'imagination visuelle du romancier"—Malraux agreed that blindness is indeed associated for him with destiny, but he immediately steered the conversation away from the purely personal: "Il n'y a pas que chez moi. Dans la tragédie grecque l'adjectif qui accompagne destin, comme grand accompagne Zeus, c'est *aveugle*. [It's not only true for me. In Greek tragedy the adjective which accompanies destiny, as *great* accompanies Zeus, is *blind*]."

Malraux's Shamanism: Initiatory Death and Rebirth

1. Armond Hoog, "Malraux, Möllberg and Frobenius," in *Malraux: A Collection of Critical Essays*, ed. R. W. B. Lewis (Englewood Cliffs, N.J.: Prentice-Hall, 1964), pp. 86–95, cites letters from Malraux showing that he intended Möllberg to be "ideologically, Frobenius" and also argues that Frobenius had an important impact on Malraux's thinking. W. M. Frohock, *André Malraux and the Tragic Imagina-*

tion (Stanford: Stanford University Press, 1952; rpt. 1967), p. 148, affirms that Malraux read Frobenius's *History of African Civilization.*

2. Leo Frobenius, *Kulturgeschichte Afrikas* (Zürich: Phaidon-Verlag, 1933), p. 296. The French text, *Histoire de la civilisation africaine,* trans. H. Back and D. Ermont (Paris: Gallimard, 1936), p. 255, reads: "Le chamanisme de l'Afrique est de même essence que celui de l'Asie . . . son noyau consiste dans la 'puissance du moi' développée jusqu'à la formation de forces d'idées personnalisées et jusqu'à l'exercice d'un pouvoir sur ces forces . . . le chamanisme consiste dans l'opposition à l'ordre naturel de la réalité. L'homme se révolte contre la réalité." Jean Lacouture, in his biography of Malraux, compares the latter's "magical powers of leadership" in the Resistance to the gifts of the shaman. *André Malraux,* trans. Alan Sheridan (New York: Pantheon, 1975), p. 306.

3. Mircea Eliade, *Naissances mystiques: Essai sur quelques types d'initiation* (Paris: Gallimard, 1959), p. 216. English translation, slightly modified, from *Rites and Symbols of Initiation: The Mysteries of Birth and Rebirth,* tr. Willard R. Trask (New York: Harper & Row, 1965), p. 102.

4. André Malraux, *Les Noyers de l'Altenburg* (Paris: Gallimard, 1948), p. 49; hereafter abbreviated *NA.* Translations mine unless otherwise noted.

5. Frohock, *André Malraux,* pp. 138–49.

6. See for example Eliade's *Myths, Dreams, and Mysteries: The Encounter Between Contemporary Faiths and Archaic Realities,* tr. Philip Mairet (New York: Harper & Row, 1967), pp. 59ff.

7. Eliade, *Shamanism: Archaic Techniques of Ecstasy,* tr. Willard R. Trask (New York: Bollingen Foundation, 1964), p. 271. See also Frobenius, *Kulturgeschichte Afrikas,* p. 188.

8. Eliade, *Naissances mystiques,* p. 216.

9. Michel Foucault, *Surveiller et punir: Naissance de la prison* (Paris: Gallimard, 1975), p. 242.

10. *La Voie royale* in André Malraux, *Oeuvres,* vol. 2 (Paris: Gallimard, 1970), p. 163; hereafter abbreviated *VR.*

11. English translation from André Malraux, *The Royal Way,* trans. Stuart Gilbert (New York: Random House, 1935), p. 245.

12. André Malraux, *La Condition humaine* (Paris: Gallimard, 1946), p. 361; hereafter abbreviated *CH.* English translation from *Man's Fate,* trans. Haakon M. Chevalier (New York: Vintage Books, 1961), p. 303.

13. I have discussed the death-rebirth motif in these two novels more fully in my "Malraux's Early Prisons: Absurdity and Transcendence," *Mélanges Malraux Miscellany* 8, no. 2 (Autumn 1976): 20–37.

14. André Malraux, *Days of Wrath,* trans. Haakon M. Chevalier (New York: Random House, 1936), p. 23, translation of *Le Temps du mépris* (Paris: Gallimard, 1935), p. 31; hereafter abbreviated *TM.*

On Dreams and the Human Mystery in Malraux's *Miroir des limbes*

1. Page references are to the Pléiade edition of *Le Miroir des limbes* (Paris: Gallimard, 1976), abbreviated *ML*. All translations into English are my own.

2. Michael Riffaterre writes of the narrative structure of the *Antimémoires*: "The *Antimémoires* are based on analogy (the method of superimposition is identical in itself to metaphor); they are thus poetry" (*Essais de stylistique structurale* [Paris: Flammarion, 1971], p. 296).

3. For a recent study of *l'imaginaire* in Malraux, with reference to its relationship to dream, see Edouard Morot-Sir, "Agnosticism and the Gnosis of the Imaginary," *André Malraux: Metamorphosis and Imagination*, in *New York Literary Forum* 3 (1979): 85–124.

4. The reference to Malraux's serious and playful nature will doubtless bring to mind the passage in the introduction to the "Antimémoires" where Malraux specifically describes the polarity of his book as a hovering between the tragic and the fairylike, legendary domain. The global term he applies to the latter, the *farfelu*, would seem to encompass quite a bit more than mere whimsicalness, however. For an important reconsideration of Malraux's *farfelu*, see David G. Bevan, "The Archaic Smile, or Butterflies and Monsters," *Mélanges Malraux Miscellany* 12, no. 2 (Autumn 1980): 19–29.

5. I hope to complete soon a study of the dream image in *Le Miroir des limbes* as it is associated with cultures, visionaries, and adventurers.

6. Malraux's allusions to the East and to its works of fantasy (especially the *Thousand and One Nights*) are elements closely related to the dream motif but, along with references to *l'irréel* (the unreal), they are too extensive to be included within the scope of this essay.

7. A fuller reference to his father's curiosity appears in the "Lazare" section: "When he killed himself, he left on his night stand a book turned to a page where he had underlined the sentence: 'And who knows what we shall find after death?' Into the stoic shadow of suicide had crept a curiosity for the unknown" (*ML* 874).

8. In fact, the dialogue between the interrogator and Malraux given in the real-life scenario bears a very close resemblance to the one that takes place between Koenig and Kyo. The novel gives us: "'They tell me you are a communist because of . . . what is it, now . . . dignity. Is that right?' . . . 'I think that communism will make dignity possible for those with whom I am fighting.' . . . 'What do you call dignity? That doesn't mean anything!' . . . 'The opposite of humiliation,' said Kyo." (André Malraux, *La Condition humaine*, in *Romans* [Paris: Gallimard, 1947], p. 394.) This becomes, simply, in *Le Miroir des limbes*: "'But good lord, what in the hell made you get into this?' . . . 'My convictions' . . . 'Your convictions! We'll see about that!'" (*ML* 194).

9. See Ralph Tarica, *Imagery in the Novels of André Malraux* (Rutherford, N.J.: Fairleigh Dickinson University Press, 1980), pp. 141–42.

10. Bettina Knapp has looked at these dreams from a Jungian perspective, according to which there may be sound psychological reasons to justify precognitive dreaming. See "André Malraux's *Hôtes de passage*

and the Mystic World," *Mélanges Malraux Miscellany* 8, no. 1 (Spring 1976): 3–12.

11. André Malraux, *Les Noyers de l'Altenburg* (Paris: Gallimard, 1948), p. 49.

12. W. M. Frohock, *André Malraux and the Tragic Imagination* (Stanford: Stanford University Press, 1952), pp. 137ff.

CONTRIBUTORS

HASKELL M. BLOCK is Professor of Comparative Literature at the State University of New York at Binghamton. He is the author of *Mallarmé and the Symbolist Drama, Naturalistic Triptych, Nouvelles tendances en littérature comparée*, and essays on diverse aspects of modern literature.

MARY JEAN GREEN received her Ph.D. in French from Harvard University in 1974. She is Associate Professor of French and co-chair of the Women's Studies Program at Dartmouth. Ms. Green has published a number of articles on contemporary French fiction. Her book, *Louis Guilloux: An Artisan of Language*, appeared in 1980. She has been active in scholarship on the literature of Quebec and is currently working on a study of French fiction and the historical events of the 1930s.

NICHOLAS HEWITT is currently lecturer in French Studies at the University of Warwick (Coventry, England). He studied at the University of Hull and was a Kennedy Scholar at Harvard before teaching at Hull and Southampton universities. He is the author of several articles on Malraux and, with Walter Langlois, of the Malraux chapter of the *Critical Bibliography of French Literature*. He has also published a full-length study of Henri Troyat and numerous articles on Céline, about whom he is currently writing a book.

WALTER G. LANGLOIS, a graduate of Yale and currently Senior Professor of French at the University of Wyoming, has been studying various aspects of the life and works of André Malraux for more than two decades. In addition to articles in scholarly journals here and abroad, he has edited or written volumes on Malraux, beginning with *André Malraux: The Indochina Adventure*. He has had various awards, including

Rockefeller, Guggenheim, ACLS, and Camargo fellowships. Most recently, a Senior Fellowship awarded by the National Endowment for the Humanities has allowed him to complete research for a book-length study of Malraux's involvement in the Spanish civil war.

BERT MALLET-PREVOST LEEFMANS taught at Columbia University from 1947 to his death in 1980. His areas of interest included the correlations between art, science, and literature; Anti-culture; Dada; Surrealism; satire and irony; and modern drama. His more recent articles are "The Meanest Flower and Rage for Order," on Mallarmé's "Prose pour des Esseintes" (*Romantic Review*), and reviews for *Art News*. Volume 11 of *The New York Literary Forum* (1983), which included his essay "Das Und-Bild: a Metaphysics of Collage," was dedicated to the memory of Professor Leefmans.

MARY M. ROWAN received her Ph.D. from Harvard in 1968 and is now Professor of French at Brooklyn College of the City University of New York. Her published articles include studies of travel and women's writing in seventeenth-century France and have appeared in *The French Review*, the *International Journal of Women's Studies*, and *Papers in Seventeenth-Century French Literature*, among others. She is now completing a book comparing modes of discourse in the writings from salon and convent in the baroque period in France.

NORMAN RUDICH, who received his Ph.D. from Princeton in 1951, is now Professor of Letters and Romance Languages at Wesleyan University. He is the author of numerous essays on esthetics, the theory of literature, the novel, Marxism and literature and criticism, as well as of studies of Balzac, Baudelaire, Lucien Goldmann, Coleridge, and Wittgenstein. He is the editor of *Weapons of Criticism: Marxism in America and the Literary Tradition* and the coeditor of Diderot's *Premières Oeuvres*. He is currently engaged in a study of Diderot's esthetics.

ROBERT SAYRE received his Ph.D. from Columbia University and has taught at Harvard University as Assistant Professor of French Literature. He is currently living in France, teaching at the University of Paris and writing a book on the problematics and history of the sociology of literature. He has published a number of articles on Lucien Goldmann, and he is the author of *Solitude in Society: A Sociological Study in French Literature*, published by Harvard University Press in 1978.

SUSAN RUBIN SULEIMAN received her Ph.D. from Harvard University, where she is now Associate Professor of Romance Languages and Literatures. She is the author of *Authoritarian Fictions: The Ideological Novel as a Literary Genre*, co-editor of *The Reader in the Text: Essays on Audience and Interpretaton*, and translator of Apollinaire's *Chroniques d'Art*. Her essays on modern French literature and on literary theory have appeared in French and American journals and collective volumes.

RALPH TARICA received his Ph.D. from Harvard after studying in France as a Fulbright Scholar. He taught at Harvard and Brandeis universities, and is now Professor of French at the University of Maryland.

He has published a number of essays on Malraux and is the author of *Imagery in the Novels of André Malraux*, which appeared in 1980.

BRIAN THOMPSON received his Ph.D. in Comparative Literature from Harvard University, where he was a Wilson and NDEA Fellow. He has also been a Fulbright Fellow in Paris, and he has published a number of translations from French and German, including Gabriel Marcel's *L'Homme problématique* and Romano Guardini's *Christliches Bewusstsein: Versuche über Pascal*. His essays on Malraux have appeared in the *Mélanges Malraux Miscellany* and in special Malraux issues of the *New York Literary Forum, Twentieth Century Literature*, and the *Cahiers de l'Herne;* a major interview with Malraux appeared in the Malraux series published by *Lettres Modernes;* his recent essay on Mauriac as a Christian polemicist was published in *Cahiers François Mauriac*. He is currently Associate Professor of French at the University of Massachusetts at Boston.

CARL A. VIGGIANI received his Ph.D. from Columbia University and taught there before going to Wesleyan University, where he is Professor of Romance Languages and Literatures. A Camus specialist, he has published biographical and critical essays on Camus and Sainte-Beuve.

SERGIO VILLANI received his Ph.D. from Harvard University and has taught French language and literature at Dalhousie University and at the University of Toronto. He has published articles on Mallarmé, Valéry, and Malraux, and he is currently working on a study of Valéry's writings on war and power.

MARY ANN FRESE WITT received her Ph.D. in Comparative Literature from Harvard University in 1968. She is Associate Professor of French and Comparative Literature at North Carolina State University. The author of essays on Camus, Ionesco, Sartre, and Malraux, she is also the editor of *The Humanities: Cultural Roots and Continuities*. She has just completed a book on images of imprisonment in the writings of Camus, Malraux, Sartre, and Genet.

INDEX

Absurd, the, 3, 22, 26, 28, 41, 86
Action: as element in *La Condition humaine*, 50, 51, 52
Air squadron, the, 116–117, 121
Alger Républicain (newspaper), 75, 76
Algeria, 78
Algerian Communist party, 74
Algiers, 74, 75
Alienation, 64, 152, 153
Alsace-Lorraine Brigade, 6, 10, 12, 43, 185
Altenburg colloquy, 5, 171, 175, 176
Alvarez de Albornoz, 100, 105, 106
Alvear (in *L'Espoir*), 5, 135, 136, 162
Alvear, Jaime, *see* Jaime
Anarchists, 120, 129, 130; and the popular revolution, 118, 119
André Malraux and the Tragic Imagination, 19, 30, 141
Angkor Wat, 31, 34, 35, 36
Anna (in *Le Temps du mépris*), 142, 154–155, 174
Anti-destiny, 8, 28
Antifascist movement: Malraux as leader in, 94
Antimémoires, 8, 149
"Antimémoires," 181, 182, 184, 185, 190
Art, 7, 8, 26, 28, 162, 175, 176

Balzac, Honoré de, 82, 83
Banteay-Srei, 2, 34, 35
Barthes, Roland, 144, 209nb
Beauvoir, Simone de, 66, 71, 77
Benbow, Horace (in *Sanctuary*), 57
Berger (in *Les Noyers de l'Altenburg*, son of Vincent Berger), 170, 171, 175; and death and rebirth, 177–178
"Berger," Colonel, 6, 43
Berger, Dietrich (in *Les Noyers de l'Altenburg*), 170, 171, 175
Berger, Vincent (in *Les Noyers de l'Altenburg*), 29, 163, 181; and death and rebirth, 175, 176; as a shaman, 170, 171
Berger, Walter (in *Les Noyers de l'Altenburg*), 175, 176, 177
Bernanos, Georges, 77
Berneri, 119, 120
Bertoni, 120
Blindness, 165–168
Blum, Léon, 89, 90–91, 98–99
Bonaparte, Napoleon, 41
Bonneau (in *Les Noyers de l'Altenburg*), 177
Borodin, Mikhail (in *Les Conquérants*), 22
Broué, Pierre, 119, 127, 130
Bruckberger, Father, 77
Burke, Kenneth, 50

Caballero, Largo, 118
Cambodia, 2, 34
Camus, Albert: and bipolar concepts, 80, 82, 86; as pacifist, 81; political views of, 75, 76, 77, 78; relations with Malraux, 73, 75, 76, 77, 79, 84–85; on revolt and revolution, 81; views on Malraux, 83–84, 87; views of Malraux on, 77, 84–85, 87
Camus, Albert, 74
Canton, 4, 33, 181
Carnets, the, 79, 81–83, 86, 87
Casamance, Queen of, 182
Cazenave, Michel, 6
Chase, Richard, 170
Chênes qu'on abat, Les, 8
Chiang Kai-shek, 49, 126
Chiaromonte, Nicola, 94, 96
Chiaroscuro, 36–37
Cholon, 32, 34
Chomsky, Noam, 118, 121
Cianca, Alberto, 96
Cinematic technique, 32, 33
Clappique, Baron (in *La Condition humaine*), 24, 52
Claude (in *La Voie royale*), 34–35, 173
Clotis, Josette, 5, 6, 77, 187
Coindreau, Maurice, 57
Comintern, *see* Stalinist Comintern
Comité mondial contre la guerre et le fascisme (World Committee Against War and Fascism), 4, 96
Comité Thaelmann, 4
Comité de Vigilance des Intellectuels Antifascistes (Committee of Vigilance of Antifascist Intellectuals), 74
Communist party, 26, 75
Communists, 24, 128, 129, 131
Condition humaine, La, 3, 4, 23–24, 63, 83, 172; chiaroscuro in, 36–37; as classical tragedy, 58; critical views on, 21–25; on death and rebirth, 172; nameless women in, 143; as political novel, 21; sensory imagery in, 31; structural analysis of, 48–49, 51–52; Trotsky on, 126
Conquérants, Les, 3, 4, 23, 24, 47; cinematic technique in, 32–33; critical views on, 21–25; nameless women in, 142; as political novel, 21; sensory imagery in, 31, 32, 33; Trotsky on, 4, 18, 126
Cosmic tree, *see* World tree
Cot, Pierre, 91, 92, 93, 94, 96
Council of Ministers, 99, 102, 104, 105, 107–108, 109

"Creative élites": theory of, 28
Curtis, Eugene, 44

Daladier, Edouard, 91, 96
Death, 3, 8
Death and rebirth, 170, 171, 172, 173, 174, 175, 176, 177–178
De Gaulle, Charles, 6, 7, 40, 43, 78, 85, 181
Delbos, Yvon, 92, 104
De los Ríos, Fernando, 97
Despair: as element in *La Condition humaine*, 49
Destiny: and blindness in Malraux's work, 160, 161, 162; defined, 160
Diaz, José, 119
Don Quixote, 176
Dorenlot, Françoise, 7
Dostoevski, Feodor, 82, 83, 170
Dream metaphor, the, 181, 182, 184
Dreams: and destiny, 183, 184, 185

Einstein, Albert, 189
Eliade, Mircea, 169, 171
Ellipsis, 31, 38
Ellora, caves of, 182
"Enfance d'un chef, L'," 64–65
Eroticism, 145–146
Escadrille España, 5, 12, 90
Espoir (film), 5, 76, 77
Espoir, L' (Man's Hope), 5, 6, 90; critical views of, 26, 122–124; metaphysical aspect of, 115; military emphasis in, 126, 128, 131; nameless women in, 143; as political novel, 21; role of popular revolution in, 120; views of, 113–114
Etranger, L' (The Stranger), 74, 76; Malraux's views of, 76, 85
Etre et le néant, L' (Being and Nothingness), 67
Eyes: Malraux's preoccupation with, 162–164, 165

Fascism, 5, 64, 66
Fascists, 93
Faulkner, William: as tragic novelist, 56; Malraux's view of, 57
Fellow traveler, 126, 132, 133, 135, 138
Ferral (in *La Condition humaine*), 24, 53, 54, 150–151
Fetterley, Judith, 141, 156
Foucault, Michel, 172
France, 9, 196n9; diplomatic preparations, 108–109; military preparations, 159–163; political opinions

on Spanish uprising, 97–98, 99; as refuge for antifascists, 93
Franco, 118, 119, 120
French Popular Front, 102–103
French Revolution, 41, 42
Frobenius, Leo, 169, 213n2
Frohock, W. M., 21, 23, 24; on the absurd, 141; approach to Malraux's novels, 16, 17, 19, 20; on La Condition humaine, 25–26; on Les Conquérants, 22; on Malraux as critic, 57; on Malraux as poet, 19–20, 26, 180; on Malraux as shaman, 190; on Malraux's Spanish experience, 90; on Malraux's use of ellipsis and cinematographic imagination, 31; on the shaman, 170

Gaillard, Pol, 135
Galante, Pierre, 43
Gallimard (publishing company), 76
Gallimard, Gaston, 76, 84
Gallimard, Janine, 77
Gallimard, Michel, 76, 77
Gallimard, Pierre, 76, 77
Garcia (in L'Espoir), 120, 121, 132, 133, 134, 135, 146–147
Gardet (in L'Espoir), 162
Garine, Pierre (in Les Conquérants), 11–12, 13, 22–23, 29, 44–47, 164; and the absurd, 3; and illness, 33
Genetic structuralism, 16, 17, 24
Gide, André, 4, 5, 18, 76, 82, 84, 85
Giral, José, 90, 91, 99
Gisors (in La Condition humaine), 24, 37
Gisors, Kyo or Kyoshi, see Kyo
Gisors, May, see May
Giustizia e Libertà (GL; Justice and Liberty), 94–95, 96, 101, 102
Goethe, Johann Wolfgang von, 170
Goldmann, Lucien, 18, 20, 21, 22, 24, 117; approach to Malraux's novels, 16–17; definition of the novel, 17; on development of the novel, 18; on eroticism in Malraux's works, 146, 210n10; on L'Espoir, 114, 126; on La Condition humaine, 25–26
Grabot (in La Voie royale), 3, 31, 161, 164
Greenlee, James, 44, 155
Grenier, Jean, 74, 76, 80, 84, 85, 86, 87
Gris, Ramon (in "Le Mur"), 64
Groethuysen, Bernard, 76, 85
Grover, Frédéric J., 76, 84
Guernico (in L'Espoir), 146–147

Half-breed, 37, 38
Hankow, 49
Heidegger, Martin, 18
Hemmelrich (in La Condition humaine), 147–148
Hernandez (in L'Espoir), 67, 68, 69, 135
Hölderlin, Friedrich, 170
Homage to Catalonia, 127
Homme révolté, L' (The Rebel), 81; Malraux's view of, 84
Hong (in Les Conquérants), 33, 37, 53
Hong Kong, 33
Hope, 50, 53, 162; as element in La Condition humaine, 49
"Hôtes de passage," 181
Human action, 64, 71
Human fraternity, 4
Humanism: in Malraux's work, 20–22, 23, 27–28

Ibbieta, Pablo (in "Le Mur"), 64, 65, 66, 67, 68
Idiot, The, 176
Illness: as Malraux's metaphor for Asia, 33
India, 182, 183
Indochina, 2, 94
Indochine (newspaper), 2, 34
Indochine enchaînée (newspaper), 2, 34
International, the, 24
Irréel, L', 8
Italy: and Spanish rebels, 103–104

Jackson, Gabriel, 118
Jaime (in L'Espoir), 116, 117, 160–162
Jaipur, 182
JCI (Juventud Comunista Ibérica), 119
Jeune Annam movement, the, 2

Kafka, Franz, 82
Karlitch (in L'Espoir), 135
Kassner (in Le Temps du mépris), 163, 173–174
Kassner, Anna, see Anna
Katow (in La Condition humaine), 4, 6, 24, 29, 53, 54, 148–149; critics' view of, 25; and ritual death, 173
Kierkegaard, Sören, 88
Klein (in Les Conquérants), 33, 142, 164
Kline, T. Jefferson, 8
Kobe, 70; and the element of time, 65
Koestler, Arthur, 77, 82
Kuomintang, the, 24

Kyo (in *La Condition humaine*), 4, 6, 25, 29, 37, 70, 151–154; and revolutionary action, 24; and ritual death, 173

Lacouture, Jean, 7, 30, 71, 74, 126
Lagrange, Léo, 93, 94, 95, 96; and military assistance to Spain, 97
Langlois, Walter, 30
Lawrence, T. E., 44
Lazare, 8, 172, 189
"Lazare," 181, 186, 187
Leclerc (in *L'Espoir*), 116, 117, 161
Leclerc, Annie, 140, 141
Left, the, 6
Léonard (in *Les Noyers de l'Altenburg*), 177
Levin, Harry, 19
Light in August, 59–60
Ligue Française des Droits de l'Homme (French League of Human Rights), 77
Lottman, Herbert, 74
Lukács, György, 18, 24, 28
Lunes en papier (*Paper Moons*), 19, 170; critical views of, 21; Frohock on, 20

MacGovern, John, 129
Madura, 182
Magnin (in *L'Espoir*), 116, 120, 121, 135, 136–137
Malraux, Clara, 2
Malraux, Roland, 186
Malraux par lui-même, 58
Man: mystery of, 179
Manuel (in *L'Espoir*), 121; as a Communist, 132, 133; as a leader, 114–115
Marcuse, Herbert, 134
Martin du Gard, Roger, 76, 78, 85
Mauriac, François, 78
May (in *La Condition humaine*), 4, 142, 151–154; and revolutionary action, 24
Maya (illusion), 182
Melville, Herman, 83
Méry, Hubert, 181, 183
Métamorphose des dieux, La (*The Metamorphosis of the Gods*), 182
Michelet, Jules, 42
Mirabeau, Victor Riqueti, Marquis de, 170
Mirbal, Juan, 64, 65
Miroir des limbes, Le (*The Mirror of Limbo*), 78; discussion of death and rebirth in, 188; discussion of dream

and reality in, 182–183; discussion of Malraux as a mystic in, 180; dream metaphor in, 181–183, 184; mystical experiences in, 187–188; and poetic tone of, 180
Möllberg (in *Les Noyers de l'Altenburg*), 169, 170, 176
Monin, Paul, 2
Monnaie de l'absolu, La, 8
Montherlant, Henri de, 84
Moreno (in *L'Espoir*), 66, 67, 70
Mouches, Les (*The Flies*), 71, 72
"Mur, Le" (The Wall), 63, 64, 65
Mystic: Malraux as, 180
Mythe de Sisyphe, Le (*The Myth of Sisyphus*), 74, 76, 83; Malraux's view of, 84

Narada (in *Le Miroir des limbes*), 182
Nausée, La (*Nausea*), 83
Négus, le (in *L'Espoir*), 135, 136, 137
Nietzsche, Friedrich, 175
Nihilism, 75, 82
Nicolaïeff (in *Les Conquérants*), 3, 23, 33, 47, 142
Nobel Prize, the, 79
Non-Communists, 128, 129
Non-Stalinist Marxists: and the popular revolution, 118, 119
Nouvelle Revue Française, La (*NRF*; periodical), 57, 63, 66, 76, 85, 88
Noyers de l'Altenburg, Les (*The Walnut Trees of Altenburg*), 5, 7, 172, 181; critics' views on, 26; nameless women in, 143–144; as a political novel, 21; shamanism in, 170

Ogasawara, Shinichi, 7
Ollivier, Albert, 41
Ong, Walter J., 157
Orwell, George, 119, 127, 128, 131

Parain, Brice, 76, 85
Paris, 55
Parole de Femme, 140
"Passion," 50, 52, 54
Paulhan, Jean, 76, 85
"Perception," 50, 54
Perken (in *La Voie royale*), 3, 31, 34, 35, 163, 172–173
Peste, La (*The Plague*): Malraux's view of, 81, 84, 87
Phnom-Penh, 2, 31, 34
Pia, Pascal, 75, 76, 85
Picon, Gaëtan, 58
Place: as element in *La Condition humaine*, 50, 51

Poe, Edgar Allen, 170
Politics: role of in Malraux's works, 19–20, 22, 23, 27
Ponge, Francis, 77
Popular revolution, the, 127, 128; Malraux's view of, 187, 188; views on, 118–119
POUM (Partido Obrero de Unificación Marxista), 13, 119, 120, 121, 128–130
Pradé (in *Les Noyers de l'Altenburg*), 177
Proletarian revolution: in Malraux's work, 27, 28
Proletariat, the, 6
Proust, Marcel, 83
"Purpose," 50, 52, 54
Pushkin, Alexander, 170

Quest for Myth, The, 170
. . . *qu'une larme dans l'océan*, 59

Rebbecci (in *Les Conquérants*), 142
Republican air force, *see* Spanish Republican air force
Republican cause: Malraux's involvement in, 5
Resistance, the, 43, 44, 76; Malraux's involvement in, 6; Sartre's involvement in, 71
Révolte dans les Asturies (*Revolt in the Asturias*), 75
Revolution: in Canton, 3, 4; as concept for Malraux, 22, 29, 41
Rite of initiation, the, *see* Death and rebirth
Robbe-Grillet, Alain, 18
Robespierre, Maximilien de, 170
Robinson Crusoe, 176
Rosselli, Carlo, 94, 95, 96, 101
Royaume farfelu: critics' views on, 20–21
RPF (Rassemblement du Peuple Français), 77

Sade, Marquis de, 83
Saigon, 31, 33, 34
Saint-Just, Louis Antoine de, 40, 42, 43, 44; as model for Malraux, 43, 44–46, 47
Sanctuary: Malraux's view of, 56–57; concept of tragedy in, 57–60
Sartoris, 59
Sartre, Jean-Paul, 5, 62–63, 77, 82, 83; and human action, 71; on political action, 71

Scali, Luigi (in *L'Espoir*), 135, 136, 161, 162
Sensory imagery, 31, 32, 33, 34, 35
Serge, Valérie (in *La Condition humaine*), *see* Valérie
Shaman, the: defined, 169
Shamanism, 26, 169, 170
Shanghai, 4, 49
Showalter, Elaine: on women, 156–157
Sierra de Teruel, see *Espoir*
Soir Républicain, Le (newspaper), 75, 76
Souen (in *La Condition humaine*), 163
Spanish civil war, 5, 62, 89, 117, 120, 126–127, 128; effect on Sartre and Beauvoir, 66; Malraux's view of, 121; Sartre on, 65
Spanish Communist Party (Partido Socialista Unificado de Cataluña; PSUC), 118, 127, 183, 185
Spanish Republic, the, 89, 99, 144–146
Spanish Republican air force, 5, 91, 92, 94
Sperber, Manès, 59, 77, 82
Stalinism, 126, 128, 130, 134, 135, 138
Stalinist Comintern, 125, 127
Stalinists: activity in Spain, 128–129
Stendhal, 83
Stieglitz (in *Les Noyers de l'Altenburg*), 175
Surnaturel, Le, 8
S/Z, 144

Tchen Ta-eul (in *La Condition humaine*), 24, 37, 49, 50, 51, 52
Tcheng-Daï (in *Les Conquérants*), 33
Temps du mépris, Le (*Days of Wrath*), 4, 7, 58, 63; and death and rebirth, 172, 173–174; influence on Camus, 74, 75, 83, 84; nameless women in, 143; as political novel, 21; and the revolutionary fraternity, 64; Camus's theatrical adaptation of, 75; views on, 26
Tentation de l'Occident, La (*The Temptation of the West*), 3, 80, 82, 115, 170
Tête d'obsidienne, La, 8, 9
Théâtre de L'Equipe (Group Theater), 76
Théâtre du Travail (Workers' Theater), 75
Thémime, Emile, 119
Theory of the Novel, 18
Thomas, Hugh, 118
Time: as element in *La Condition humaine*, 50–52, 54, 55

Towards a Sociology of the Novel, 17

Tragedy: Faulkner's view of, 59–60; in Malraux's fiction, 58; in Malraux's view of the novel, 57, 58, 59

Trotsky, Leon, 18, 22, 126; criticism of *Les Conquérants,* 4

Valérie (in *La Condition humaine*), 53, 54, 142, 150–151

Vannec, Claude, *see* Claude

Vargas (in *L'Espoir*), 120, 121

"Venice," 175

Verve, 160

Viezzoli, Giordano, 95, 96

Virile fraternity, 4, 28, 155, 162; Camus's view of, 81; and sense of communion, 154, 155

Voie royale, La (*The Royal Way*), 3, 7,

23; and death and rebirth, 172; nameless women in, 143; sensory imagery in, 31, 34, 35

Voix du silence, Les (*The Voices of Silence*), 8, 19, 123, 124, 160

War: as concept for Malraux, 122

Warrior (*guerrier*): defined, 116–117

Wilkinson, David: on *L'Espoir,* 113–114

Women: in Malraux's novels, 144–145, 147–149, 150

World tree, 170, 171

Ximénès (in *L'Espoir*), 114, 115, 133, 136

Zola, Emile, 18